A History of Walford and Bishopswood

A History of Walford and Bishopswood
a South Herefordshire Parish

compiled and edited

by

Virginia Morgan & Bridget Vine

Walford Parish Residents Association
in association with
Logaston Press

WALFORD PARISH RESIDENTS ASSOCIATION
Millennium Committee

LOGASTON PRESS
Little Logaston Woonton Almeley
Herefordshire HR3 6QH

First published by Logaston Press 2002
Copyright © to be shared between
Walford Parish Residents Association and the authors:
Virginia Morgan, Bridget Vine, David Walshaw and Sheila Walshaw 2002
Copyright © illustrations as per individual credit 2002

ISBN 1 873827 87 3

Set in Times by Logaston Press
and printed in Great Britain by
MFP Design & Print, Manchester

Cover illustrations:
Front: Kerne Bridge looking north-east towards Bishopswood & Walford
(photograph by Andrew Anderson, Bishopswood)
Rear: (clockwise from top left): view from Howle Hill across Coughton;
Great Howle Earthwork; Hom Green; Deep Dean
(photographs by Chris Barron, Walford)

Contents

*This engraved spoon was presented by the Parish Council
to every child under the age of 12 years in the parish,
and also to pupils attending Walford School but living outside the parish,
to commemorate the Millennium*

ACKNOWLEDGEMENTS

The editors would like to thank the following people (all resident in Walford Parish unless otherwise stated) who have provided assistance, information, photographs and access to a range of material, without which this publication would not have been possible:

Mr. Edward (Ted) Allen, Mrs. Wendy Alston, Mr. and Mrs. Paul Baker, Mr. George Baldwin, Dr. Nick Barton (Oxford), Mrs. Mary Bevan, Mrs. Glennys Bickmore, Mrs. Liz Boynton (Ross), Mrs. Barbara Brain, Mr. Cecil J. Bromhead (Harrogate), Mr. Basil Brown (Mitcheldean), Mrs. Joyce Bundy, Mrs. Ruby Burford (Ross), Mr. N. Burston (formerly Director of Roads for Ross District), Mr. and Mrs. Ray Cawthorn, Mr. Richard Chinn, Mr. and Mrs. Robert Chinn, Mr. and Mrs. William Chinn, Mrs. Margaret Claxton, Mr. and Mrs. Sidney Cobb, Mr. Jack Coombes (Ross), Mrs. Bernice Cooper, Mr. and Mrs. Roy Cope, Mr. and Mrs. John Corbett, Mr. and Mrs. Bill Cubberley, Mr. Mansel David (Ross), Mr. Barry Davies (Newlands), Mrs. Doreen Davies (Newnham-on-Severn), Mr. John Davies, Mrs. Jill Draper, Mrs. Sanna Drummond, Mr. Reg Duberley (Ruardean), Mr. Barry Eachus, Mr. and Mrs. Lyn Edmunds, Mrs. Cicely Edwards (Ross), Mr. and Mrs. Dennis Edwards, Miss Elizabeth (Bessie) England (London), Mrs. Joan Evans (Ross), Mr. and Mrs. John Exton, Mrs. Jennifer Freeman, Mr. and Mrs. Jack Foster, Mr. John Gabb (Ross), Mr. Andrew Gardiner (Ruardean), Mr. Colin Greasley, Mrs. Marjorie Green (Ross), Mr. Robert Green (Ross), Mrs. Libby Greenway (Peterstow), Mrs. Cynthia Griffiths (Ross), Mrs. Joan Griffiths, Mr. Martin Griffiths (Ross), Mr. John Hall (Ross), Mr. Donald Hamar, Mrs. Ann Harris, Mr. and Mrs. Adrian Harvey (Kings Caple), Mrs. Irene (Bunny) Haunton, Mr. Harvey Hemms (Ross), Mr. Jason Hicks, Mrs. Doris Hindmarsh, Mrs. Heather Hoddinott, Mr. and Mrs. Bernard Howls, Mrs. Heather Hurley (Hoarwithy), Mrs. Dorothy Jenkins (Ross), Mrs. Ada Jones (Ross), Mr. George Jones, Mr. Michael Jones (Mitcheldean), Mrs. Eunice Jordan, Mrs. Joan Joseph, Revd. Tony Kelk, Mr. Jethro Kirk

(Hereford), Mrs. Gina Lane (Ross), Mr. Peter Lee (Bridstow), Mr. Alan Lewis, Mr. and Mrs. John Lewis, Mr. Joe Lewis (Pontshill), Mrs. Roz Lowe (Goodrich), Miss Gina Marchetto (Ross), Mrs. Phyllis Marshall, Mrs. Madeleine McAdam (Symonds Yat), Mrs. Margaret Merrick, Mrs. Gwen Morgan, Mr. Mark Morgan (Bridgend), Mr. Mervyn Morgan, Mr. Timothy Morgan (Bristol), Mrs. Anthea Myers, Mrs. Peggy Nelson, Mr. Gerry Nicholas (Plymouth), Mr. Harry Paar (Essex), Mr. Alex Perry, Mrs. Jackie Perry, Mrs. Sheila Pimblett (Southampton), Mrs. Ann Powell (Coalway), Mrs. Pauline Powell, Dr. John Powell (Ross), Dr. Colin Price, Mr. J. Randall (formerly Head of Highways, Hereford County Council), Mr. Eric Rawlins (Ross), Mrs. Jean Reeves, Mr. Alan Ricketts (Coleford), Mrs. Heather Roberts, Mr. Jack Roberts (Cinderford), Mrs. Joyce Roberts, Mrs. Nancy Roberts (Milton Keynes), Mr. Steven Roberts (Walford School Headmaster), Mrs. Ann Shawcross, Mrs. Mary Sinclair-Powell (Ross), Mrs. Jill Smart, Mr. Colin Smith (Ross), Mrs. Dot Smith (Ross), Mr. Gerald Smith, Mr. Guy Smith, Mr. Francis Suttill, Mrs. Margery Spencer, Mrs. Jane Sweet-Escott, Mrs. Adeline Tarry (Derby), Mrs. Beryl Taylor, Mr. John Teiser, Mr. and Mrs. Jim Tonkin (Wigmore), Mr. Edward Watson (Ross), Mr. James ('Chappie') Webb, Mrs. Irys Wesson, Mr. and Mrs. Stanley Wheway, Mr. Barry Whitby, Mr. Jeremy Whitehouse (Ross), Mrs. Margaret Wilce (Ross), Mrs. Sheila Williams (Redditch), Mr. Richard Worrall, Mr. and Mrs. Ivor Worsfold (Ross), Mr. and Mrs. Richard Yemm.

For their specific contributions of advice, artwork and text for the publication:
Mr. Andrew Anderson for the photograph on the front cover
Mrs. Liz Baker for the drawings of the Churches and Walford Halt
Mr. Chris Barron IT advisor and for the digital photography
Mr. Peter Draper for the graphic design of the cover
Mrs. Jackie Perry for the drawing of the Parish Map
Mr. and Mrs. David Walshaw for their texts on Houses, Post Offices and Shops, and River, Road and Rail in addition to much invaluable local history information
and particularly to Mr. Geoff Gwatkin (Ross) for the 'pull-out' reproduction of the Walford Parish Tithe Map.

Thanks are due to a number of individuals and organisations for permission to use illustrations as indicated in the relevant caption and where their copyright is retained. Where acknowledgement may not have been fully given under the illustration, we would like to acknowledge the following: p.4: Ross-on-Wye and District Civic Society; pp.6 and 7: Dr. Nick Barton of Oxford; p.30: Revd. Tony Kelk, Vicar of Walford Parish Church; p.46: Trustees of the Jane Clarke Charity; pp.44, 47, 49, 180 and 181: Herefordshire Council, Department of Education.

To the following Organisations:
Clwyd-Powys Archaeological Trust for information
Herefordshire Council Archaeology Department for assistance
Herefordshire Council Research Department for information
Herefordshire Nature Trust for information
Herefordshire Record Office and the staff for assistance in finding
        documentary information
Herefordshire and Worcestershire Group for Regional Importance of
        Geological and Geomorphological Sites (R.I.G.S.)
Ross Gazette Office for access to their records
Ross Heritage Centre for information
Ross Library and the staff for assisting with searching for local history
        information
Walford Parish Council for financial assistance with research costs
Walford Parish residents for their information in the Millennium Housing
        Questionnaires
Walford Women's Institute for access to their local history accounts
        produced in 1954/5 and 1965.

Also to the publisher, Andy Johnson of Logaston Press, for his guidance, understanding and patience.

Finally, the Millennium Committee of the Walford Parish Residents' Association would like to acknowledge the generous grant aid awarded from the National Lottery Grant 'Millennium Festival Awards for All' Programme which made this publication possible.

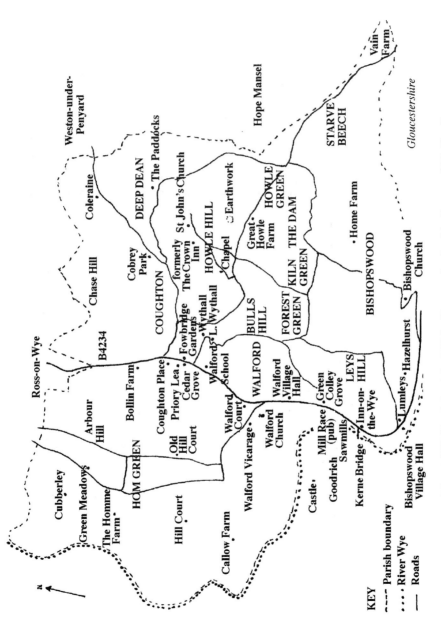

Map of Walford Parish, 2002. (Drawn by Jackie Perry of Walford)

INTRODUCTION

This is an account of the history of a South Herefordshire parish with several settlements in its diverse landscape. The acreage has increased over the years with a total of 4,977 acres in the civil parish in the year 2001. The map opposite shows the boundaries and main features of the parish.

The members of the Committee of the Walford Parish Residents' Association first put forward the idea of setting down the history of Walford and Bishopswood at their AGM in the autumn of 1999. The award of a 'Millennium Festival Awards for All' National Lottery Grant in the year 2000 enabled the idea to become a reality. Walford Parish Council were also generous in providing funding to help with some of the research costs.

The text has been compiled from many hours of research in the Herefordshire Record Office and the Ross Library, memories and narratives from local residents and also the many papers, photographs and snippets of information that have kindly been made available to the editors by members of the local community and from farther afield.

Inevitably, with an account such as this, there will be omissions and inaccuracies but it was felt important to publish before the start of the new millennium became too distant a memory. All the material used for the publication will be lodged at the Herefordshire Record Office for future reference. Should readers feel they wish to contribute further to the information about the parish, they are welcome to contact the editors so that additions can be made to the reference material.

The editors wish to convey their warmest thanks to everyone who has contributed to the publication of this book, in whatever way, with particular appreciation for the help of their patient partners and the publisher, Andy Johnson, of Logaston Press.

We hope you enjoy reading this book.

Virginia Morgan & Bridget Vine
April 2002

CHAPTER I
Geology and Archaeology

The geology of Walford and Bishopswood is complex and varied. The river Wye winds through the area, with this parish on its eastern side, and enters the Forest of Dean plateau at Kerne Bridge, to the south. Most of the river plain is Lower Devonian Old Red Sandstone, laid down c.400 m.y.a. (million years ago) with alluvium bordering the river. There is a band of very hard Quartz Conglomerate (sometimes called Pudding Stone) emerging from beneath the coal measures in the Forest of Dean and running through Mitcheldean, Wigpool and Hope Mansel to traverse the northern flanks of Howle Hill and the lower part of Bulls Hill, crossing the Wye just south of Kerne Bridge to continue along the Wye Valley. With this feature as a margin, the higher areas locally are based on Tintern Sandstone (Upper Devonian c.340 m.y.a.) and above that Carboniferous Limestone (c.300 m.y.a.). Howle Hill, which is a syncline (a downfold in the strata), is formed from a more recent sandstone which contains coal. This latter formation is called the Trenchard Coal measures.

Looking at a map of the geology of the parish (Sheet 233) one can see that the Tintern Sandstone generally surrounds the Carboniferous limestone areas, which in turn surround the Kiln Green, Howle and Coal Hill areas. There is, however, a 'tongue' of Tintern Sandstone along the Dry Brook in Bishopswood all the way from the river Wye, in the south, up to the Oxlet. Unfortunately there is no official geology map available for the northern part of this parish, but W. Dreghorn's *Geology explained in the Forest of Dean and the Wye Valley*, published in 1968, is a useful guide.

The Old Red Sandstone was laid down when this part of Britain lay near the Equator. Later, with progressive movement of the plates on the crust of the planet, the area moved north. This explains the colour of this Devonian period rock, which was deposited in desert conditions. These tectonic movements were accompanied by energetic upheavals in the shape of volcanoes, earthquakes and mountain formation. There were also extreme climatic changes

1

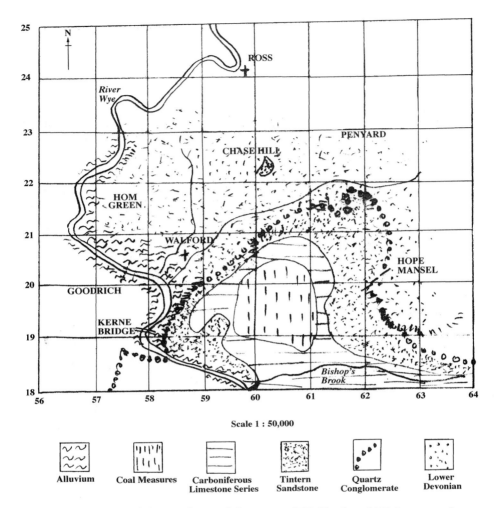

Scale 1 : 50,000

| Alluvium | Coal Measures | Carboniferous Limestone Series | Tintern Sandstone | Quartz Conglomerate | Lower Devonian |

An indication of the geology of the area of Walford and Bishopswood,
by Virginia Morgan

with resultant freezing and melting, the latter resulting in inundations. The rocks were often faulted and folded, and periods of deposition alternated with those of erosion. All these factors make the interpretation of the geology a job for experts; this account will attempt to simplify the picture.

There were several Ice Ages in the last million years. The Anglian one (350,000 to 250,000 years ago) resulted in glaciation on a broad north/west front as far south as Cheltenham in this part of the country, during which time this area was covered with ice. The most recent Late Devensian glaciation, lasting for approximately 15,000 years (from 30,000 years ago), ended on a irregular line running north of Birmingham, dropping south through Hereford, before looping westwards to cross the Bristol Channel south of Newport. South Herefordshire was south of its limit, but the climatic conditions would have been extreme.

Information has been kindly supplied by the R.I.G.S. group for Herefordshire and Worcestershire (Regional Importance of Geological and Geomorphological Sites) which explains some of the complexities. The original course of the Wye, locally, would have been south from the 'horse-shoe' bend at Ross, through the Coughton Marsh region. The marshy area is explained: 'Blockage of the valley by ice, or perhaps even a glacial lake as the ice melted, would cause the river to divert to a different route, resulting in the pronounced meander. .... The result is a large, flat area which is poorly drained, hence the marsh today.' Another meander is postulated by William Dreghorn in his book mentioned above. He thinks that a massive meander originated in Ross, then flowed in an easterly direction through the Weston-under-Penyard area, Bill Mills, behind Cobrey around the lower slopes of Chase Hill and through Tudorville in a north-westerly direction back to Ross to rejoin the main stream. The present Castlebrook stream is a tame remnant of this loop. He suggests that the meander was 'cut off within the last few thousand years in an inter-glacial period when the climate was much wetter and the erosive powers of rivers much greater'. Certainly the surge of water along the main road between Walford and Ross in a heavy rainstorm gives credence to the ancient route of this meander. The river Wye, famous for its scenic qualities, is reputed to have been called the Vaga—the wanderer—by the Romans.

With water as the theme it is interesting to note the numbers of wells and known springs in the parish. Among the old field names there at least 50 with water connotations, among them: Marks Well, Rogers Well (or Rudges Well) Beeches Well, Napple Well, Three Wells, Well Meadow and Well Piece. Springs exude from the side of Bulls Hill most years, and in wet weather others appear in unexpected places, sometimes causing severe landslips. Pool Meadow, the Waterfalls, Spout Meadow, Boggy Piece, Slippery Orchard, Pleasant Springs, Sharmans Pool Patch and Sinkway Piece are among these field names, and can be traced with the aid of the 1840 Tithe Map and its accompanying Apportionment. Another intriguing water feature is the sink-hole at Dunderhole Farm which is where 'a stream of water of considerable size goes into the earth (supposed to be a disused mine) and re-appears at about a mile distant and thence flows into the river Wye'. One explanation of the name is 'thunderhole', from the tremendous noise as the water disappears.

Water and the underlying strata provided the essential ingredients of the early industries of iron-smelting and the more recent one of lime-burning in Bishopswood and Walford.

Rollo Gillespie of R.I.G.S. has kindly provided detailed information on the unusual structures underlying Howle Hill. In his words 'The Lower Dolomite,

Whitehead Limestone and Drybrook Sandstone are missing at Howle Hill and the Lower Trenchard Coal Measures lie unconformably on the Lower Limestone Shales'. An unconformity is the actual physical break between two series of rocks. It represents a long interval of time between the two different types of sedimentation, so that, in the case of Howle Hill a very old rock formation (*c*.340 m.y.a.) immediately underlies a much more recent one (*c*.260 m.y.a.) and the intervening layers have been lost, either through folding and erosion, or through denudation and erosion of the 'sandwich' interior. This juxtaposition of lime sources and coal extraction proved very useful to our ancestors. The report continues: 'This led to a mutually supportive mining/quarrying industry for lime burning in the 19th century. Around 17 quarries were in use, and the Causeway Quarry (O.S. 603203) is the last remaining substantial exposure of the north edge of the Lower Limestone Shales which stretches through South Wales'. Both R.I.G.S. and the writer believe that the few remaining lime kilns (at least 10) in the parish should be protected for future generations.

The earliest evidence of man in this area is from the Upper Palaeolithic time, the most recent period of the Old Stone age (*c*.12,000 years ago). With the improving climatic conditions this period merged into the Mesolithic period, the 'Mid' Stone Age, around 8,000 years ago. In the words of Dr. Stanley Stanford 'Thus *Homo Sapiens sapiens*, emerging as a distinct species by 35,000 or 40,000 bc seems to have been in occupation of north-west Europe during the final

One of the lime kilns in Walford in 1992 (top), with its charge hole (below). (Photos by Virginia Morgan, courtesy of Ross-on-Wye & District Civic Society)

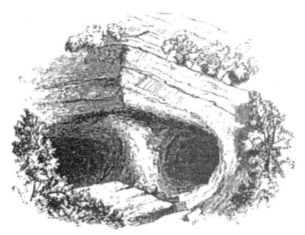

King Arthur's Cave, Great Doward from Forest of Dean *by H.G. Nicholls, 1858*

phase of the last ice-age'; ('bc' means uncorrected radiocarbon analysis, i.e. plus or minus 40 years). As England was then joined to the Continent, in the summer months migrating hunters could have traversed the land, using their flint tools to skin and butcher their prey. Dr. Stanford continues: 'there may have been long periods when a local retreat of ice allowed the hunters to establish them-selves permanently, for centuries possibly, on the edge of the forest or in the shelter of caves'. The nearest evidence of such occupation is the series of caves and rock shelters in the Upper Wye Valley, with the most famous example being King Arthur's Cave on the lower slopes of the Doward, Whitchurch.

This double-chambered cave was investigated by the Revd. W.S. Symonds in 1871/72 and photographs exist showing the workman barrowing soil out of the cave. His team excavated down to three metres, finding bones of extinct species, like the woolly rhinoceros and mammoth. In addition, remains of other ice-age fauna were found, including the cave lion, hyena, horse, bison, great Irish deer and reindeer. Some of these finds can be seen in Hereford Museum.

Several other excavations have been carried out in this area, with the most recent series of investigations and trench excavations (1993/97) led by Dr. Nick Barton and Dr. Alison Roberts, who had a team of diggers, geologists, botanists and experts in small mammal and snail analysis. Flint artefacts and remains of red deer were found in a well stratified layer, radiocarbon dated to about 10,000 bc. Much interesting material was recovered from areas that had been disturbed by the previous digs, and/or mining activities in the cave; this was achieved through careful observation while sieving the sediments. The most exciting finds came from a compact area on the inner side of one of the chambers; in the Director's words: 'these deposits yielded an exceptionally rich quantity of finds including lithic artefacts, faunal remains in various conditions of preservation, Bronze Age pot sherds and three Mesolithic perforated marine shell beads ... the discovery of these artefacts also provides the first tangible links between the human activities at this cave and at Madawg Rock Shelter'. The last named

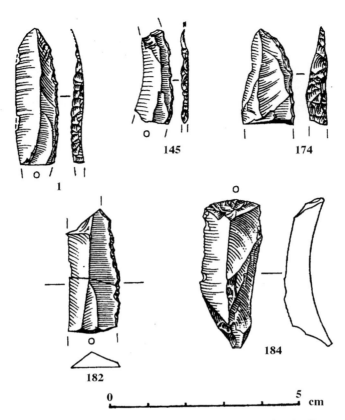

Flint artefacts recovered from King Arthur's Cave
in Dr. R.N.E. Barton's excavation of 1995

rock shelter is near King Arthur's Cave, to the south-east, and was one of the 20 sites examined by this team, 12 of which provided locations with archaeological and palaeontological deposits.

In 1997 several perforated cowrie shells were found in Madawg; these were identical to those from King Arthur's Cave in the previous year. Additionally, several Mesolithic microliths were recovered from Madawg. A charred sloe stone and a charred hazel-nut shell were radiocarbon dated, one dating from between 8,780 and 8,640 years before the present. It was surmised that the cowrie shells had been for decoration, as each one was pierced in two places, as if for adornment. With the discovery of so many Late Palaeolithic and Mid- to Late Mesolithic tools, carefully made for specialised jobs, the conclusion that skilled and intelligent humans had lived, or camped, in these caves and rock shelters seems indisputable. The nearest available deposits of easily-worked, high-quality flint-stone is over 100 miles away, so planning and possible barter or trade is also indicated.

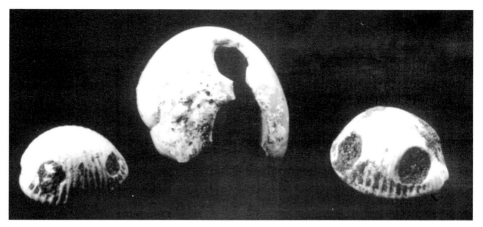

Perforated marine shells, two cowrie and one periwinkle (Mesolithic) recovered from the alcove in the Second Chamber, King Arthur's Cave, 1996. (Courtesy of Dr. R.N.E. Barton)

As the climate improved mixed woodlands became established and the hunter/gatherers were no longer dependent on their caves or shelters, and could roam further afield. Evidence of their activities in the form of crafted tools have been found, but in this area only those made of stone survive. There are many reports of Mesolithic finds in the Forest of Dean, and at Skenfrith and Llanishen near Monmouth. Near Ross, single, isolated small stone tools have been found on Chase Hill, and at Great Howle in this parish, Meolithic material was found near the spring area which feeds the Lodge Grove Brook. This last location was selected by the Neolithic and Bronze Age people who followed on, and, in the first century A.D., by a family involved in ironworking.

The next period, the Neolithic (*c*.6000 to 4000 years ago), is characterised

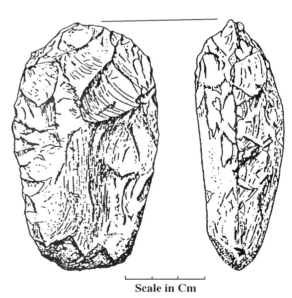

Scale in Cm

A polished Neolithic stone axe (rhyolite) found at Bulls Hill, Walford, by Mervyn Morgan in December 1992

by the establishment of settled farming. Longer, slimmer axes made from flint or other igneous rock are found dating from this time, and in 1992 a polished axe/adze was dug up by Mervyn Morgan in the grounds of Westfield House, Bulls Hill. It is made of a volcanic material, rhyolite, and was probably carried from the North Wales quarry near Penmaenmawr. In Neolithic times axes were hafted, or fitted to a handle, for more varied uses.

Nearby his wife found a flint knife. Both could originally have been unearthed, without appreciating what had been found, when a large underground water cistern was installed by the owner of the neighbouring property in the early 1900s, only to be reburied.

The Archaeology Department of Herefordshire Council has a valuable record of all archaeological finds, with details of their provenance and type. This is available for public scrutiny, and they are always anxious to have any new finds or sites reported to them. With their permission items found appear in the following two tables as the Sites and Monuments Record for Walford Parish. Some items are noted from *The Archaeology and History of Ancient Dean and the Wye Valley* by Bryan Walters (pub, 1992):

PERIOD	TYPE	PLACE FOUND	S.O.No.	DATE OF ENTRY IN RECORD	REFERENCE
Mesolithic	flint arrow-tips	The Park Great Howle	614189	1985	The *New Regard* Journal
Mesolithic	tools (not detailed)	Great Howle near spring of Lodge Grove Brook		*	*
Neolithic	flint scraper	Farm Homme Green	580222	1989	J. Dinn, Heref. City Museum
Neolithic	flint flake	Farm belonging to Mr. Boynton	593226	1952	H. White 1989 & TWNFC 1952
Neolithic	axe/adze rhyolite	Bulls Hill	566203	1992	H.M. Morgan
Neolithic	flint knife	Bulls Hill	566202	1994	C.A.V. Morgan
Bronze Age	Bronze spear-head	Coughton Marsh during draining	588214	*c.*1871	TWNFC, in Glouc. Museum
Bronze Age	hoard of four axes	Bishopswood area	*	1993	SMR Heref.
Bronze Age	discoidal flint knife	Walford	584227	*	J. Dinn 1989 text Heref. City Mus.
Bronze Age	flint barb and tang arrow-head	Old Wood	616185	1985	*New Regard*
Bronze Age	earthwork circular tumulus	near Walford Court	588206	investigated 1970	N. Bridgewater
Iron Age	NO RECORDED FINDS although the Great Howle Hill earthworks site is sometimes referred to as an Iron Age Hill Fort (see above opposite)				

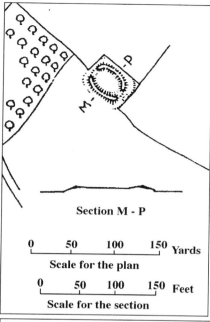

Section M - P

0   50   100   150 Yards
Scale for the plan

0   50   100   150 Feet
Scale for the section

The plan of the possible Iron Age hillfort on Howle Hill, reproduced from the RCHM Vol. II.

The earthworks at Howle Hill (SO 611 201) are sometimes described as Great Howle Camp. The Sites and Monuments record describe the site as 'a roughly rectangular enclosure with rounded angles and rampart with openings, perhaps modern at NW and SE ends'. Another entry reads: 'the enclosure is more oval than rectangular with indications of a ploughed out ditch and strength of the bank, both exterior and interior, where best preserved, which suggest possible remains of a ring motte. The openings are modern lowerings of the bank'.

PERIOD	TYPE	PLACE FOUND	S.O.No.	DATE OF ENTRY IN RECORD	REFERENCE
Roman	coin hoard (Appx. 18,000 coins)	Bishopswood	598185	1895	Hereford Museum (part of collection)
Roman	pottery and parts of roof tiles	Old Wood, nr. Lodge Grove and brook	619190 & 613187	1985	*New Regard*, 1985
Roman	pottery	Lodge Grove Wood	610190	*	Description Hereford Museum
Roman	pottery fragment	farm belonging to Mr. Boynton	593226	1952	H. White, 1989 & TWNFC, 1952
Roman	coin, AD 340	*	596204	1956	finder A.T. Jones of Bulls Hill TWNFC, 1956
Medieval	lynchets five terraces	Castle-Brook Farm	608216	before 1932	RCHM Vol. II
Medieval	ruined chapel	Coughton	594212	before 1754	Taylor's map of Herefordshire
Medieval	earthworks, deserted medieval village	Homme Farm	578222	before 1932	RCHM Vol. II p.167
Medieval	cross, octagonal shaft, C14/15	Hom Green	579221	*	H&W records
Tudor	love token (Henry VIII)	*	588206	since 1999	found by metal detectorist
C19/20	limekilns (10)	mainly on Howle Hill	various	post. med.	*Lime kilns in Walford Parish* pub.1993

* = details not available

The industrial archaeology of the parish will be described in more detail in the chapters on Agriculture and Industry.

Chapter II
History

The name Walford, it is thought, derives from *Walecford*, the 'Welc(s)h ford'. This ford could have been the ancient one near Flanesford, known as Priory Ford, or alternatively the one across the river Wye opposite Goodrich Castle. The route across the ford might have come from *Ariconium*, Weston under Penyard, to continue to Monmouth, or *Blestium* as it was known by the Romans. Several authorities think that earlier British trackways can be traced along a line from Merrivale, Ross, to Arbour Hill, behind Old Hill Court and on to the Goodrich crossing. As outlined in chapter five the road from Ross through Hom was turnpiked after the Turnpike Act of 1749 and the line down to the riverbank, under Goodrich Castle, is still known locally as Boat Lane.

The Revd. Thomas Dudley Fosbroke, a respected antiquarian, was the curate and, later, vicar of St. Leonard's Church, Walford, and St. John the Baptist Church, Ruardean, for 32 years, until his death on 1 January 1842. Among his works is one, published in 1821, entitled: *Ariconensia, or Archaeological Sketches of Ross and Archenfield*. This contains notes on places of local interest, among them the Roman settlement which some think was the precursor of Ross on Wye, *Ariconium*, in Weston under Penyard and Bromsash. This large complex has only been partially excavated, but it has yielded considerable evidence of iron-working, in the form of scoriae (slag waste after a metal is smelted out of its ore) and forges, in addition to the foundations of other large buildings and tessellated pavements. Founded *c*.A.D.50, it has been described as the Merthyr Tydfil of the Roman occupation of Britain. It was a military fort as well as a settlement and industrial site. Fosbroke validates its importance by quoting the *Anglo-Saxon Chronicle*: 'In this year 418 [A.D.] the Romans collected all the treasures of Gold which they had in Britain, and part they concealed in the ground that no man might afterwards find them. And part they carried with them into Gaul'. (The word 'gold' is figurative in that the chroniclers meant wealth rather than the actual precious metal). He then attests to the quantity of coins discovered at *Ariconium*, before continuing: 'we are to expect coins at such places as were of great note in the year 418 when the Romans on leaving the island hid their treasure, and the greater the towns were the treasure is so much the larger, and consequently more coins are discovered in or about such towns as were of more considerable note'.

This has direct relevance to the large hoard of coins found at Bishopswood in 1895. Around 18,000 coins were found in three earthenware urns on the property of Harry McCalmont, then owner of Bishopswood Estate. His workmen were clearing an area close to All Saints' Church, Bishopswood, when they came across the first of three jars among a heap of stones about 23 cms. below the surface. The jars were 32 cms. high and nearly 13 cms. across the mouth and base, and had been enclosed by rough walling. The owner of the land kindly gave the find to the Woolhope Field Club.

Subsequently, a coin expert examined 17,550 of the copper coins and pronounced that all but three of them had been minted in the Constantine period (A.D.290-360) and many had Christian symbols, so that they must have been deposited after A.D.340. Eighty-four coins were given to Hereford Museum, some to that at Gloucester and 135 to the museum at Newcastle on Tyne. The coins were minted at a variery of places, including one at Alexandria, one at Carthage and 583 at Trier; 384 were illegible. A resident in Bishopswood, Colin Greasley, has pointed out that the coins were generally of a low denomination and could have come from an army paymaster's paychest.

Other significant Roman coin hoards found in Herefordshire were on Coppett Hill, and in Combe Wood, near Aston Ingham, in 1855; in the latter find several thousand small brass coins were concealed in two chests, ready for transport. Many

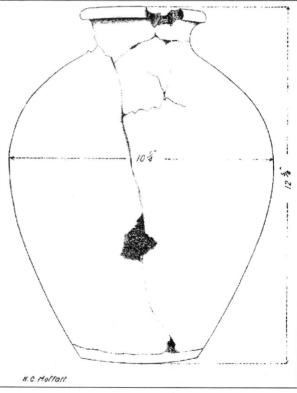

Jar which contained Roman coins found on the Bishopswood Estate in 1895.
(From TWNFC, *Vol.XIX)*

coins had also been excavated at *Ariconium*, but their interest was outshone by the 'urns, statues, bronzes, earrings, fibulae (a decorative brooch of safety-pin form), pins, nails, keys ... and a large bronze head with ram's horns' found in the vicinity.

The picture of the period before and after the Roman occupation of this area is hazy. The tribe to the west of the Wye were the Silures, and those in the area we now call Gloucestershire were the Dobunni; it is thought that Central Herefordshire was occupied by the Decangi. The hill fort on Chase Hill, Ross, (22 acres) was probably the stronghold of the tribe (possibly the Decangi) that controlled this part of the county. Christianity came here before the Romans left Britain. The British kingdom of Ergyng was the legendary birthplace of Saint Dubricius and part of this large territory became Archenfield which was situated on the west bank of the Wye, stretching from the Monnow to Wilton. St. Dubricius (about 450-522A.D.) established a college at Hentland which, by tradition, catered for 1,000 scholars. He became Bishop of Llandaff and, later, Archbishop of Caerleon, retiring to a monastery on Bardsey Island.

The Saxon invaders reached the Wye *c*.590 when Hereford city was founded. Under Penda the land east of the Wye became part of his kingdom of Mercia. Archenfield, on the west of the Wye, came to act as a 'buffer' zone between the Welsh and the English, its men holding a formidable reputation for courage in adversity.

From Saxon times the tenants-in-chief who held their manors from the king were expected to build a church on their manor, to install a priest and to provide him with enough land to make his living. This was called Glebe land and in Walford it extended from the Church as far as the land, given in 1873, by the Church authorities for the new National School, now Walford Primary School. It also included the land on the opposite side of the B4234, on the site of the yard used by Symonds the Builders, now a new, small housing development. Other pockets of glebe land are detailed in the church terriers described on pp.18-19.

The church was frequently built close to the dwelling of the lord of the manor, and his tenants made up the congregation. It is quite possible that the original manor was centred on Walford Court. The parish, the area under the spiritual care of the parson, was often linked with the manor where there were many years of uninterrupted family 'lordship' and was often delineated by a substantial hedge. The fields on the 1840 Tithe Map are reminders of these times, with fields called 'innage' (in hedge) running parallel to the present ecclesiastical boundary.

There is a theory that the great earthwork built on the orders of Offa, King of Mercia, in the latter years of the 8th century A.D. came through this parish. This 80 mile long Dyke was intended to demarcate the boundary between the Anglo-Saxon kingdom of Mercia (the present Midlands was the centre of Mercia) and the British kingdoms in what is now Wales, and was a huge effort of engineering. If King Alfred's biographer, Asser, can be believed, the Dyke ran from 'sea to sea', that is from the Dee estuary in the north to the Severn estuary in the south. However, modern historians place the northern end of this huge linear earthwork at Treuddyn, near Wrexham, running south to Rushock Hill in Herefordshire. South of that point there are many gaps and there is continuing debate about the authenticity of the stretches of earthwork to Lydbrook and on to Sedbury Cliffs, both in Gloucestershire. One theory describes a route in this district from the Cleeve (Ross) across Duxmere (*dic-moer*, 'the Dyke boundary'), to the Vine Tree Inn on the Walford Road. The supposed trace disappears until a bank forming a hedge on the breast of Leys Hill, which continues into Bishopswood above All Saints' Church. Again the traces disappear but the name Marstow (Ruardean) is significant as the Dyke was a 'mark', or boundary. On this alignment a mile of the Dyke reappears near the site of Lydbrook Viaduct to continue to Collins Grove. Much of the route was demarcated with holly trees, and again this name is a pointer as *celyn* (hollies) may have been transmuted into Collins. Wherever possible natural features, like rivers or cliffs, were used as the barrier. This stretch ended on the edge of Coldwell Rocks, a substantial 'mark'. This route is described by James G. Wood in the *Victoria County History of Herefordshire*, published in 1908, but is disputed by most of the other experts on the Dyke.

There were both royal and episcopal manors before the Normans arrived, and Walford was one of the latter when the Domesday Survey commissioners started their country-wide survey. This has provided historians with an invaluable account of the time and was completed *c*.1086.

Walford was in Bromsash Hundred and belonged to the Canons of Hereford; the entry outlines the manor:

> In Walecford [Walford] are 7 hides paying geld [tax]. On the demesne is 1 plough and there could be 2 more. [There are] 6 villeins and 4 bordars with 5 ploughs. There are 14 acres of meadow and 3 hayes. The villeins pay 10s. for the waste land.

Originally a 'hide' was the amount of agricultural land that could be cultivated in a year using one plough with an eight-ox team, but later historians believe that it was an area varying between 120 and 180 acres depending on the place and the date. The demesne was land in the occupation of the lord of the manor, and the villeins and bordars were peasants subject to him. A 'haye' was a hedged enclosure. The waste land was common land on which the local people could graze their animals, with allocations of numbers of stock to each family.

Under Saxon rule districts had been divided into Hundreds and periodically the men of each hundred gathered at their moot to make judicial or administrative decisions. These moots were situated at memorable places such as fords, ancient burial places or barrows, and landmark trees. Many of the hundreds were named after trees, such as Bromsash (Brooms Ash) and Greytree. At the time of the Domesday survey, Bromsash Hundred comprised 22 'manors', four of which—Whittington, Walford, Ross and Upton Bishop—belonged to the Church of Hereford under Bishop Robert de Loisinga. At a later date Bromsash Hundred was absorbed into that of Greytree.

The manorial system is complicated. Fortunately, in his unpublished manuscript (written in 1983) Jonathan Claxton of Walford gave an explanation. In his words:

> The rulers of the various regions granted their lands in 'manors' to 'tenants-in-chief'. In return these tenants paid as rent a limited period of military service each year, accompanied by their armed retainers. The tenants were also responsible for local administration, and for settling cases brought to the ruler's courts. Disloyalty to the ruler meant the loss of their manors, and at the death of a lord of the manor, the heir, if approved by the ruler, would have to make a payment of what might be called death duties. These tenants-in-chief granted some of their land to their armed retainers, who in turn gave service to the lord of the manor, and also administration and court service at manorial level, e.g. at Ross. Agricultural work was carried out by the villeins (farmers) who produced their own and their landlord's food supplies, and paid some money rent for their holdings. The villeins were not allowed to leave their holdings, or the manor, unless they could buy their freedom from this restriction. This buying of freedom, or 'manumission', was possible and a fairly regular rate was charged. All tenants, of any variety, had to pay some type of death duty before they could succeed to the holding. This was the system in operation in late Saxon times but nearly all the Saxon tenants-in-chief lost their estates after the battle of Hastings.

The various estates of Herefordshire were divided amongst the King, the Bishop and Canons of Hereford, Roger de Laci and Ralf de Mortimer and other marcher lords. Walford was 'held of' the Bishop and Canons of Hereford and this continued until the reign of Elizabeth I. The bishops, while lords of the manor, received all the rents from the land in addition to part of the income from the cornmills, fishponds and dovecotes. The *Red Book*, compiled for the Bishops of Hereford in about 1285, contains much detail about the administration of these manors.

The Bishop of Hereford could lease out his manors, and it is recorded that this was done on several occasions. Hugh de Walford, in 1182 had this privilege, in return for a 'knight's fee'. This fee varied on the quality of the soil, which had to be sufficiently fertile to allow a knight and his family to subsist for one year.

Three other de Walfords are mentioned in an account by W.H. Cooke: Thomas, who did military service for King Henry III; John who, in 1282 'accompanied the King's forces into Wales for the period of 40 days, with a horse fully caparisoned, as tenant by knight-service to Bishop Cantilupe'; and Henry who was the witness to a deed of release relating to a house in Walford, in 1336.

In 1422 the Bishop leased the lordship of Walford to a kinsman, John Thornby, with permission to farm the land for life, with a rental of 50s. 4d. and 'an instant payment of twelve pennies'. Other tenants were John Chambers (1441) for a period of 20 years, rental 12d., and his tenancy was followed by those of John Warner, John Tremayne and John Hunter, the last named the bishop's 'beloved servitor'; his lease began in 1516.

The area in and around Ross was divided into the manor of Ross Borough (*Rosse Burgus* in the *Red Book*) and Ross Foreign (*Rosse Forinsecus*). Ross was one of several market towns in Herefordshire and each of these was surrounded by an area of agricultural land; in this district this was Ross Foreign. Ross Foreign was a separate manor and stretched from Bishop's Brook in the south, to the southern limit of Brampton Abbotts in the north. The western boundary was the Wye and to the north-east Upton Bishop and so included much of current day Walford Parish. Both these manors were under the lordship of the Bishop. However, Linton, to the east and south-east, belonged to the King, and by 1285 he had granted it, together with Eccleswall and some land and a mill at Coughton, to the Talbot family. Up until 1885 Coughton Marsh was still partly in the manor of Ross Foreign and partly in the manor of Eccleswall.

In 1559 Queen Elizabeth I took possession of the manors of Ross Borough and Ross Foreign. Initially she granted Ross Foreign to Edmund Downing and Henry Best (in 1588), but they assigned their interest to the Queen's favourite, Robert, Earl of Essex. In 1595, on the request of Essex, all the Crown lands in both Ross and Walford were granted to Sir Gelly Meyrick and Sir Henry Lindley. However, the Earl of Essex fell from favour, and was executed in 1601; Meyrick shared the same fate. Subsequently the manors of Ross Borough and Ross Foreign passed into separate hands, the former going to Sir Henry Lindley and the latter to Thomas Crompton.

On Elizabeth I's death in 1603 Essex's widow bought both manors for £7,000 and in due course they passed to her son, the 3rd Earl of Essex. When he died without children they passed to his sisters, one of whom was Lady Frances Devereux, Marchioness of Hertford. Her husband was restored as 2nd Duke of Somerset in 1660 with the return of the monarchy after the end of the Civil War. Lady Frances, by then the Dowager Duchess, had Ross Market House built around 1670. On her death in 1674 the manors were inherited by the 4th Duke of Somerset who died in the following year. The manors descended to the husband of the Dowager Duchess's grand-daughter, the 1st Viscount Weymouth. The estates stayed with this family until the death of the 3rd Lord Weymouth (who became the Marquis of Bath in 1789) and in 1818 the latter's son auctioned both manors.

The family names become more familiar at this stage. In 1818 Captain Kingsmill Evans bought Ross Borough and Ross Foreign for £4,400, and on his death they passed to his sister's son, Kingsmill Manley Power. In 1865 the Ross Town Commissioners bought from Manley Power of Hill Court all his rights as lord of the manor of Ross and thus they became owners of the Manor Pound (near the Pound Inn, now the Royal Hotel), the Market House and the Market Tolls. According to Mrs. Leeds of Ross, a respected historian, the sum agreed upon was £1,000 but the purchase was not completed until the 1880s with the Town Commissioners paying interest until the completion of the deal.

The care of the parish woodlands was of prime importance and they were highly prized both for the opportunities they provided for the 'chase' and the value of the timber. Heather Hurley and Pat Hughes, in their book *The Story of Ross,* point out that the Bishop of Hereford kept the woodlands 'in his own hands' and they were not in the rent roll. The woods at Chase Wood and Penyard, Tedgewood (Upton Bishop) and Bishopswood were owned by the Diocese of Hereford. In 1228 the King ordered a 'perambulation' (an ordered walk or survey by foot) to establish the boundaries between the Bishop's territory and his own. Comments from Revd. T.D. Fosbroke are relevant when he describes a 'Chace' as 'a spot of ground where animals were preserved for the sake of hunting, and legally recognized by Royal Grant, Privilege or Prescription. It differed from a Park in being unenclosed and from a Forest in smaller extent, the latter of which belonged to the Kings only'. Recent research reveals that some of the land for the 'chace' was frequently open grassland as dense woodland would have prevented sighting and hunting the deer.

The protection of the woodland was sometimes the responsibility of a member of the bishop's household. The household roll of Bishop Swinfield describes a daring depredation on the night of Wednesday in Whitsun week, June 1305 when 'a party of 16 in number entered the wood within the Manor of Ross and, in spite of the Bishop's servants, felled and carried off his trees'. There was immediate retribution; the guilty parties were denounced by name in the churches of Walford, Ruardean, Weston, 'Castle' Goodrich and Hope Mansel on every Sunday evening. Communion was denied to them, until they had sworn an oath that 'they would transgress in this manner no more and had submitted to the exemplary punishment of walking once round the Church of Ross in their shirts on a Sunday and once round the Market on a Market-day'. The ringleaders of this gang were named as Thomas and John Clarkson, of

Mitcheldean, and they were ordered to bring into Ross churchyard the trees they had felled and removed.

In 1441 Alexander Jordan, one of the Bishop of Hereford's valets, was made the keeper of the wood, 'commonly known as Bishops wood', receiving among his remuneration, a robe equivalent to that of other valets in the episcopal household, to be presented every Christmas. Subsequent custodians of the wood and 'chase' of Bishopswood were John Grey, gentleman, (in 1513), and Richard Willison, gentleman, who was described as the *custos* of the woods, and paid a rent of £4. A directive from the Bishop was issued in 1523 to inform all the parishioners of Walford, Goodrich, Bridstow and Foy that to capture and carry away hawks in the 'Chace' of Bishopswood was forbidden, and that offenders would be fined for this offence.

There must have been several other instances of trespass, because other attempts to exercise the right of 'estovers' are recorded, under which local free-holders were permitted to take reasonable quantities of fallen wood as fire-wood. 'Pannage' was another privilege whereby the freeholders' pigs could roam and graze on acorns in the due season.

In an attempt to prevent these incursions the Lord of the Manor and his wife (the Earl of Clanicarde and Lady Frances), together with Robert, Earl of Essex, took a case for judgement in Chancery against the trespassing free-holders. In 1614 a compromise was decreed; the estimated 2,000 acres of Bishop's Wood, formerly part of the waste land of the manor of Ross Foreign, was to be divided between 'Noble Parties' and the freeholders. Under this arrangement the litigants were to have half of the common, free of manorial rights, and the respondents were to enjoy their half of the 'said ground or wood called Bishop's Wood and the wood thereupon growing, with the appurtenances, without lett or interruption of the then owners of the Manor'. The names of the freeholders were listed; they included John Stratford of Walford, Esq.; John Markey, William Kyrle, John Dew, Lumley Dew, all of Walford, Gentlemen; Margaret Rudhall, of Rudhall, a spinster and gentle-woman; and several yeomen, among them Richard Clarke, Edward Yemm, Walter Harris, James Hardwicke, John Croose, Thomas Griffiths and John Seymour, 'all of Walford'.

Two terriers detail the site, boundaries, acreages and occupiers of land and property which was administered by the incumbent of the church in 1614 and 1635. The first begins: 'A Terrier of all the Howses Gleebe Lands and Teithinges belonginge to the Parsonage of Walford in the Countie of Hereford according to the presentment of Gregory Burghill clearke, [and] James Hardwicke and Launcellot Pierce, Churchwardens of the same Parish'. (The vicar was described as a clerk in those days.) There are 14 'items' which include the Parsonage 'with Two Barnes, One Beastehowse and One Stable thereunto belonginge' and several pieces of land with field names which occur again in the Tithe Map drawn up in 1840. Among these are the Moores, the Wariffield, Catlands, the Bromage and Stony Furlongs. Additionally the terrier claims most of the 'Teythe, Corne and Haye within the parishe of Walford and Ruardyne'. An additional list detailing all the houses, land and tithes belonging to the Vicarage of Walford was attached, with the same signatories and date. This has only four items: the Vicarage with one barn and one stable 'thereunto adjoyning', a half-acre close, the churchyard, estimated to contain one acre, and the private tithes of the parishes of Walford and Ruardean together with all the tithes of the hay and corn from the private landowners.

The later Terrier of 1635 is entitled 'A true coppie of the terrier of Glebe Lands and porcions of tythe belonging to the Vicaridge of Walford in the Diocese of Hereford taken by the Churchwardens, and some others of the said parishe'. The first item describes a dwelling house of three bays and a barn and stable of two bays, together with a garden and a 'little plot of meadowe ground adjoyninge, conetyning both about halfe an acre'. The signatures are those of the Vicar James Westphalen, and William Hodges and William Fisher, both Churchwardens. The 50 items that follow all relate to the tythes due on different parcels of land, and in many cases the landowners are mentioned. These include Richard Clerke 'the elder' who had land 'lyinge by the high waie leadinge from Homme to Goodriche passage'. He also owned half an acre near The Hope (Hopes Wood is above the present Daycroft Farm). Other landowners were James Kyrle, John Markey, Lord Viscount Scudamore, Edmund Harris and 'Mistris Dewe'. The last named lived at 'Withall Crafte'. The Wythall or White Hall was then called White Croft. One of the occupiers of land belonging to Viscount Scudamore was a Richard Chinne. 'Cowghtons Cross' and 'Cowghtons Mill' are noted in the details of tithes due, with several allusions to the 'Chappell' where the land was in the possession of Mr. Stratford. The last item reads: 'The tythe of one acre of arable land of the land of Widdowe Smith lyinge in a place called Withall Crafte neare Puestie'. This place name is particularly interesting as the hamlet of Pusty (or Pewsty) no longer exists (see also pp.150-151) where the map shows its location below the lower slopes of Bulls Hill towards the stream behind Walford School).

Other old field names in the parish are recorded in a lease dated 1715 which 'recited' the surrender of a former lease by Mary Phillips, widow of Stephen late Chanter to John Kyrle Esq. in November 1710. The parcels of land detailed include the Moores, Stowfield, Quarry Field, Church field, Lower Bromidge, and 'one acre lying nearing Goodrich Boat with the lands of the Honourable Markey on all or most parts thereof and also one other plot called Higgins Plott'. The document concludes 'all which premises are situate lying and being in Walford aforesaid ... and are part and parcel of the Revenues of the said

Walford and Bishopswood. Part of Bryant's map of Herefordshire, 1835

Chantership and were formerly in the possession of Sir Edward Harley Knight decd. ... excepting one barn'. The signatories are Mr. Bond and Mr. Seymour of Walford.

Ross, only a short distance away, was badly stricken by the plague in 1637, with 315 deaths recorded on the ancient cross in Ross churchyard, but no records have been found of Walford being similarly afflicted. The earlier country-wide outbreak of the Black Death, as it was called, or bubonic plague, in 1348, which killed over one third of the population of England and swept through to Wales in 1350, may well have affected this area.

The Civil War that raged between 1642 and 1651 had repercussions in this parish. Walford Court was designed to resist attack. The historian-vicar of Walford, the Revd. Fosbroke, provides more detail: 'It consists of a succession of walled courts commanding each other, and there is no approach to the

20

house but under direct and flanking fires from behind walls and out-houses. In the orchard, behind the house, is a mount for a magazine, upon which a cannon might be placed for discharging grape'. It was the son of the owner of this house, Colonel Robert Kyrle (1613-1669), who attracted more attention because he changed sides twice. There were few families among the landed gentry of Herefordshire who supported the Parliamentarians, but the Kyrles were among these, both the family at Much Marcle and here in Walford. After serving with the armies in Germany and Holland, Robert Kyrle took the commission of Lieutenant in the forces of Parliament, and was soon promoted to Captain. After 'assisting' in the capture of Hereford in October 1642 (and becoming the Commander of Horse) he became conscience-stricken and joined the King's army based at Oxford. Promotion followed and he was appointed Lieut.-Colonel in the garrison of Monmouth. While leading a party out of town for provisions they were set upon by Col. Massey with his Roundhead troops. In order to avoid retribution for his treachery, Robert Kyrle practised another one—he offered to march in front of the enemy's troops. On his approach, thinking Kyrle was leading his own troops, the guard let down the drawbridge. Col. Massey's troops followed and demanded the town for Parliament. In the words of a contemporary report, the ruse was successful: '... the garrison was so exceedingly amazed that some of them fled away and left their arms, and the rest called out for quarter ...'. Robert Kyrle was appointed Governor of Monmouth and its castle and Parliament discharged him from 'all delinquencies committed by him since 1642'. In subsequent years he worked hard to reconcile the Commonwealth authorities with the Royalists and actively co-operated in the restoration of the monarchy.

An account of a perambulation of the bounds of Bishopswood, dated 1683, gives the names of places and people, whilst the whole document provides a valuable insight into the past. The walk took place in November 1682, and many of the subscribers' names are familiar: Richard Bond, John Young, Walter Cubberley, John Croose and Thomas Wensley among them. The preamble reads:

> Whereas severall of the freeholders and others of ye Parish of Walford within ye said Mannor having enclosed severall parcels of land out of a certaine Comon belonging to the said freeholders of the said parrish called Bishopswood into theyer owne freelands and tenantcyes adjoining to the said wood and digged up their hedges betweene their said lands and the said Comon whereby the antient bounds thereof in all likelyhood would have been lost if not timely prevented.

A Court leet (hearing or inquiry) had been held to hear the grievances and it was apparently decreed that the subscribers to the petition should walk the bounds of what they considered to be the Bishopswood freeholders' land to assess any incursions or encroachments. They met at 'the mouth of the lane entering into the said common at Bulls Hill' and detailed very carefully their route until they returned to their starting place. As Colin Greasley notes, this survey traces the boundary of the common together with the names and locations of inhabitants around the boundary at that time, and gives a picture of the pattern of scattered independent settlements that are evident today.

The chief activity in this large parish has always been agriculture, whether for subsistence by the smaller land-users on the higher ground, or for profit and prestige by the large estate owners on the fertile lower land. Chapter six provides more detail on this. The other source of income was the establishment of iron-working in the Bishopswood area from the 17th century with the more recent quarrying and lime-burning industries. These are covered in chapter seven.

In the early 19th century a large estate at Bishopswood was created by the ironmaster, William Partridge. This included land in Walford, (previously part of Ross Foreign), the ironworks and land in Bishopswood and Ruardean formerly belonging to the Foley family, and also land in Ruardean which had formerly belonged to the Clarke family of Hill Court, Walford. From then on most of the Bishopswood woodland was managed by the estate owners.

In these times of stress among farmers and anxiety about the future within the tourism industry, it is interesting to read of the admiration of this area by visitors in earlier days. In 1797 Samuel Ireland published his *Picturesque Views on the River Wye* and describes the 'enchanting views passing from one bend of the river to another'. Among these he included Ross, Walford Church and Goodrich Castle and the surrounding country 'which, at a happy distance, combine to form a landscape of peculiar richness and beauty'. He continued, after describing Goodrich Castle, 'the country on the opposite side of the river towards the village of Walford is peculiarly beautiful'. The juxtaposition of industry did not seem to detract from the views.

His verbal journey down the river flowed on: 'Here the Wye in a long and serpentine reach, appears in a perspective point of view and affords a pleasing and happy termination to the scenery; its banks are screened on the south, by an extensive coppice wood, and on the north by fertile meadows rising towards Bishopswood, from which a considerable iron furnace in the vicinity derives its name. From the stone quarries in this neighbourhood the new bridge at Bristol was principally erected'. This quarry was near the road to Courtfield from Goodrich; the stone was oolitic limestone.

As the feudal system was gradually replaced, the administration of the parishes came under the authority of the Vestry with Justices of the Peace as local arbiters of the law. The 'Vestry' consisted of the vicar and two church-wardens, one of whom could be appointed each year by the vicar. However

No. on Register.	NAME OF VOTER.	PLACE OF ABODE.	BAILEY.	CROFT.	BIDDULPH.	BLAKE.
	WALFORD PARISH.					
	Voters in respect of Property, including Tenant Occupiers, at a Rent of £50 and upwards.					
828	Blake, Rev. Aldrick	Old Hill, Walford			..	
832	Bevan, James	Howker's-green			..	
834	Brown, John	Ley's-hill	..			
835	Bailey, William	Walford			..	
843	Cox, Amos	Howl-hill, Walford			...	
848	Gwatkin, Richard	Walford	..			
850	Green, William	Walford			...	
852	Greenway, Thomas	Walford			...	
853	Greenaway, William	Lime Tump	..			
854	Howells, George	Ley's-hill, Walford			..	
855	Hardwick, Nathaniel James	Bolling			..	
856	Hancocks, Arthur Annesley	Upper Weston, near Ross			...	
857	Howls, Gilbert	Walford	..			
859	Holder, Henry	Walford			...	
860	Harris, Richard	Walford			...	
861	Harris, Henry	Howl-hill			...	
866	Jones, Edward	Vine-tree			...	
867	Jenkins, Thomas	Walford			...	
868	Little, Thomas	Quabbs			...	
869	Little, Thomas	Baches, Walford			...	
871	Loveridge, Richard	Walford	..			
872	Morgan, William	The Tump, Walford			...	
873	Meredith, Thomas	The Quabbs	..			
874	Meek, James	Mayo's Kiln	..			
875	Mason, Edward	Whitchurch			...	
876	Morgan, Thomas	Howl-hill			...	
878	Partridge, John	Bishop's Wood, near Ross	..			
881	Power, Kingsmill Manley	Hill Court, Walford			...	
883	Patterson, James	Station-street, Ross			...	
884	Price, Ephraim	Ley's-hill			...	
889	Robinson, Thomas	Waterloo-villa, Gloucester			...	
890	Roberts, Richard	Mayo's kiln			...	
891	Russell, James	Walford	..			
893	Scudamore, Richard	Walford			...	
894	Simmonds, William	Ley's-hill			...	
895	Smith, Samuel	The Lodge			...	
897	Smith, William	Walford			..	
898	Stonhouse, Rev. Arthur	Walford			...	
899	Smith, John	Howl-hill	..			
900	Thayer, Isaac	Walford			...	
903	Tomkins, William	Walford			..	
906	Thirkill, Thomas Pulvertoft	The Hill, Walford			...	
907	Turnock, Joseph	Ross	..			
908	Taylor, Charles	Walford			..	
909	Thorney, William	Coughton			..	
910	Webb, Henry	Walford				...
911	Woolley, John	Forest-green, Walford				...
912	White, George	Forest-green			..	
913	Williams, William	Oxlet			..	
914	Whittingham, William	Slad			..	
915	Webb, Benjamin	Oxlet				...
918	Wood, Thomas	Warryfield, Walford			..	
921	Williams, John	Oxlet			...	
922	Webb, James	Oxlet			...	
927	Whysom, John	Oxlet				...
928	Young, Frederick	Walford				...
929	Young, William	Tumps				...
931	Young, Amos	Old Winsleys			..	
	Voters as Occupiers of Rateable Value of £12 and under £50 Rental.					
934	Blakey, George	Walford	..			
935	Blakey, Robert	Walford	..			
936	Baldwin, Edwin	Walford	..			
939	Hartland, Edward	Walford	..			
941	Morgan, James	Walford	..			
943	Phillips, William	Walford	..			
944	Phelps, Henry	Walford	..			
945	Ricketts, Loftus	Walford	..			
946	Rawlings, Henry	Walford	..			
948	Wheeler, Thomas	Walford	..			

both were usually elected, annually, by those parishioners who were entitled to vote in the parliamentary elections.

Initially the meetings were held in the church vestry, but records show that around 1840 they were held at the Travellers' Rest (now Barn House), Coughton, and, on other occasions, at Brook Farm, near Walford Church.

The franchise was initially restricted to the wealthier landowners and freeholders, or tenants paying at least £50 per year in rent or holding a long lease. In 1867 the rent qualification was reduced, but at no time, until complete parliamentary enfranchisement in 1928, could all women vote.

The first voters' register was made in 1843. In this parish there were 139 eligible voters in 1835, 102 in 1852, 98 in 1857, 112 in 1861 and 103 in 1868. In Walford the parish electors also chose a Parish Clerk and a Sexton, with two men to act as Overseers of the Poor and others as

Extract from the Poll (the list of those eligible to vote) for Walford Parish for 1868 (HRO)

Waywardens. The Overseers collected the Poor Rate, which was assessed on the value of agricultural land, and this was used to maintain the poor and sick in the parish. There was a workhouse on Howle Hill, and relief was sometimes made available as food to those at home who could not work. However, from the establishment of regional Poor Law Unions (after 1834) all the parish revenue raised had to go to the central pool administered by the Ross Board of Guardians, where Walford Parish had two representative Guardians; an Assistant Overseer continued to report any cases of need or poverty to the Vestry meetings.

The Local Government Act of 1894 altered this system and from that date elected Parish Councils dealt with civil affairs, with the Vestry continuing to look after ecclesiastical matters. All male parishioners over the age of 18 were entitled to vote and it was decided that there should be 13 Parish Councillors to look after the large civil parish of Walford and Bishopswood. In 1895 this comprised 4,340 acres with a total population, as recorded at the 1891 census, of 1,116 (which included 386 people in Bishopswood).

Since 1974 Walford Parish Council has had the same status as Ross Town Council. Every year the councillors decide on a precept to cover the expenditure anticipated in the forthcoming 12 months. They are always conscious of the need to keep the precept within reasonable limits as a proportion of the funding has to be met by their parishioners; this sum is collected as part of the Council Tax demand. The Parish Clerk deals with all the decisions made at council meetings, in addition to other parish matters. The most recent Chairmen of Walford Parish Council are listed below:

1957	Revd. John Thackwell
1961	Major J. Gaskell
1978	William Chinn
1981	Sidney Cobb
1982	Harold Spencer
1985	Edward Sainsbury
1993	Gordon Keay
1994	Eric Drummond
1996	Edward Sainsbury

CHAPTER III
The Churches and Chapels

For centuries the village church has typically been a focus of rural community life striving to provide for and assist with the spiritual and practical needs of the parishioners. In a rural parish such as Walford the housing has always been scattered over a wide geographical area with the farms and estates of the 'big houses' occupying large portions of the land. The churches and chapels were, and remain, important in providing a community meeting place both for religious worship and social activity.

The civil parish of Walford currently has three church buildings, all with a history to tell: St. Michael and All Angels in Walford, St. John's on Howle Hill and All Saints in Bishopswood. Previously there was a small church at Hom Green (a private chapel on the Hill Court estate formerly belonging to the Trafford family) and several chapels in the parish: the Plymouth Brethren Chapel on Howle Hill, the Baptist Chapel on Leys Hill and the Wesleyan Chapel at Kiln Green.

The Ecclesiastical Parish of Walford-on-Wye lies in the Diocese and Archdeaconry of Hereford and the Deanery of Ross and Archenfield.

The *Victoria County History of Gloucestershire - Forest of Dean*, published in 1998, notes that Ruardean church, in neighbouring Gloucestershire, was a chapel of Walford in 1291. The precentor (the leader of the congregation) of Hereford Cathedral was appropriator and patron of the vicarage. The precentor obtained a curate or chaplain for Ruardean chapel in the early 16th century but the vicar of Walford disputed and claimed that right in 1523. The disagreement was resolved in 1535 and the vicars of Walford, or more usually their curates, served the chapelry. Ruardean remained a chapelry of Walford until 1842 when it was constituted as a separate benefice in the precentor's gift.

Between 1842 and 1917 the patron of the living of the parish was the Bishop of Worcester, since when the living has been the responsibility of the Lord Chancellor. *Littlebury's Commercial Directory* for 1876 shows that the living of Walford was stated to be the grand sum of £242, gross, with a residence (the vicarage), a grant of £41 and about 17 acres of glebe (land attached to the benefice) from the Ecclesiastical Commissioners.

Walford parish church stands on the site of an earlier wattle and daub Saxon church which was dedicated to the Saxon saint, St. Leonard. The present building is Norman in origin and its central part is thought to be one of the oldest in Herefordshire. The church is built of local sandstone, ashlar and rubble but the mason's identity is unknown. An anonymous mason's mark can be seen on the south wall just east of the porch.

The church currently consists of a chancel with three bays, a north chapel, a nave of four bays, a north aisle, north and south porches and a northern tower. The footprint plan shows the main features of the church and the different ages of the structure of the building, the oldest dating from the 12th century.

The Report of the Royal Commission on Historical Monuments, South West Herefordshire, 1932, gives a comprehensive description of the main architectural features of the church.

From the back of the church looking to the east end, the chancel and arches can be seen to be offset. This arrangement represents the image of Christ on the cross where his head would have been tilting to one side of his body. The

This line drawing of Walford church is by the Revd. Michael Lapage for his booklet about the church published in 1985

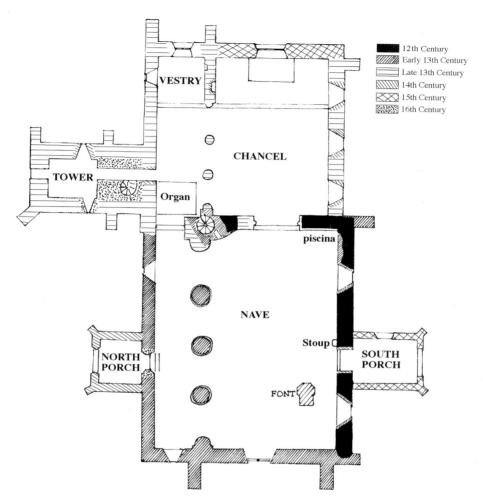

*Footprint Plan of Walford Church; Scale (Approx) 8 feet : 1 inch
Compiled from the booklet* The Church of St Michael and All Angels,
Walford *by Revd. Lapage, published in 1985 and the* Report of the Royal
Commission on Historical Monuments, South West Herefordshire, *1932*

chancel arch is relatively low and this makes it difficult for sound to carry from
the choir to the nave. Opposite the north porch door is the octagonal 15th-
century font with a Tudor rose decoration.

Originally there was no north porch to the building and entrance was
through the south porch and door from a path leading across the churchyard
and over a stream. There is a holy water stoup (stone basin) just inside the south
porch. The latter is now used as a room for the choir and the entrance to the
church is by the north porch.

It is likely that the altar originally stood where the lectern is, near the piscina in the south wall. The piscina is a stone recess, usually decorated, containing a basin and traditionally used for washing the communion vessels. The corbels (projecting stone blocks as a support for timber) of the east and south walls are still visible jutting out from the present walls.

Prior to the Reformation and Cromwell's time, there was a rood screen right across the chancel arch with room for people to cross. A rood is the cross of Christ, a crucifix, and was typically hung from a large central screen across the chancel arch in pre-Reformation times. There was usually a

The 15th-century font in Walford church (Photo Bridget Vine)

platform over the rood screen, called the rood loft. A small access door above the pulpit is all that remains of the rood loft. The loft entrance is behind the pillar next to the organ.

The north aisle was originally the private or Chantry chapel of the de Walford family who held the knight's fee of Walford in the reign of Henry III. The knight's fee was a landholding sufficient for the knight and his family to subsist for one year.

This chapel later became the Kyrle chapel. The Kyrle family held the manor of Walford Court from the late 1400s and the chapel was handed over to the church in 1887. The late 16th-century funeral helm of Lieutenant-Colonel Kyrle hangs on the east wall of the nave above the low and narrow chancel arch, and is thought to resemble that worn by Louis XIII.

Either side of the helm are two hatchments with the arms of the Clarke family of Hill Court. The Clarke family was descended from the Kyrle family but died out in the mid-18th century through the male line. The church owns the Corunna Medal of Lieut.-General Sir Manley Power, KCB, KTS, who was Lieutenant Governor of Malta from 1819 to 1825 and owned both Hill Court

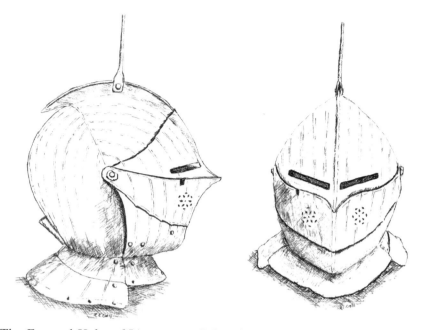

The Funeral Helm of Lieutenant-Colonel Kyrle, about 1600, which hangs over the chancel arch in Walford Church. (Line Drawing by Mr. R. Cross in Walford Women's Institute Local History of Walford, *1954/5)*

and Walford Court, two of the larger houses in the parish. There was a lineage connection between the Manley-Power and Clarke families.

The north aisle with its arcade of four pillars with capitals decorated with leaf carvings and pointed arches was added to the nave in about 1235 during the Early English architectural period. The aisle was continued east to form a north chapel and the present organ chamber. The windows are pointed and the point of the east window is not in line with the top of the arch and the chancel is not in line with the nave. The walls are approximately three feet thick and originally there was a separate square tower with two bells which may have been used as a place of refuge in times of strife.

The church was in a dilapidated condition by 1430 and general repairs were necessary. The east wall of the chancel was rebuilt and perpendicular Gothic windows were added along with a passage connecting the north tower to the main building through the north chapel. In 1517 the building was damaged by an unusually severe flooding of the nearby river Wye.

In 1754 a gallery was erected in the west end of the church. This addition was made possible by a subscription of £38 17s. The church register of the time shows a record of 37 'kneelings' in the gallery appropriated to the subscribers. Up to about 1830 there was a whipping post near the avenue where the lime trees now grow in the Road of Remembrance.

The north porch was a later addition and, as previously mentioned, stands slightly out of true with the tower and main body of the church. Unfortunately the tower was struck by lightning in February 1813 and was severely damaged—the spire collapsed into the churchyard, the tower split, all the windows were smashed and the bells fell down. One of the bells that survived was taken to Hope Mansell church which was, at that time, also the responsibility of the vicar of Walford. There are only two bells now, each bearing the inscription 'John Rudhall fecit [made me] 1824'. The larger tenor bell sounds G, weighs about 1/2 ton and measures over 3 feet in diameter. The other bell sounds an octave and a semi-tone higher and weighs about 1 cwt. and measures over 1 foot in diameter.

The church building was as it is now except for several phases of maintenance and the extensive 1887 restoration to be described later. A local benefactor, Miss Mary Beatrice Philips who lived at Hazelhurst, Bishopswood, contributed to several of the church restoration projects and also donated the organ in 1887 which is still in use. In 1865 the old timberwork in the roof was uncovered (and seen to be in sound condition) when the lathe and plaster were removed.

In 1886 the Revd. George Kewley launched a successful campaign to raise over £1,000 to restore the nave and the aisle. The minutes of the vestry meeting

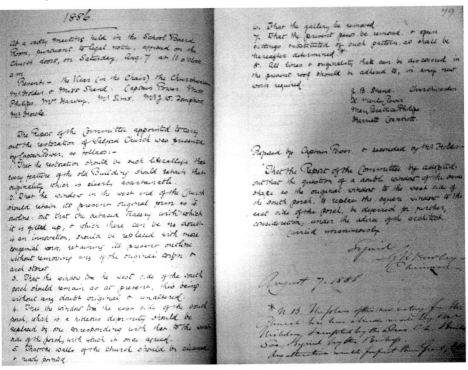

Extract from Walford Vestry Minutes
with details of the proposed restoration, August 1886

held on 7 August 1886 give the report of the committee set up to carry out the restoration works. The record states that 'the restoration should be such literally that every feature of the old building should retain that originality which is clearly ascertainable' and that 'all lines and originality that can be discovered in the present roof should be adhered to, in any aspect of work required'. The minutes further detail the specific changes to be made to the structure of the windows and redecoration of the walls, for the removal of the gallery (previously erected in 1754) and the pews to be replaced by open seating. The restoration of the chancel was carried out under the supervision of the lay rectors who were responsible to the bishop for the upkeep of the chancel and vicarage. The church tower was also restored at a later date

By 1887 the extensive restoration programme was completed and the church was dedicated to St. Michael and All Angels. Sadly the vicar was ill at the time of the dedication service and died a week later.

In 1900 a lych gate was erected (at a cost of around £70) in the vicar's memory. The gate bears the inscription: 'To the glory of God, and in reverent memory of His servant, George Robinson Kewley, born 21st November 1821, died 6th September 1887, Vicar of Walford 1884 to 1887, this lych gate was rebuilt 1900'. At that time the church was reached by a footpath leading from the road and across a field to the lych gate.

After the First World War the Parochial Church Council purchased the field adjacent to the church. In 1923 the churchyard was extended and a Road of Remembrance created and planted with lime trees. More detail on this is given in the chapter on War and Peace.

In 1947 mains electricity was installed to the church building and an electric blower provided for the organ. Three years later Mrs. Guy Trafford funded the restoration of the sundial in the churchyard. Also in 1950, new wrought iron gates and stone piers were added at the entrance to the Road of Remembrance, the gates being given by Lieutenant-Colonel L.D. Frewen, DSO, who had lived at Old Hill Court, Walford, and the War Memorial Committee presenting the stone piers on behalf of the parishioners. These provided a memorial to those who had lost their lives in the Second World War and were dedicated on 24 September by the rural dean, the Revd. Prebendary P.A. Lushington.

Maintenance work was discontinued for a short time after the Second World War. In 1953 the Diocesan Architect confirmed concerns that the timbers supporting the church roof required repair and the stone roof tiles needed replacing. A church reroofing appeal was started in 1954 and raised the required sum of £1,000 to enable the work to be carried out, the Dean of Gloucester holding a service of thanksgiving and dedication in 1955 following the completion of the repairs. There are no current plans for maintenance work.

There are several notable monuments and memorial tablets inside and outside the church of which the following are examples:

- a tablet in the chancel, inscribed in Latin, erected in 1681 to the vicar, William Adams, who was continuing to use the Book of Common Prayer at the time of the Reformation contains the words '*insultantibus Ecclesiae Anglicanae hostibus*'—'let us in the Anglican church not be insulted by the enemy'. The inscription concludes 'Go, tourist, and if again there be times of persecution, do thou likewise'.

- a monument on the west wall to the Reverend John Beeston, vicar for just one year in 1810, and also his family.

- a stained glass window at the west end of the church commemorates the eldest and youngest sons, Richard and Frederick, of Mr. and Mrs. Butt of Holcombe, Bulls Hill, who were both killed in action in France during the First World War.

- in the Kyrle chapel a memorial to the Clarke family (husband and wife, Joseph and Jane, and their children Richard, Joseph, John, Stephen and Henry) erected by Kingsmill Evans Esq. in 1821 and one for Kingsmill Evans himself, of the Hill Court, who died in 1851 '... in humble hope of salvation through the mercy of God ...'.

- a brass with the Collins arms and quarterings and inscriptions for John Stratford Collins of The Wythall, who died in 1859, and his wife Edith and four sons and six daughters.

- another tablet is to the memory of the learned Thomas Dudley Fosbroke, the antiquary, curate and then vicar of Walford from 1810 until his death in 1842 at the age of 72 years: 'for 32 years he faithfully discharged the duties of those parishes ... in the literary world he had attained a high degree of eminence as a scholar, an antiquarian and a local historian'.

- Revd. Richard Greenaway, vicar of Walford from 1681 until 1745 'a sound and learned divine, and great admirer and strenuous defender of the doctrine and discipline of the Church of England; he bequeathed some considerable legacies to charitable uses, and particularly one of £60 to this parish'.

- Mary Beatrice Philips who died in January 1898: 'built and endowed St. John's Church in this parish in 1875 and was a generous benefactress to this church at its restoration in 1887'. Miss Philips was not buried in the parish she had endowed so generously but at Abbey cwm hwr in Radnorshire.

- a marble monument to Ferdinando Stratford-Collins Esq., son of John Stratford-Collins, J.P. and chairman of Walford parish council for 21 years who died at Lincoln Hill in March 1919.

The current vicarage was built in 1960 and is located next door to the church. There were previously two earlier vicarages in the parish. One, now a private house called The Old Vicarage, was built in 1860 and situated about 1/4 mile from the church near the village school. The other, built *c*.1704, is now called Hunsdon House and is situated in Daycroft Lane.

Researches have provided a list of the clergy and parsons of Walford since 1226. There have been several notable vicars serving the parish:

- Richard Greenaway was vicar of Walford from 1681 until 1745 and also served neighbouring Ruardean but was suspended in 1739 for failing to attend an episcopal visitation.
- The antiquarian and county historian Thomas Dudley Fosbroke also served Ruardean and Walford until 1842. His book, *Ariconensia: or Archaeological Sketches of Ross and Archenfield*, was published in 1821.
- Kentish Bache was vicar from 1887 until 1916 and worked long and hard to resolve a complicated dispute over a legacy intended to provide a curate's living at St. John's on Howle Hill.

In 1874 Miss Philips provided funds for the building of a chapel, St. John's Church, and a nearby schoolroom on Howle Hill. The land was provided by Samuel Buttermere who lived at The Paddocks, Deep Dean, and he also

1226 Thos, persona de Waleford	1754 Guy Hill
1256 Godfry Giffard	1769 John Barroll
1309 Wm de Rowardin	1810 John Beeston
1347 Nicholas Botolph	1811 John Theodore Archibald Reed
1349 John Hony	1830 Thomas Dudley Fosbroke
1387 William Tregase	1842 Arthur Stonhouse
1396 John Jay	
1421 Walter Packer	Walford separated from Ruardean by order in
1436 William Miles	Council
1441 John Seycell or Cecil	
14-- Thomas Seymour	1884 George Kewley
14-- Thomas Worthe	1887 Kentish Bache
1509 John Moreton	1916 Charles Henry Cook
1526 Thomas Lee, M.A.	1817 Theodore Emmott
1530 William Warnecombe	1920 Robert Dixon Rosby Greene
1558 Richard Kyrle, B.A.	1929 Richard Lavers Kemp (Hon. Canon of
1604 George Burghill	Manchester)
1616 Rowland Burghill	1934 Thomas Mendus Williams
1633 James Westfaling	1947 Joseph Walter John Thackwell
1634 Gregory Burghill	1961 John Glendwr Owen
1635 Jonathan Buckley	1971 Kenneth James Till (Chaplain to the
1647 Giles Workman	Queen)
1655 Thomas Worthe	1979 Michael Clement Lapage
1662 William Adams	1989 Paul Tarling
1681 Richard Greenway	1997 Michael Anthony Kelk
1745 Walwyn Morgan	

List of the Vicars of Walford

St. John's Church, Howle Hill.
(Drawn by Liz Baker)

donated the stained glass window at the east end of the building. The chapel is a Chapel of Ease and the building is dedicated, but not consecrated, and is only licensed to hold services. It was built of stone quarried on Howle Hill and dedicated to the Apostle St. John the Evangelist.

The architectural style is Early English and the architects were Messrs. Haddon Brothers of Hereford and Malvern. The builder was William Griffiths of Lea in Gloucestershire and the building was erected for a cost of around £1,300. Mr. Symonds the coachman to the vicar at the time, Revd. Arthur Stonhouse, drove the Bishop of Hereford up to Howle Hill to lay the foundation stone. There is an adjacent schoolroom, built at the same time as the church, which was only used until the late 1880s after the school in Walford had opened.

The church opened in 1875 and consists of a nave, chancel, sacristy and a south facing porch. There are choir stalls in the chancel and the church can accommodate a congregation of around 130. The organ, made by Messrs. Banfield of Birmingham, was erected in 1888.

In 1930 the interior of the chapel was redecorated and the organ over-hauled. Part of the organ overhangs the north choirmen's seat, in three semi-turrets, and the organist now sits on the opposite side of the chancel, with the light from the south window behind his back. The organ pipes are of high quality metal being three-quarters tin and one-quarter lead. In the year 2000 members of the congregation arranged a Millennium Exhibition of the local history of Howle Hill and its church and local craft work. In 2001 the Diocesan Architect reported that both the church and school room buildings urgently needed extensive refurbishment and were unsafe to hold services. The Parochial Church Council took the decision to close the buildings for public use until further notice. A service of closure was held in St. John's schoolroom on 9 December 2001.

For the 31 years between 1875 and 1906 seven curates were appointed to St. John's and lived in various houses on Howle Hill: the Revd. Messrs. Lucas, Bowstead, Reece, Bowen, Shepherd, May and Richards.

In 1885 Miss Philips established an endowment of £150 to provide a stipend for a curate. No curate was appointed from 1906 until 1919 when the Revd. Mr. Church was the last curate in the parish.

The building of All Saints Church in Bishopswood was started in 1841. The work was funded by John Partridge, a former High Sheriff of Monmouthshire and the son of William Partridge, a local iron-master and owner of the former Bishopswood estate. The church was consecrated in 1845 and an incumbent provided. Both William and John Partridge are buried in the churchyard together with other members of their family who lived locally.

The first full time incumbent was the Revd. Robert Collins who was licensed on 17 September 1845. Also during this year, the ecclesiastical parish boundary was altered. As mentioned earlier, the parish of Walford had previously included neighbouring Ruardean as well as Walford, but Ruardean was excluded when the new boundary was defined. In 1845 Bishopswood became a separate ecclesiastical parish formed out of portions of the parishes of Walford and Ruardean.

The first entry in the Baptism Register was dated 26 December 1841. There were 36 baptisms in the parish before the church was consecrated and it is thought they were carried out at the vicarage. This was formerly called Lower Coppice but is now known as Bishopswood House. Members of the Church of England worshipped there whilst Roman Catholics attended services at the Catholic church on the Vaughan estate across the river from Kerne Bridge at Coppett Hill near Goodrich.

The Bishopswood church registers show that for 20 of the first 50 marriages, the bride and groom were unable to sign their names. Also, for 20 of the first 50 burials, the deceased were under the age of 15 years.

The church was built of stone with a slate roof and originally comprised a nave, porch, small belfry in the centre with a single

All Saints Church, Bishopswood.
(Drawn by Liz Baker)

bell and an organ. It was left as built for the 35 years from 1845 until 1880 when several changes were made by the vicar and the churchwarden, Richard Scudamore. For a cost of around £200 the west end gallery was taken down, the pulpit removed and a new one erected opposite on the north side of the church, the font was repositioned at the west end, all the choir stalls and pews were renewed and the organ moved to the north side of the church.

The church as built had an English oak ceiling and fortunately this was not affected by all the changes. The ceiling has over 40 roof bosses: 33 in the nave and chancel and 10 plus 10 halves in the sanctuary ceiling. It has been said that choirboys bored by the sermon used to raise their heads to the ceiling and count the roof bosses. There are no stained glass windows in the church. Commemorations to those who lost their lives in the First and Second World Wars are described in the chapter on War and Peace.

Local recollections in the 1920s and 1930s recall how church festivals used to bring the community together in celebration, with old and young working alongside each other to decorate their church with flowers, greenery and other materials collected from the surrounding countryside. There were regular processions from the neighbouring parish of Goodrich through to Walford with the proceeds of the collection being donated to the cottage hospital in Ross and the local nursing associations who provided health care for the community.

The 100th anniversary of the consecration of the church was in 1945 but the church service book only shows, for 18 May 1945, a record of a service to commemorate Deliver in Europe (D.E.) Day. Clearly the recent war was uppermost in people's minds as no mention was made of a celebration of the centenary of the building of the church.

1845	Robert Cave Wood Collins
1849	William Watkins Deering
1851	William Wade Wait
1852	Henry Watson
1857	Thomas Hawley Edwards
1871	Henry Delacour de Brisay
1872	Octavius James Ellis
1879	Charles William Neville Custance
1885	Robert William John Smart
1889	Frederick Hooper Aldrich-Blake
1898	Herbert Martin Maynard
1906	Thomas Cole
1917	Arthur Wynne Thomas
1922	Henry Jabez Jerrom
1924	Albert Henry Bromfield
1929	Harold Flitcroft Hutton
1939	Robert Noble Beasley
1942	Willie Ellam
1949	Joseph Walter John Thackwell

with Walford and Howle Hill

1961	John Glendwr Owen
1971	Kenneth John Till
1979	Michael Clement Lapage

with Goodrich, Marstow and Welsh Bicknor

| 1989 | Paul Tarling |
| 1997 | Michael Anthony Kelk |

The Vicars of Bishopwood

The benefice was joined with Walford in 1948 and the vicarage was sold as a private house, now called Beverley House. A problem worthy of note was entered in the vestry minutes for 1955 of 'destruction done to harmonium and hassocks by mice'. A preparation called 'Scram' was recommended to resolve the problem. During the 1960s the Revd. John Owen used money left to the church by Miss Hoitt to carry out a range of improvements and redecoration. Apart from the installation of electricity and central heating at that time, the church has remained relatively unchanged since then. Stephen Jayne sang in the church choir all his life and was Churchwarden for 32 years. After his death his wife, Edith, became a Churchwarden for 18 years. Their daughter, Margery, now Spencer, played the organ at Bishopswood for over 50 years from 1940 until 1998.

The church celebrated its 150th anniversary in 1995 and several projects were arranged to commemorate the occasion. Special services were held in the church and conducted by the Bishop of Hereford. A name board was commissioned to list all the vicars of the church from the time of the consecration; the average stay of a vicar seems to have been around six years.

For the millennium year 2000 members of the congregation were invited to stitch commemorative kneelers and the 40 names of the contributors are listed at the rear of the church. Also that year a flower festival was held and the money raised enabled the organ to be serviced and overhauled.

There have been old and new church buildings at Hom Green. According to W.H. Cooke in his *Collection towards the History and Antiquities of the County of Hereford Volume III in Continuation of Duncumb's History*, the old chapel was erected in the 12th century by Bishop William de Vere and dedicated to the Paraclete (the Holy Ghost). It was a small structure, in the form of a parallelogram, and only survived until just after the Reformation when it became derelict. The foundations are no longer in evidence but a cross was present near the site as late as 1932 and

The cross in the wood at Hom Green. (Courtesy of Walford W.I.)

Hom church around 1950. (Courtesy of Walford W.I.)

referred to as 'The Cross in the Wood' in Alfred Watkins' book *The Old Standing Crosses of Herefordshire*. The exact origins and history of this cross are unknown.

The new Hom church was built in 1905 and the architect was Bodley, a locally (and internationally) renowned architect, who was also involved in the design of the Liverpool Anglican and Washington cathedrals. This was originally a private chapel and associated burial ground for the Trafford family on their Hill Court estate. It comprised a nave, chancel and bellcote. The building is divided into two naves by tall octagonal piers along the centre of the building and the windows all have triangular heads to their lights. The chapel was sold with the estate to a commercial enterprise, Rehau, in 1994. Rehau have recently refurbished the building to provide facilities for corporate entertainment.

The Plymouth Brethren Chapel on Howle Hill was established in 1865 through the efforts of two brothers, Edwin and Julius Isbell. Edwin Isbell was a doctor in Hereford and Julius Isbell lived at Chasewood Cottage, Walford, following his return from sheep farming in Australia. Julius was very concerned for the spiritual welfare of the local people of Coughton and Howle Hill and started an afternoon religious meeting on Howle Hill. He was also mindful of the lack of available education for local children who often started work at 10 years of age as formal education was not compulsory. Sunday School and religious services were held for a while in a barn at Edgehill Farm.

In 1865 the Isbell brothers funded the building of a chapel and schoolroom on Howle Hill along with the Baptist church in Ross. The building was used for

Howle Hill Brethren Chapel Sunday School in the 1920s. Left to right:
Back Row: ?, Marjorie Kearsey, Joyce Stacey, ? Burford, ? Burford,
Laura Young, Clive Powell, Miss Cowmeadow, Janet Williams
Middle Row: ?, ?, ?, Iris Stacey, Clara Young, ? Burford
Front Row: Carrie Spencer, Dick Stacey, Richard Young, ? Holloway,
Ruby Jones, Jimmy Hughes, Peter Lane, Leslie Lane.
(Courtesy of Joyce Roberts)

daily, free, school sessions and weekly Sunday School as well as church services. Later there was a monthly women's meeting. A Mrs. and Miss Sage were caretakers for the chapel and schoolroom and lived in an adjoining cottage.

Over the years, the Sunday School used to arrange annual outings for the children. On their return tea was provided in the Chapel Hall often accompanied by home baked bread provided by Mr. and Mrs. Hickling (from Nottingham) who ran the chapel for 16 years. Their leadership was followed by Mr. and Mrs. Albert Attenborough (also from Nottingham) and then lastly Mr. and Mrs. Archer Bird of Ross-on-Wye who retired through ill-health. In 1966 the chapel was reroofed by Mr. Bullock of Ross.

The first schoolmaster in the schoolroom was Mr. Tarry who also became pastor at Leys Hill Chapel. The next teacher, Mr. Devinner, increased the school numbers to over 100 but this put an increased demand on the resources of the Isbell brothers. Edwin Isbell contacted a George Muller in Bristol who was known to be prepared to assist the funding of such institutions. Mr. Muller was able to support the school and chapel until the time of the establishment of the Government Board Schools.

One notable pupil of the school was Harry Whittaker, of Bulls Hill. He showed an aptitude for learning and after receiving private tuition from the vicar he worked as a teacher in a private school. He then qualified in Latin and Greek and subsequently became a clergyman in the Church of England. He continued his studies and later qualified in medicine.

Although the school closed in 1882, chapel services continued until 1998 which was an unbroken service to God for 136 years. The chapel and associated cottage were then sold as a private dwelling.

Leys Hill Baptist Chapel, now a private house, was situated along a lane, Old Chapel Lane, just off the Bulls Hill and Kerne Bridge Road on Leys Hill. There was a burial ground associated with the chapel.

The chapel was established following the arrival in the district of Thomas Wright, a member of North Wales Baptist Church who went out into the community as a minister, a post funded through the trustees of Edward Goff. The will of Mr. Goff, who lived in London and died in 1813, also provided for the establishment of 32 free schools in Herefordshire and the surrounding counties to be set up for poor children 'without distinction'.

The chapel was built in 1832 and had an initial congregation of eight members. Up until 1894 the chapel had its own ministers and then became a part of the Ross Baptist Church and received preachers from Ross and other areas. On Good Friday in 1931 the congregation celebrated the 99th anniversary of the chapel.

The master at Leys Hill was paid £50 per annum and given rent free housing in return for providing tuition in reading, writing and arithmetic during the week and religious instruction and preaching on Sundays. In 1836 there were 49 pupils at the chapel school which remained open until 1847.

Chapel funds were raised by the congregation for general maintenance. In 1951 a special appeal was launched and successfully raised the £100 required to redecorate the interior of the building. Services at the chapel continued until the 1960s and in 1962 the chapel was sold as a private house.

From the time it opened the chapel had an associated Sunday School which met regularly. The Secretary and Treasurer of the chapel, Miss Roberts, was a teacher at the Sunday School for 20 years from the 1930s until the 1950s. Unfortunately nobody succeeded her and so the Sunday School was closed.

The Wesleyan Methodist Chapel at Kiln Green is now a private house called Yew Tree Cottage. The chapel was described in *Lascelles Commercial Directory and Gazetteer* of Herefordshire for the year of 1851 as 'situated on the hill at Kiln Green, a neat little stone building'. The chapel was in regular use for worship for more than 100 years with services being taken by circuit preachers on Sundays at 10.30am and 2.30pm. In 1977 a planning application sought to convert the chapel into a private dwelling after it had ceased to be a place of worship.

The civil parish of Walford currently has two churches: St. Michael and All Angels in Walford and All Saints in Bishopswood. These two churches, together with those at Goodrich, Marstow and Welsh Bicknor, made up the Kerne Bridge Group of churches within the ecclesiastical parish. From May 2002 ecclesiastical boundary changes will be implemented so that Walford will be joined to the Ross Team Ministry of the Diocese of Hereford. Bishopswood will join a grouping with other churches to the south and west of the parish. There is no curate in the parish and from May 2002 there will be no resident vicar.

The current service structure came about in the 1950s when the Revd. John Thackwell became vicar of Walford and Bishopswood. Weekly services are held at Walford, Bishopswood and Goodrich churches with services on alternate Sundays at the church of Marstow. Special services are held for Harvest Festival and the other church celebrations throughout the year.

Before the provision of the organ for Walford parish church in 1887 by Miss Philips, the church music was provided by a harmonium. The Walford Women's Institute Local History dated 1954/5 lists the organists up to the 1950s as follows: Miss Shand of Old Hill Court, Miss Collins of the Old Vicarage, Miss Cook daughter of the Revd. Charles Cook, Mr. Willoughby who became organist in Ross, Mr. Barnacle who had been organist at Hereford Cathedral, Mr. William Symonds a churchwarden, Mr. Tarry the headmaster, Mrs. Robinson from Goodrich and Sir James Almond who lived in Walford following his retirement from the Indian civil service.

The Revd. Kentish Bache, vicar of Walford from 1887 until 1916, was an accomplished musician and acted as his own choirmaster and organist for several years. He was also musical director for the Howle Hill String Band which was formed in the late 1890s and is mentioned in the chapter on Recreation and Social Life.

In the early 1960s the organist at Walford church for four years was John Handley, son of the headmaster, until he went to teacher training college. Mrs. Margaret Claxton took over from him and played the organ until the year 2000 when in her 90s. Barney Bell also played during that time until in 1986 Paul Baker took over from him. Today he shares the position with Frances Harwood who also plays at Bishopswood church.

Each of the churches had a choir in the first half of the 20th century although women were not admitted until 1930. In the 1930s and 1940s the choirs of both Walford and Bishopswood were awarded prizes in county competitions. The choir ceased at Bishopswood in the 1960s and today there is only a choir at Walford church.

There were several organisations associated with the parish church: the Sunday School, the Mothers' Union and the Young Men's Club. No records concerning the running of a Sunday School attached to the parish church seem to exist although memories go back to back to the turn of the 20th century. After the Second World War numbers began to increase and activities such as summer outings and Christmas parties were arranged. Mention has been made earlier of the outings arranged on Howle Hill by the Brethren chapel.

The Mothers' Union was started in Walford in the late 1920s by Mrs. Kemp, wife of the vicar from 1929 until 1934, who also embroidered the Mothers' Union banner which stands in the chancel of Walford church. During the war the Union lapsed and was restarted in 1947 by Mrs. Thackwell, wife of the vicar at that time. A Young Wives group was started in 1951. Both have now ceased and were replaced by the Churchwomen's Fellowship which holds monthly meetings in the village hall.

The Church of England Young Men's Club was a social club which ran from 1934 until the outbreak of the war. The vicar, Revd. Mr. Williams led the group which was held in a room at the vicarage. In the 1960s a youth club met in the schoolroom next to the church on Howle Hill.

The Pathfinders Hut near the Walford church lych gate was erected during Revd. Michael Lapage's incumbency with much practical and financial help from parishioners. This is still used for activities for the younger members of the parish.

In common with other village facilities such as post offices and shops, the number of religious buildings in Walford has declined over the years as the worshipping population has contracted. Many of the redundant places of worship have taken on new roles as private dwellings and availability and adequacy of funding for maintaining the existing church buildings and making religious provision is constantly presenting challenges.

At the start of the 21st century, the church holds its place in this rural community and remains important in providing a community meeting place both for religious worship and social activity.

CHAPTER IV
Care of the Sick and the Poor

Prior to the 1900s there were few state provisions for healthcare, education and assisting those in need, apart from some locally provided facilities for education and Poor Law assistance. The less fortunate residents of rural communities such as Walford and Bishopswood were dependent on the generosity and support of the church and the owners of the 'big houses' and estates to improve their lives. These benefactors and philanthropists were respected members of the community and through their 'gifts' they provided opportunities for those less fortunate than themselves in the form of education and other support that would not otherwise have been available.

One of the earliest records of parish benefactions can be seen in the vestry of Walford church. A board, dated 1765, and entitled 'Benefactions to the Poor of the Parish of Walford' lists personal bequests and charitable gifts from several individuals for the benefit of the parish:

- the will of Joseph Clarke left £100 (at £5 per year) to teach poor children to read.
- members of the Stratford family: Elizabeth, Martha, Hester and John, left a range of amounts from £20 and £300 for charitable uses.
- the Revd. Richard Greenway, vicar of Walford from 1681 until 1745, left the annual interest from the sum of £60 to be paid to 10 of the poorer households who paid rent to the church.
- a parish flock in the hands of the administrators of the late William Chinn at the Bollin Farm.

The will of John Stratford, proved in 1739 and named on this Board of Benefactions, stated that through his sister Elizabeth's will £100 should be used by his trustees to benefit four poor households in the parish. Unfortunately the legacies detailed in the will were never actioned and so this bequest was lost.

Provision for the poor was originally a parish responsibility and, from the time of the 1601 Poor Law, workhouses were set up in communities usually through the sponsorship of the local church. A parish could rent a premise as a workhouse and employ a workhouse keeper. The disadvantaged could live there and would be found work to help pay for their keep. Unfortunately administration was sometimes lax and some workhouses were often referred to as 'houses of terror or debauchery' which rather detracted from their charitable and moral purpose.

In 1723 legislation (9 George I) enabled a parish to set up a workhouse either on its own or with a neighbouring parish. The individual workhouses were financed by local ratepayers and were only available to parishioners who could prove their entitlement

The Vestry Benefactions Board, dated 1765, hanging in Walford Church.
(From Walford Vestry)

through poverty and parish settlement. Provision for the poor was funded through poor relief, Justices of the Peace setting a local poor rate which was levied on occupiers of land and property in the parish. Paid Overseers collected the funds and along with the churchwardens determined who would receive this poor relief. The workhouse could also be used to temporarily house vagrants in need.

The census returns for Walford for the years of 1871 and 1881 list the occupants and the existence of a property called The Workhouse on Howle Hill. The remains of this tiny cottage are still visible and, if it was indeed a parish workhouse, it is likely to have fallen into disuse for this purpose in the 1830s after changes to the Poor Law. No records have been found relating to this property or the administration of a parish workhouse in Walford.

In 1834 the Poor Law was amended and the care of the poor was transferred from the ecclesiastical parishes to Boards of Guardians newly constituted by the merging of parishes for Poor Law purposes into nearly 600 Poor Law Unions. Each Union was controlled by a Board consisting of parish representatives who were elected by the major ratepayers. Any previously existing parish work-houses in the area were replaced by Union workhouses. Sometimes when local help could not be provided, the Board arranged for the emigration of younger paupers in the hopes that they would find a new and prosperous life abroad.

The Union workhouse for this area was in Ross and The Ross Civic Society 'Pink Publication' Number 11 documents its administration. The workhouse was supervised by a board of guardians, called the Guardians of the Poor, who were elected annually on a restricted property based franchise. Within the workhouse the Master and Matron reported to the Board at their fortnightly meetings. The Guardians were assisted by a Clerk who had a paid post whilst the Treasurer and the Guardians were honorary posts. Outside the workhouse the Relieving Officers, one for each of the four districts within the Union, iden-tified the poor who were not eligible to enter the workhouse but needed 'out relief', usually given in the form of bread, money, clothes or shoes. Overseers of the Poor were resident in each parish, the role being an honorary parochial post typically held by the Churchwardens (unpaid) and others in the parish appointed by the Justices (paid). The Overseers collected the rate levied on the occupiers of property (the Poor Rate) which was used to assist in the mainte-nance of the paupers in the parish. The Churchwardens were also responsible for liaising between the parishioners and the church authorities, accounting for the expenditure of the church rate and supervising the education and relief of the poor in collaboration with the Overseers. Directories (eg *Lascelles*) for this parish area for the late 1800s list local people who held official posts in the parish on behalf of the Union. Walford was one of the largest parishes in the Ross Union and was represented by two elected Guardians.

In the late 19th century several charitable institutions existed in Walford and these helped to provide for some of the poor and the educational needs of the community. *Cassey's Directory* in 1858 states that 'there are charities of about £20 yearly' but does not give the sources. The 1876 *Littlebury's Directory* states: 'The charities belonging to the parish amount to about £7 10s yearly'. The charitable sources of this benefit are also not named.

The *Jakeman and Carver Directory* for 1890 and the *Kelly's Directories* for 1895, 1905, 1913 and 1934 all list: 'the charities are in the hands of the official trustees and consist of an educational charity of £269 6s 4d invested in $2\frac{3}{4}\%$ Consols (consolidated stocks), founded by the late Joseph Clarke and a clothing charity of £256 16s 11d, invested similarly, and founded by the late Miss Jane Clarke, Hill Court'.

The generosity of several local individuals and estate holders in the parish provided the following assistance:

- the Jane Clarke Charity; a clothing charity for women
- the Joseph Clarke Charity; an educational charity organised under the

Endowed School Commissioners
- Beatrice Philips Trust; administered by Queen Anne's Bounty
- the 'Lost Charities' of Richard Greenway and Richard Bond
- the Robert Holme Storey Charity; to provide for the poor and needy
- the Charity Field at Coughton Marsh
- the Goff Baptist Chapel and school at Leys Hill.

The earliest records available for charities in Walford parish relate to the two bequests for charitable provisions made by Joseph and Jane Clarke, husband and wife, who lived at New Hill Court in the late 1700s. The family memorial tablet in the north chapel of Walford church gives an indication of the nature of this community spirited family: 'Jane, last survivor of that truly respectable family long famed for their extensive charity and unbounded benevolence, who died at the advanced age of 96 years ... her kindness universal friendship permanent and charity unbounded in life ... for what seemed more than mortal excellence ...'.

The Jane Clarke Charity was a clothing charity for women founded from an initial bequest of £256 16s. 11d., and was used to purchase wool, hemp or flax to be distributed to the poor women of the parish to enable them to make clothing. The charity was distributed at Christmas and administered by the vicar and churchwardens; the minute books of the church vestry meetings detail the annual awards and fund statements for the years from 1879 until 1895. Clothing tickets for the value of 7s. 6d. were issued to around 20 parishioners each December.

Under the terms of the Local Government Act of

The Clarke Charity Clothing Charity gift listing for December 1879. (Extract from Walford Vestry Minutes)

1894, the Vicar and two members of the parish council became trustees for the fund. The Revd. Kentish Bache kept meticulous records in the vestry minute book whilst he was vicar: '... Miss Jane Clarke's clothing charity for the year ending 31st December 1896, £256 16s 11d in the 2³/₄% Consols the income of which is paid quarterly by the Official Trustees of Charitable Funds to the Vicar of Walford's Charity Account at the National Provincial Bank in Ross. The Chairman of the Parish Council, John L. Bennett, and Parish Councillor, John Collier, met the Vicar at the vicarage on 8th December 1896 and agreed the issue of 18 clothing tickets valued at 7s 6d each'.

The chairman of the parish council in 1919 was Robert Pashley, another local benefactor, and he queried three previous annual credits to the account. It transpired that these payments should have been made to the Jane Clarke fund. At this point the charity commissioners agreed the trust should have a parish councillor as one of its trustees to oversee the process and prevent the fund ceasing in the future.

The number of recipients varied each year and one year the gift took the form of a blanket distribution. The gifts helped provide an additional extra at Christmas despite the gradually improving living standards. The fund exists to this day with a residual balance of around £140.

The Joseph Clarke Charity was originally established in 1732 when Joseph Clarke's will provided the annual sum of £5 for the instruction of poor children. The payment was charged upon the estate of Kingsmill Evans Esq., a relative of the Clarke family. A small school was provided in Coughton for the instruction of eight to ten children and their mistress received the £5 as an annual salary payment. An extract from the Hill Court papers describes the bequest to be given in two half year's payments of £2 10s.

In 1853 Kingsmill Evans advised the parish vestry that the school had ceased and that there were accumulated funds he wished to make available to the community. The school was formally closed when the Elementary School opened in Walford in 1874. The fund then became administered by the parish and was an organised charity under the Endowed School Commissioners. In

A receipt, dated 1/5/1810, for the instruction of the poor children in the parish under the Joseph Clarke bequest of 1732. (HRO)

1872 a trust was formed and representative governors appointed. This was the only educational endowment in the parish and a trust fund with an annual income at that time of £16 3s 4d was established from the following sources:

- a rent charge from the Hill Court estate of £5 per year.
- the Official Trustees income from $2^1/_2$ % Consols (nominal value) £269 6s 4d yielding around £6 14s 8d per year at that time.
- Herefordshire County Council 3% Savings Bonds (nominal value £147 15s 4d, book value £95 5s 0d) then yielding around £3 8s 8d per year.

The scheme expired on 31 December 1953 but was renewed for a further three years by the Education Committee. Along with school funds, the endowment enabled the purchase of a sound film projector in 1954 which was regularly used for school lessons. In 1955 the income was regulated by the Herefordshire Education Committee with the gifts designated as follows:

- £5 for school prizes for general school work.
- £5 for a scholarship or exhibition for a promising pupil(s) to attend secondary or higher education.
- the balance to be awarded for other purposes deemed appropriate by the Managers under the terms of the Charity, Clause 23, dated 8 August 1872.

The Walford school log books regularly documented the award of the school prizes and scholarships which were presented at a special award ceremony as is shown in the sample entry for 1923.

Miss Mary Beatrice Philips was an extremely generous benefactor in the parish in the late 1800s. Her funds enabled the building of St. John's Church on Howle Hill and she also founded a trust fund with an annual income of £10 for repairs to this church and gave an endowment, initially of £150, for a curate's stipend. Both these bequests were administered by Queen Anne's Bounty, a fund established in 1704 to receive and use ecclesiastical dues previously annexed by Henry VIII. These funds had become the property of Queen Anne and were used to supplement the incomes of poor clergy. In 1948 Queen Anne's Bounty and the Ecclesiastical Commission were combined to form the Church Commission.

The charity fund of Robert Holme Storey, owner of the Bishopswood estate in the 1920s, was derived from the proceeds of the sale of the Bishopswood schoolmaster's house when the school closed in 1956. The interest from the fund investment was used to provide for the poor and needy of the parish. A regular occurrence was the gift of food hampers to the over 80s each Christmas. The fund still exists with a residual balance of around £800.

The Report of the Commission for Inquiries concerning Charities in England and Wales (County of Hereford) refers to two 'lost charities' in the parish: those of Richard Greenway and Richard Bond. Revd. Richard Greenway was vicar of Walford from 1681 until 1745 and left, in his will, a gift of £60 to be paid over to the churchwardens for investment. He directed that the annual interest from this investment should be paid for ever on St. John Baptist's and St. Thomas' Day to 10 poor households not on the poor register of the parish. The money is said to have been placed in the hands of a solicitor in Ross who died insolvent and thus the fund was 'lost'.

The £1 annual bequest of Richard Bond can be found referenced in the 1837 Charity

Wednesday, 28th March: The disposition of annual income for this School, as decided by the Education Sub-Committee appointed to determine in which ways these funds, a charge on the Hill Court Estate, should be employed — will be as follows for at least the next 3 years: "(1) A sum not exceeding £5 yearly to be devoted towards a School Lending Library — (2) A sum not exceeding £5 a year to be expended for School Prizes, such prizes to be given not for regular attendance but for general school work" (3) "The balance of the annual endowment to be devoted towards a scholarship or an exhibition to a promising pupil or pupils at some place of higher education, to be approved of by the Managers; or in the event of no child of sufficient merit being forthcoming, or of a sum being still unexpended, the managers to be empowered to expend the same in any one of the ways approved of by Clause 23 of the scheme of the charity dated 8th August, 1872." Note is made here, as elsewhere, of the very liberal and generous spirit in which Mr. Guy Trafford has acted in the matter.

The educational bequest for provision of school prizes for pupils of Walford school. (Extract dated 28 March 1923, from Walford School log book)

Commission Parliamentary returns (no dates provided) as having been directed by his grandfather's will. The Bond family owned Cobrey Park at Coughton from around 1670 until 1776. The legacy had been withheld and no information was available to indicate its whereabouts; thus it was recorded as 'lost'.

The Charity Field at Coughton came into being when 31.7 acres of Coughton Marsh was enclosed under the 1861 Inclosure Act 'in trust for the labouring poor of the parish of Walford'. Most of the land was divided amongst the 24 freeholders of the parish who had previously owned rights of common pasture on the marsh. Just over 2 acres was given in trust to the Churchwardens and overseers of the poor and their successors to be let out in 1/4 acre allotments to the 'labouring poor'. Allotment wardens were responsible for the area and all the plots had to be fenced within 12 months and were allocated such that one side adjoined the 30 foot public road and carriage highway to be constructed as access to the land.

The parish church vestry minutes for the years 1865 to 1889 record the letting of the 1/4 acre allotments and also mention complaints about the poor

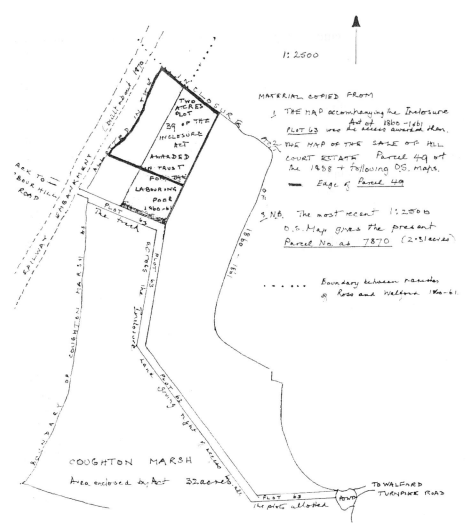

Copy of the Map of the Walford Charity Field at Coughton Marsh.
(Drawn by Jonathan Claxton and reproduced by kind permission of the
Trustees of the Walford Relief in Need Charity)

state of the road and fences and payments made to carry out the necessary repairs. In 1873 the vestry wrote, without success, to the Ross Highway Board to request a bridge or culvert at the point where the stream crossed the road. The allotment wardens were subsequently ordered to provide a culvert. By 1889 all applications to rent allotments had ceased and the 2 acres was let out for grazing until the early 1990s.

In 1894 the newly constituted Walford Parish Council continued this practice and in 1981, through the efforts of Jonathan Claxton, set up the Coughton

Marsh Access Committee to secure legal access in perpetuity. This was necessary as, because of land exchanges, the shape of the charity field had altered (although the acreage remained the same) and in consequence the allotments no longer adjoined the public access road.

In the early 1980s the parish council ceased to be custodian trustee of the land under the requirements of the Local Government Act 1972 whereby a parish council was prohibited from holding property in trust for a charity for the relief of poverty. At that time the name of the charity was changed on the advice of the Charity Commission to the Walford Relief in Need Charity and new trustees were appointed.

In 1996 the field was sold by the trustees to the Herefordshire Nature Trust so that it could be preserved as a nature reserve. The funds resulting from this sale are on bank deposit and administered by three trustees, all resident in the parish, and one of whom is a parish councillor so that the parish interest is represented. The nature reserve is accessed across private farmland and prior to the sale, the landowner (also one of the trustees) had agreed to a right of way being created to the field to enable access by members of the parish and the Nature Trust in perpetuity.

Towards the end of the 19th century charitable funding was supplemented by the state benefits that were becoming newly available to assist those in need. The welfare reforms of the early 20th century helped relieve poverty to a certain extent, measures such as government provision of old age pensions in 1908 enabling the elderly to retain some degree of independence. Additionally families were becoming more prosperous and elderly parents could remain at home with their children.

The numbers entering such institutions as the workhouses gradually began to decrease and vagrancy reduced with the outbreak of the First World War and the opportunities for work provided by the increased numbers of unskilled jobs available. However, there was a further surge in poverty and vagrancy after the Second World War.

In these days of the welfare state, 'modern day poor relief' is provided through the means-tested system of benefits aimed at keeping people in employment and thus in receipt of an income to enable them to provide for their own daily needs.

In respect of medical care, there has throughout the ages always been a range of home medicines and local cures available for treating a range of ills. These home-made mixtures were often regarded as being worse than the ailment they were intended to heal and rarely had little beneficial result.

Formal medical treatment has only been available, free to all, comparatively recently. The services of a doctor were previously only available to those with the funds to pay and thus were out of reach of most of the working people in the parish. Chemists could be paid to make up bottles of 'this and that' to help, more by luck than judgement. Individuals more generally had only such as hand-me-down potions and the use of talismans and songs to assist a cure. Herbal remedies probably provided the most optimistic outcome and sometimes certain individuals in a community were sought after for their 'healing touch'.

The mentally ill were the responsibility of the parish and were initially resident in licensed private houses in the parish and subsequently in county lunatic asylums. These institutions were regularly inspected by a medical practitioner. There were asylums in Whitchurch, Hereford and Abergavenny and the parish paid the keep of its pauper 'in-mates'. The workhouse accommodated those who were mentally ill and presented no risk or danger either to themselves or the other residents. In 1904 a Royal Commission recommended that all the mentally ill poor should be cared for under the provisions of newly established Lunacy Authority Councils rather than by the workhouse system. In 1913 this duty of care was transferred to county councils.

In the 1800s the 'village woman' (typically an unqualified nurse-midwife) carried out the beginnings of community health care. Mrs. Ann Young was the

'midwife' on Howle Hill and the surrounding area from the late 1800s until 1924 when she was in her 70s. She lived and worked in the district and was described by Fred Druce in his book *The Light of Other Days* as 'a rough diamond'. She walked to visit all her patients and helped them as best she could with the limited resources of the time. Typically she was paid a fee of 5s. or as much as 7s. 6d. if the patient could afford it—or nothing if they couldn't!

The paupers of the parish under the care of the Ross Union workhouse fared quite well as they received medical care from the Medical

Mrs. Ann Young of Howle Hill.
(Courtesy of Fred Druce, Ross)

Officers, medical practitioners employed on a contract basis by the Board of Guardians of the workhouse. The sick and poor of the parish could apply either for medical relief to enable them to purchase treatment at home or to the workhouse to be admitted for treatment. The Ross Union workhouse records indicate that the disabled, visually, hearing and speech impaired were well cared for and often sent to specialist homes outside the area for care or to take up apprenticeships as appropriate. The workhouse paid subscriptions to the hospitals used for treatment provision.

The Ross Union supplied basic medicines and 'bandages, leeches and syringes where ordered by the Medical Officer'. The workhouse dispenser could earn much needed funds for the workhouse by selling drugs and so was urged by the guardians to keep the dispensary well stocked. Medical officers received fees for attending cases in the Union district and in 1839 a fee of 8s 6d would have been charged for attending family cases in Walford parish.

In the early 1900s only the wage earner (usually the man) in a family was entitled to free health care as a result of paying a National Insurance contribution from his wage. Dependants were left to fend for themselves and could only receive medical treatment by payment. Often the wealthier in the parish assisted in supporting those of lesser means to obtain medical treatment—for an annual donation, such residents were often allowed a quota of letters for an introduction for poorer residents to obtain medical treatment. Older residents can remember visiting such a house to obtain a letter of referral to the local hospital to enable someone to obtain appropriate medical treatment.

Fortunately there were several community groups to help the sick and needy. Organisations such as the Ancient Order of Foresters, the Oddfellows' Club (the Loyal St. Michael's Lodge of the Independent Order of Oddfellows, founded in 1880) and other Friendly Societies were concerned with providing sick benefits in kind, and later in cash, to help the sick and needy. Each Court of the Foresters (the local one was Court Garron of Goodrich) appointed and paid a fee to the local doctor to attend to its members. 'Woodwards' were also appointed to ensure that sick members observed the rules and did not go to work whilst they were ill and claiming support.

Annual parish parades were organised in the community to help boost funds and raise awareness of the benefits of belonging to such groups. All the parish organisations and members from clubs in adjoining villages dressed up and rode on horseback and decorated lorries in the fundraising parade.

The Sunday Parade became a hospital benefit and was called Hospital Sunday. After the introduction of the 1912 National Insurance Bill all the different Orders joined in the Sunday procession which took place on the first Sunday in August. The financial resources of all these groups were combined and a local doctor retained by members' subscription until 1948 and the introduction of the National Health Service as we know it today. A precursor to the

National Health Service of today was responsible for medical care and sickness benefit was given at about 10 shillings a week.

The annual Hospital Parades helped raise community funds in the 1920s to assist local medical care provision such as that available at Ross Cottage Hospital and through the local nursing associations. The church services that took place after the parade were held alternately at Walford and Bishopswood churches.

In the 1920s local Women's Institute groups were instrumental in setting up the nursing associations which served local areas. The Bishopswood and Walford Nursing Association was established in 1928 to provide care in the community through the funding of a district nurse. Fundraising events were vital to the success of the nursing association and the group often received support from local church service congregation collections.

On 5 August 1928, Bishopswood parish arranged a parade including all the local Friendly Societies and a procession with band from Goodrich to Bishopswood, taking a collection along the way for the Ross Cottage Hospital. The Ancient Order of Foresters joined in on horseback in fancy dress, including the characters of Robin Hood (Br. G. Gwatkin), Little John (Br. H. Dobbs), Maid Marion (Mrs. G. Smith) and Will Scarlet (Br. L. Williams). At Kerne Bridge, parishioners from Walford joined the procession which continued to Bishopswood church for the service.

Mrs. Joyce Roberts, who has lived all her life (nearly 90 years) on Howle Hill, recalls in her oral history record *Life on Howle Hill in the 1920s* how neighbours always helped each other when ill: 'The news of someone ill or in need of help was enough to start a collection or similar. Illness especially and folk needing hospital admission, meant a visit to one of the local gentry known to support the hospital, to ask for a letter which hopefully gave early admission for treatment. This usually meant a trip with my mother to visit the house which would hopefully give help ...'.

Mrs. Roberts' memories further describe several useful home remedies: 'most minor illnesses and accidents were home treated. For boils and carbuncles they applied a bread poultice, very hot soap and sugar poultice. Boiled onions were used for sore throats. Blackcurrant, elderflower, camomile and peppermint teas were used for colds, and the men's special cure was toast and cider. Brimstone and treacle, or senna were used for constipation cure, and houseleek poultice for earache. A bandage of brown paper soaked in vinegar was used to cure headache and the blue bag was always on hand for wasp stings. Infectious illness brought isolation and sheets steeped in disinfectant hanging over the bedroom door. Isolation often lasted 3 weeks'.

As previously mentioned, the nursing association funds were used to provide a district nurse for Walford and Bishopswood. Nurse Alice Hill was the first district nurse in the parish from 1924 and her own account of her work can be found recorded in the Walford Women's Institute *Walford Within Living Memory* compiled in 1954/5: 'I became District Nurse and Midwife of Walford and Bishopswood in 1924. I followed a Mrs. Ann Young who was then over 70, I nursed her in her last illness. I admired her courage and work for she must have walked hundreds of miles to her patients, stayed with them and did her best, which was wonderful, for the fee of 5s. or 7s. 6d. and sometimes nothing. Great credit was due to her.

'I was presented with a second-hand push bike and then taken around the hills which was my district. Did I push the bicycle? Oh no! I found all the little lanes and walked. It was a hard furrow to plough at first as the folk appeared to be frightened of the uniform. One doctor informed me that, if I had worn a bonnet and shawl and white apron, all would have been well, any way I persevered and I believe won their trust. It was the ante-natal visits they could not understand as I believe Mrs. Young would meet them and take names and maybe not see them again until called, but, praise be, all that is altered now.

'In 1927, I acquired a Frances Bennet motorcycle, 1½hp. It was a joy to climb the hills without effort. The only drawback was that, after reaching the top, I had to let it cool before starting again. I had three in 12 years and was given £1 10s. per annum, for three years, for the upkeep, and then it was raised to £2 10s.

'In 1937, Mrs. Hann, of Hazelhurst, Bishopswood, held a Garden Fete and Sale of Work to raise funds for a small car. We got over £100 and so I was presented with an Austin 7 Tourer. [Nurse Hill still owned the car in 1955 after she had retired.] Also the Women's Institute gave me a lovely motor rug, made from cured rabbit skins ...

'By that time my district was extended to Goodrich and Hope Mansell, then the war came and the screened lights. How I dreaded night calls, especially when it was Coppett Hill or Huntsham Hill! Still I enjoyed it and made a great many friends. The folk were grand to work for and I think they were all satisfied customers ...'.

Nurse Hill was followed by Nurse Alice Watkins who came to the district from Hereford in 1952 and lived in a house provided for her at the newly built Coughton Place development. She shared the house with a friend, Nurse Morgans, who worked in Ross. The two district nurses lived all their working life and subsequent retirement in the community they served.

When Nurse Watkins started work, communications were very different from those of today—few cars, no mobile phones and few telephones in the area at all. The district nurse worked very much on her own and needed to be self-reliant and think on her feet, dealing with each situation as best she could. Nurse Watkins' own account gives an insight into the demands and scope of her work through the middle part of the 20th century: 'I first came to Walford in October 1952 to live in Coughton Place having been appointed by

Herefordshire County Council to work as the District Nurse/Midwife/Health Visitor in Walford and surrounding villages. And so I was privileged to become involved in the lives of the people of Walford "in sickness and health"—through trials and tribulations—joys and sorrows—from birth to death—until my retirement in 1980.

'My duties consisted of general nursing of all illnesses, acute or chronic, minor or terminal. Surgical dressings of all kinds again minor to major. Periodic injections for whatever—monthly or otherwise—and any other problem or complaint that arose. I carried out a full range of health visiting duties—child care—school nursing, care of the elderly—health education and attendance at clinics. And in between came the midwifery—full ante and post natal care—home confinements and again health education.

'In all disciplines I worked in close co-operation with colleagues—GPs, local hospitals, school teachers, social workers and others as well as local voluntary organisations. As the years progressed nursing treatments and procedures changed—as it should be—helped by the coming of more nursing aids and equipment and of course disposables.

'Midwifery changed dramatically—all (or almost all) confinements taking place in hospital with early discharge for care at home. Eventually all midwifery care was taken over by the maternity unit with midwives from the hospital doing the home visits.

'Health Visitors and District Nurses became GP attached—caring for the patients from a practice rather than in an area. More and more treatments were carried out at the surgery and less and less in the home.

'I was attached to what is now Alton Street Surgery and relinquished my health visiting duties except my care of the elderly and lonely people of Walford. Administration changed from Local Authority to Community Trust. Thus the familiar sight of the District Nurse driving or walking round the village was consigned to history'.

Nurse Alice Watkins, the district nurse in Walford from 1952 to 1980. (Courtesy of Walford W.I.)

Nurse Watkins not only tended the sick in the community but used what must have been her very limited spare time to be active as a Parish Councillor, School Governor and in supporting various social and fundraising activities. She assisted in the running of the youth club and for over 15 years was part of a committee working tirelessly to raise funds to enable a village hall to be built in Walford. Alice Watkins died peacefully in Ross Community Hospital in July 2001.

Basic medical care was provided for pupils attending the village schools from around 1909 through the regular medical inspections conducted by the school dentist and nurse. Mention is made in the chapter on education of the range of illnesses that kept pupils from attending their lessons.

There was a severe outbreak of diphtheria in the parish in 1908 when many young people died. It was thought that the outbreak was started by a letter from Birmingham to Walford as both the writer and recipient subsequently had diphtheria. An outbreak of scarlet fever in 1916 resulted in the closure of the school for 10 weeks.

There was, and still is, no resident village doctor; the nearest being GPs located in group practices in Ross and Drybrook. A pair of cottages at Forest Green have been called Doctor's Place for over 100 years but there seems to be no traceable medical connection on record. Hospital facilities for the area were, and are, available in Ross and further afield in Hereford and Gloucester.

The Community Health Trusts deliver healthcare from group GP practices in Ross and Drybrook with the sick being required to make appointments to attend the practice surgery rather than being visited at home (which is possible in emergencies). This can be difficult for the infirm of the parish who may not have access to transport as readily as they used to. Local organisations such as the Women's Royal Voluntary Service based in nearby Ross, can provide transport to enable people to attend medical appointments. As an alternative to visiting the local surgery, prospective patients can also obtain medical advice in the home — not from a visit by a practitioner but by telephoning for medical advice from the NHS Direct service or searching for information on the Internet.

The town of Ross is well provided for as regards choices for medical treatment. In addition to the national health facilities provided from the GP practices, the community hospital and the dentists, there are several 'alternative health practitioners' offering a range of treatments at a price. Aromatherapy, reflexology, chiropractic and medical herbalism to name but a few are all available and take their place alongside conventional medical care. Several alternative practitioners are resident in Walford parish and carry out home visits, working on a self-employed basis.

Rural communities such as Walford experience many trials and tribulations and there are several organisations that can provide support and assistance where required. In 1992 the Herefordshire Rural Stress Action Group, was the first of its kind in the country. The group is a free and confidential service open to everybody in the countryside where sometimes people may feel very isolated in coping with their difficulties. The stresses and strains in farming due to a range of difficulties have been well documented over recent years and it is a sad fact that nationally there are around 70 suicides by farmers every year. In Herefordshire there are currently around 30 contacts a week to the Rural Stress Information Network. Whole families need support as they feel isolation and distress at the thought of the difficulties that may lie ahead.

In 2001 the County was in the grip of a foot and mouth outbreak which wreaked havoc on rural life. There are also many other on-going difficulties relating to issues such as reductions in rural transport and the closure of village shops, schools and public houses all of which provided a useful focus for a community. All these matters cut away at the fabric of rural life and their importance should neither be forgotten or underestimated.

CHAPTER V
River, Road and Rail

The lines of communication of the Walford and Bishopswood area are, as is common, largely dependent on the natural physical obstacles between one place and another. In this case these are the River Wye, together with its tributary streams, and also the higher areas between valleys, which almost form a plateau. South from Ross the river runs through a flood plain and the parish of Walford lies largely on the left bank with Goodrich to the west. The area known as Coughton Marshes can now be be used for agriculture following drainage and reclamation.

In respect of water transport and communication, the River Wye has never been very suitable for navigation with unpredictable currents and shallows and occasional sudden floods. In the introduction to his articles on the Kerne Bridge, John van Laun refers to attempts to improve the situation from 1662. Navigation along the Wye was made possible through an Act of Parliament in 1695 and by 1727 coal from Lydbrook could be transported by river to Hereford.

Barges were used to transport materials upstream—initially towed by men in harness; one man pulling one ton of cargo! In 1808 an Act was obtained to build a horse towing path from Lydbrook to Hereford, completed at a total cost of £5,000. Two horses towed each barge and when Kerne Bridge was built there was a walking way under the second arch of the bridge. The remains of this tow-path can be seen in the footpath which runs on the Goodrich side of the river up to Ross, although it seems to have disappeared further north.

Part of Walford parish is situated in the Wye Valley Area of Outstanding Natural Beauty which was designated in February 1971 so that the year 2001 was its 30th anniversary. The river valley has not only natural beauty and is rich in wildlife but also has many historic buildings and 'early on became associated with' the concept of 'the Picturesque' style of art. The river has lofty banks and many twists and turns so providing a succession of views and perspectives. The picturesque style was based on a set of rules by which the traveller could

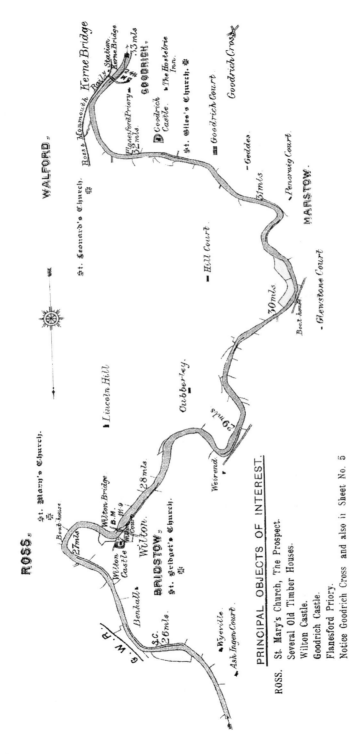

Stooke's Tourist Map of the River Wye, 1892; Ross to Goodrich

PRINCIPAL OBJECTS OF INTEREST.

ROSS. St. Mary's Church, The Prospect.
       Several Old Timber Houses.
       Wilton Castle.
       Goodrich Castle.
       Flanesford Priory.
       Notice Goodrich Cross and also in Sheet No. 5

gain the greatest satisfaction from a vista. However, the resulting pictures were not always topographically accurate.

In the 18th century the Revd. William Gilpin popularised the Wye Tour thus making it an essential experience to paint, write and generally enjoy the beauty of the landscape alongside the river. Gilpin's interest arose from a boat trip he took in 1770 on the river Wye from Ross to Chepstow. His journey was described in his book *Observations on the River Wye*, published in 1782. The Revd. Thomas Fosbroke also wrote about the Wye and the locality in his book published in 1826.

The first Wye pleasure boat was built in 1745 by John Egerton, son of the Bishop of Hereford and appointed to the benefice at Ross. A pleasure boat was typically rowed by two to six men and was equipped with awnings, lockers, food and a central table at which writing, sketching and dining took place. The fare was one and a half guineas for each leg of the journey: Hereford to Ross, Ross to Monmouth and Monmouth to Chepstow. By the end of the 18th century, Ross had become the centre of the fashionable 'Wye Tour'. The surrounding area had become a popular tourist area with the artists and poets of the time, such as Wordsworth, who visited to enjoy the 'picturesque' scenery. Wordsworth is said to have met the girl who became the subject of his poem 'We are seven' in the Goodrich area in 1793.

In June 1870 members the Woolhope Naturalists' Field Club and their wives took the Wye Tour to visit the new railway tunnel at Kerne Bridge. The account of the day out says that 'precise and careful arrangements had been made ... there was a pleasant breeze upon the water, but a clear proof of the sun's heat on shore, ... was afforded by the different herds of cattle bathing themselves in the cool water'. The party stopped the boats in the parish to disembark and walk up to Goodrich Castle and then continued by river to a point about one mile below Kerne Bridge.

Stooke's 'Tourist map of the River Wye' from Hereford to the Severn in 1892 provided detail of the principal places of interest along the route of the river as well as noting the salmon catches to Ross. However, by the late 1800s the Wye Tour was declining in popularity.

As well as being an obstacle in its own right, the Wye also floods fairly frequently so that routes through the parish generally avoided any low-lying ground. Some of the worst floods were in 1735, 1795, 1852, 1947 and 1963, and parish churches, which are often located by the river, were badly affected. In 1815 Eusebius, son of the Revd. John Beeston, vicar of Walford for just one year in 1810, was drowned in the Wye aged only 26.

In October 1883 there was a huge tidal wave in the Wye and Severn. The text from a pamphlet of that year reads: 'the tidal wave up the Wye is so high that I have never yet heard any contradiction of the statement that with the sole exception of that in the Bay of Fundy in Nova Scotia, it is the highest in the world'. At the Anchor Inn at Tintern the 1883 tidal mark is shown five feet up the kitchen wall. In 1963 the second highest flood in living memory submerged the station platforms cutting off Kerne Bridge completely.

Weirs had been built along the river, probably since Roman times, to assist river navigation and also fishing but a lock had to be provided with each. In the 1600s these flash locks raised the water level so that boats could move upstream, whilst the flush (or flash) of water released when the lock was opened enabled a boat to be carried downstream over any shallows below the weir. Later, more complex pound locks were built on the Wye to assist the development of trade with the city of Hereford.

The river has long been a valuable asset for fishing and one local Walford resident, Robert Pashley, who started fishing in 1897, was known as 'the Wizard of the Wye' because of his prowess at salmon fishing. His catches are documented in H.A. Gilbert's book *The Tale of a Wye Fisherman*.

In the latter part of the 19th and early 20th centuries, the coracle was commonly used for fishing on the river. The coracle is a small, oval craft propelled by a paddle and able to take just one person. It was an extremely light vessel made from wooden lathes and calico or hide coated with pitch or tar. The last person to be use one on the Wye was William Dew of Kerne Bridge, grand-father to Nancy Bromfield who previously lived in the parish. Mr. Dew made his own coracles (calling them truckles) and regularly sailed on the river until about 1910. Following his death in 1931, his coracle was given to Hereford Museum by his daughter in 1935 and is now in St. Fagan's Folk Museum, Cardiff. These days the river is easily accessible on foot, canoe, bicycle and car but no longer by rail, as will be mentioned later in the chapter.

As has been mentioned earlier, the river tends to flood fairly regu-larly and this affects the routes of pathways which generally avoid the low-lying ground. The type of soil and rock on which the track lies also influences their capability to carry traffic (at least before the advent of tarmac), a notable example being the brick clay

William Dew and his coracle.
(Courtesy of Walford W.I.)

underlying what is locally known as the 'Dirty Road' (between Howle Cross and the New Buildings at Forest Green) and other paths lying off this road. The latter often become mudbaths in wet weather.

Not much is known about early tracks in the area. Jonathan Claxton, in his manuscript work, 'Ross Borough and Foreign', describes the large hill fort on Chase Hill: '... from the style of ramparts and gateway it was built (or rebuilt) 4 to 500 years before the Roman invasion of 43AD. This fort would have given refuge to several hundred people together with their flocks and herds and there are many tracks and footpaths leading up to the top of the hill.'

In Roman times iron was known to be an important asset and the Forest of Dean was one of the areas worked for ore. The chief area used for smelting was known as *Ariconium*, now identified as a site near Weston-under-Penyard just beyond the parish boundary in Gloucestershire. To smelt the Forest of Dean iron ore a great deal of timber would have been used (as charcoal) for fuel; this was available either from the Forest or the well-wooded area just to the north of Ross around Upton Bishop. The smelted metal would have been taken away by pack horse, sled or cart, or sent to some place where the heavy material could be taken by water transport: *Blestium*, on the site of present-day Monmouth, or Lydney, perhaps, to avoid the rapids at Symonds Yat. All these considerations also influenced the much later ironworks at Bishopswood, where the furnaces had originally been erected in the reign of Charles II.

From 1809 a large network of tram roads existed in the Forest of Dean to transport coal, iron ore, stone and other goods, and a branch road was built in 1810 from Lydbrook to serve the ironworks at Bishopswood, which by then belonged to the Partridge family. Smelting ceased at Bishopswood in 1814, and bar iron for working was transported there from Lydbrook until about 1817, when the works finally closed.

There was a well-established shipping place at Lydbrook, with an incline from the tram road to the river, the remains of which are still visible. At the Bishopswood end the tram road reached the river at both Bishopswood and Cinderhill wharves. Near the county boundary of Herefordshire with Gloucestershire there is a tunnel for the tram road under the present Bishopswood to Lydbrook road, the B4234. This tram road ended immediately opposite at the riverside in Cinderhill wharf, while Bishopswood wharf was slightly further downstream.

Only very slight signs remain of either wharf these days. There was yet a third wharf, approximately half a mile further south, at Wyelands. This house is now demolished but was near the present site of the Severn & Trent water extraction plant. The wharf was built by the Lydney Trading Society in the 1820s, but it is believed to have closed in the early 1840s.

To return to the Roman iron smelting at *Ariconium*, some of the cinders and slag produced found a use as road metal, for which function it is apparently

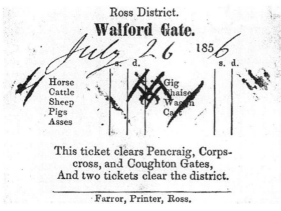

Toll Gate Ticket, Walford Gate, 1856.
(Hereford City Library)

excellent. One of the routes which it is thought was used to transport the ore and smelted iron (and which may have been an earlier British trackway) was the route along the gravel terrace of the River Wye (via Alton and probably Lincoln Hill) to the shallow river crossing at Goodrich. This crossing was originally known as the Wal- or Welsh- ford, and later as Goodrich Boat. It was still important until the building of Kerne Bridge (opened in 1828) and the later arrival of the local railway (1873). Heather Hurley, in her book *The Old Roads of South Herefordshire*, notes that the ferry was still in use in the early 20th century; it was mentioned in the Ward Lock Guide of 1914/15. The route through Hom Green to Goodrich Boat and on to Monmouth was one of those which became a turnpike road from Ross after 1749 when the Ross Turnpike Act was passed.

Before the Turnpike Acts, road maintenance had been carried out by individual parishes under the terms of the 1555 Highway Act, which had transferred the responsibility from manors to parishes. By the early 1700s, the state of the roads was becoming so deplorable that a new method of financing the work (pioneered in the east of England) was adopted nationally. Groups of trustees, comprising wealthy local residents and parsons, sought approval by Act of Parliament, which empowered them to oversee the maintenance of the roads and to charge tolls towards their upkeep. The tolls set locally in the Act of 1749 were lower for carts carrying lime or coals (a maximum of 8d.) than for other carriages (which were charged a maximum of 1s.).

The income from the tolls, after deduction of costs for repair and administration (including the wages and accommodation of the toll keepers), went towards repaying any mortgages taken out to cover the costs of road repairs and building the toll houses—a term originally of 21 years, though this often had to be extended. The account book of the Ross Turnpike Trust between June 1857 and May 1859 gives details of the amount spent on the maintenance of the Walford Road for each month in comparison with the other turnpike roads from Ross which went to Gloucester, Hereford, Ledbury and Monmouth. Expenditure on the Walford road was consistently higher than on any of the others, often twice as much or even more. As could be expected, it was also much higher during the winter months. The hedges were cut once a year, either in July or August.

Page from Ross Turnpike Trust accounts book for 1857-9.
(Courtesy of Martin Griffiths, Ross)

The accounts indicate that there were three regular maintenance men, each paid between 2s. and 2s. 6d. a day, with a variable number of extra men hired to break stone at 1s. 2d. per yard, with others 'raising stone' at 7d. a yard. The stone came from two quarries: that of Mr. Bennett, which was probably near the bottom of Whitings Lane, and that of 'John Partridge Esq.', which would have been somewhere on the Bishopswood estate. The copy from the account book shows the format of the record made for the Walford Road from January to February 1859.

Several turnpike roads passed through the parish and the official description according to the original Act of 1749 read:

> ... the Road leading from the said Town of Ross, by Coughton's Chapel, to a Place called the Quern, in the Parish of Walford, being Three Miles or thereabouts; and also the Road leading from the Town of Ross aforesaid, to Goodrich Boat, being Two Miles, or thereabouts ...; and also the Road leading from the said Town of Ross, along Puckeridge Lane, to a Place called Dib Dean in the Parish of Walford, being Three Miles, or thereabouts ...

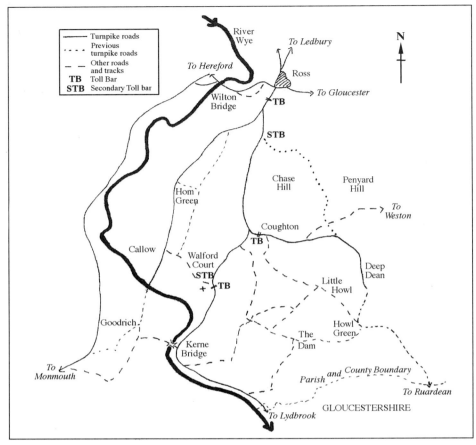

Map of Turnpike and other roads in Walford. (Drawn by Sheila Walshaw)

Routes could be, and were, altered to improve roads. The Ross to Ruardean route, for instance, originally went past Hill Farm, between Chase Hill and Penyard Hill, past Castlebrook and up what is now a footpath to the Paddocks before joining the Deep Dean road.

The section between Ross and the Paddocks was discontinued as a turnpike road in 1791, with closure in 1820 by an order of the local J.P.s which reads:

> being satisfied that a certain Team Road or Public Highway the whole or part whereof is called Puckeridge Lane within the said Parishes of Ross and Walford branching from or out of the Turnpike Road which leads from the Town of Ross towards Ruardean in the County of Gloucester at a certain place called Tuderville or Tudors Barn Unto and communicating with the same Turnpike Road at or near a place called the Paddock in the said Parish of Walford and being in length Two thousand seven hundred and ninety four yards is unnecessary We do hereby order the

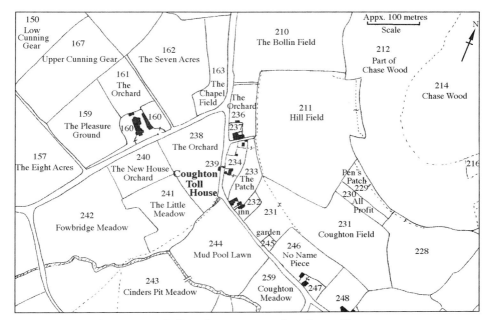

Area around Coughton corner showing toll cottage.
(Drawn by Sheila Walshaw from the 1840 Tithe Map)

same to be stopped up Reserving nevertheless to John Partridge Esquire Henry Barnett Esquire Kingsmill Evans Esquire Mr Thomas Mills Mr John Yonge Jones Mr Amos Jones and Mr Richard Addis their heirs and afsigns and their and each of their Tenant and Tenants a free Pafsage at all times for Persons Horses Cattle and Carriages through or along the Land or Soil of the said Old Highway so to be stopped up to and from their respective Lands Tenements and hereditaments adjoining such Old Highway according to the ancient usage thereof ...

In its place the section of the road between Coughton Street and the Deep Dean road became the new turnpike road, with a toll cottage just off the Coughton corner. This is currently called The Cider House but was previously known as The Pig and Whistle and the Pike House. In 1815 another Act had provided for the turnpike to continue beyond The Quern by a further 2,607 yards to William Partridge's iron furnace at Bishopswood, at a cost of £554. Various proposals were made to turnpike other routes in the parish, but none of these came into being.

Another toll cottage in Walford was on the B4234, on the north side just around the corner almost opposite the entrance to the parish church. The gate itself appears to have existed in two different positions (or possibly there were two toll bars as indicated on the 1835 map of the locality by Bryant). An earlier map of 1822 shows just one, across the road now leading to Hill Court, while

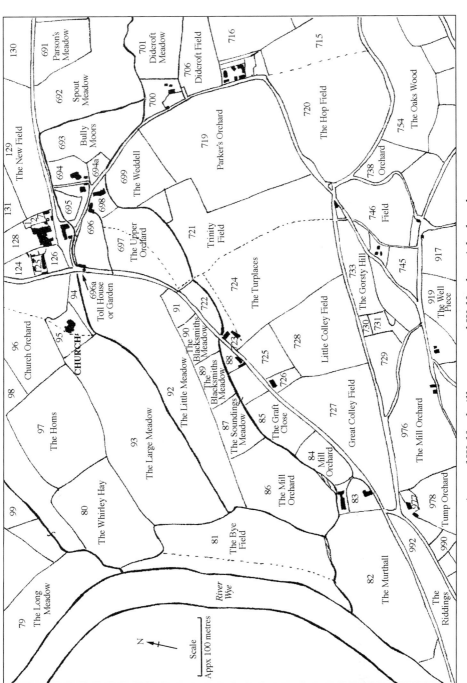

Area of Walford village around Walford parish church.
(Drawn by Sheila Walshaw from the 1840 Tithe Map)

The Goodrich Ferry
(from Picturesque Views on the River Wye *by Samuel Ireland, 1797)*

the Tithe Map of 1840 shows it on the present B road through Walford village. The change was perhaps connected with the opening of Kerne Bridge in 1828, which itself was a toll bridge.

John Partridge (then resident at Courtfield, near Goodrich, before moving to Bishopswood House in 1826) was one of the main instigators and financial backers of the Kerne Bridge project. An alternative route involving a bridge at the Goodrich Boat site had been proposed in 1824 by the Goodrich ferry company, supported by Kingsmill Evans, whose land adjoined the ferry route and who also owned the ferry. Eventually, however, Kingsmill Evans gave up his opposition to the Kerne Bridge route on 'certain conditions' and a promise of compensation, and in 1825 the Bill (4 George IV Cap. 60) was presented in Parliament, eventually receiving Royal assent in May.

The bridge and access roads were built over the next couple of years, opening in June 1828. As usual, tolls were much higher for horse-drawn carriages (6d.) than for horse-drawn wagons (4d.), other users and foot passengers. The toll for foot passengers was 1d., although payment was only levied for one journey a day. This charge was still the same in the 1920s and 1930s. Stage coaches and post-chaises, however, had to pay for each crossing. Tolls finally ceased in 1948, by which time the bridge had been taken over by the county council. Compensation was eventually paid to the ferry company, but only in 1834 after a court case.

Left: Ancient milestone indicating 3 miles from Ross which lay on the grass track between Boat Lane and the river Wye. (Courtesy of Walford W.I.) Right: Metal Milestone on the B4234, Walford Road. (Photo Sheila Walshaw)

After the railway bridge over the river was opened in 1873, pedestrians evaded the road bridge toll by crossing the river by the new route. An indignant letter from William Partridge, dated 30 August 1873, notes: 'I myself shortly after the opening of the Ross and Monmouth Line counted 12 persons crossing the railway bridge at one and the same time, to the prejudice of the Kerne Bridge Company. This practice should be put a stop to forthwith ... I am confident that the G.W.R. Company will not tolerate any such encroachment but will order their servants to summon before the Magistrates under the Railway Act any persons so offending.'

Several milestones remain in the parish and the unshaped stone milestone which used to be near the river bank on the Walford side of the former Goodrich ferry may have been an original one. Another stone used to stand exactly one mile nearer Ross against the roadside wall of Hill Court at Hom Green until around 1980. The metal mile posts still visible at The Vine Tree farm (at the Walford/Ross parish boundary), at the bottom of Bulls Hill on the Walford Road and opposite the entrance to Hazelhurst Nursing Home at Bishopswood were made in the mid-1800s by Perkins and Bellamy of Ross.

The ferry crossing at Goodrich is believed to have historical connotations. According to E. Jervoise, 'the rights of the ferry at Goodrich were given by Henry IV (then the Earl of Derby) to the ferryman who gave him the news of the birth of his son, later Henry V, and according to Heath the actual grant was then (in 1807) in operation.' The ferry was operated by means of a rope, as is the present day ferry at Symonds Yat.

The last use of a river crossing was perhaps during the Second World War, when the Felsted School for boys from Essex was evacuated to the area and occupied Hill Court and Goodrich Court across the river. A rope bridge was

*The Felsted School Suspension Bridge
over the Wye.
(By kind permission of Felsted School)*

built for the boys to cross the river for lessons. Since then, however, there has been no need for a crossing, and even the old roads down to the river are not open to the general public.

As has been said before, the river did not make a very satisfactory means of communication. When the river was frozen, in flood, or during dry weather the traffic transferred to the road (to Ross and then via Wilton Bridge), with predictable results on the surface of the latter.

Changes to the 18th century transport system came from both local and national developments. One local change came with the opening of Cats Hill in 1841 which is now the B4227. This runs from just outside the parish boundary up to Ruardean and then on to Nailbridge. This provided another, but not a significantly easier, route to Ruardean from Ross. One parishioner remembers coaxing her father's draught horses down this hill, slippery with ice, in bitter, winter weather.

The development of a national canal network in the early part of the 19th century did not really affect the parish. The nearest canal was the Hereford and Gloucester Canal, which was routed via Ledbury, with the closest point to the parish being at Newent, and so access to this did not impinge much on local traffic. However, the building of the railway system 60 years or so later did make an impact. Locally this came with the introduction of the Ross and Monmouth Railway, which opened in 1873 and is described later in this chapter.

The station at Kerne Bridge, with its goods facilities, was open until 1959. How much traffic it took from the local roads is uncertain, partly as the production from the area's limekilns was petering out during this era, whilst larger scale coalmining had not really begun. A shallow shaft and some open cast mining existed in the early 1800s at Great Howle with a larger open cast operation there run by the National Coal Board in the 1970s, when the coal was taken away by lorry via Sharman Hill.

Generally, though, railways provided enough competition for tolls to become uneconomic. The Ross Turnpike Trust finally wound up its affairs on 1 January 1873 with the maintenance of the main roads thereafter becoming the responsi-

bility of the Ross District Highway Board and then, after 1888, the newly constituted county councils. The turnpike roads generally were not as well maintained
at the end, owing to the tolls being used to repay outstanding mortgages.

In Walford and Bishopswood the road network probably did not suffer the
same neglect as in other places where railway stations were easier to reach and
the lines went to several different places. A pony and trap ensemble (or donkey
and cart) was owned by quite a few people, apart from the carriages owned by
the gentry. Fred Stacey of The Crown Inn on Howle Hill had a pony and trap,
as did Archibald England of Bulls Hill. The fact that the Parish Council erected
a horse drinking trough halfway up Bulls Hill in 1897 for Queen Victoria's
Diamond Jubilee indicates that there must have been a fair bit of horse traffic
in the vicinity. This trough was also used to water cattle in dry weather.

In 1890 the Comet Coaching Company Guide, published by Mr. Bellamy of
Ross, gave details of the coach and four that ran between Ross, Monmouth and
Abergavenny. The service passed through Walford stopping at Kerne Bridge. The
fare from Ross to Kerne Bridge was one shilling which did not compare econom-
ically with the railway fare. The coach left Ross at 10.30 a.m. and, after picking
up passengers at the railway station, arrived at Kerne Bridge at 11.15 a.m. when
the horses were changed. A carrier's cart also stopped in Walford to pick up
passengers on its journey from Lydbrook to Ross on certain days. Until the First
World War the gentry had their own horse drawn carriages and the farmers drove
dog carts and waggons. Donkey carts were also in common use at that time.

Donkey and cart near Wenslow Cottage, Howle Hill around 1920.
(Courtesy of Joyce Roberts)

The first mention of a bus service in the directories of the period was in *Kelly's Directory* for 1929. This referred to a daily omnibus service run by the Bristol Tramways and Carriage Company between Coleford and Ross, passing along the Walford main road. In the same directory

Edwards' bus. (Courtesy of Walford W.I.)

William Webb of Forest Green is mentioned as 'Haulage contractor, car proprietor and coal dealer'. Older residents remember his bus providing transportation on local market days for many years and taking miners to work in the Forest of Dean. Just after the First World War Richard Lewis of the Kerne Bridge Inn used to operate a charabanc, running trips to the Forest from Kerne Bridge on most fine afternoons. Eventually the bus was bought and turned into a lorry by Mr. George Reed of Mitcheldean. An entry in *Kelly's Trade Directory* for 1937 advertised that 'Webb's omnibus passes Howle Hill P.O. on Tues. Thurs. and Sat. for Ross'. Later this service was taken over by Edwards of Joys Green, who was operating it in 1955 and still doing so in 1965.

Nowadays H & H Coaches run one bus each way on a Thursday morning and Circle Line of Gloucester one each way on a Saturday morning. These two operators also run buses along the Ross to Kerne Bridge road, together with Duke's Travel (Ross to Coleford service) and Stagecoach Red & White (Monmouth to Gloucester), giving a total of about 13 buses each way per day. The fare, in 2001, from Ross to Walford was 75p., and to Kerne Bridge 95p., while from Walford to Coughton was 40p. and from Coughton to Ross 50p. (equivalent to 10s. in 'old money'). The figures for fares given in the 1965 Women's Institute Local History were 6d. from Walford post office to Coughton and 9d. (4p.) from Coughton to Ross!

Cars gradually became the more normal mode of transport with the result that road surfaces needed improving; any dry weather resulting in clouds of dust. The stone surface that older community members remember from their childhood in the 1920s would probably have been water-bound macadam, where crushed stone was laid, rolled and then bound with water and grit or fine dust. Spent stone from the lime kilns was frequently used for road mending in those days with the heaps of stone being dumped by the roadside for the roadmen to break up.

During the 1930s the stone road surfaces were sprayed with hot tar and then ¼in. (6mm.), or larger, stone chippings rolled into the surface. Up to 1945 the motor traffic was quite light and these sufficed. However, at the end of the war petrol became more easily available again and in addition ex-army lorries came on to the market in quantity, leading to the setting up of many small haulage firms across the country. The volume of traffic in general increased and eventually roads had to be strengthened. Tarmacadam from the Forest of Dean quarries (tar and Herefordshire stone mixed to specification) was delivered and hand-laid to achieve this. After about 1950 machines were introduced to lay the tarmac. These machines had originally been brought over from America during the war to lay aerodrome runways and about five times as much tarmac could be laid in a day with the same number of men.

When Herefordshire County Council took over the responsibility for roads, it could not afford to maintain and upgrade all the various roads that existed. Over the years not all the roads and tracks that existed were upgraded to tarmac surfaces. An example of the latter is the road down past Chadwyns (previously called Hawker's Green) and through to Dunderhole Farm. It is worth recording that the property on the opposite side of the road from Chadwyns used to be called Coldharbour; this name is usually an indicator of a Roman route.

Holes in the road surface are a perennial problem and doubtless then, as now, a heavy rainstorm did considerable damage to the road surfaces. Even where new drainage systems have been installed, as on the upper stretch of Leys Hill, water flows over the surface rather than into the ditches and grids, also a problem on Sharman Hill. Leys Hill is referred to as White's Road in the 1841 census and this name is still used by some long term residents of the area. For many years roadmen have not been employed to keep the ditches and drainage grids clear, so water can pour down the road surfaces, scouring out holes and depositing silt and grit in inconvenient places and causing a minor flood on reaching the bottom of the hill. The increased amount of car traffic, usually in a hurry, also destroys the drainage system where two cars try to pass in a place suited to one car only. At the time of writing (2001) Walford Parish Council has just employed a lengthsman to keep roadside edges clear for drainage so the situation should improve.

Along with the current network of roads there is a maze of footpaths in the parish, over 25 miles of them. Some of these may date back to medieval days, if not earlier, as they agree well with the description of the old sunken lanes as being, in Heather Hurley's words: 'created long ago before the use of wheeled vehicles when foot travellers preferred a direct line regardless of steep gradients rather than a long sinuous route'.

Other footpaths led to the churches, shops or schools and the local wells. Those to the schools were much used by children before and just after the Second World War, as local people remember. At the Walford School centenary celebrations in 1974 one elderly parishioner recalled walking down from Marling Pitts on Howle Hill to the school along these paths. Similarly the routes to Bishopswood School provided excuses for young pupils to dawdle on their way to school. Many other paths go 'round the hills'; the bridlepath (WA7O) past Marks Well and Rogers Well and linking Howle Hill with Bulls Hill is one. These routes are considerably shorter than the current roads between the two points!

The majority of the present Wye Valley Walk section in the parish between Kerne Bridge and Coughton Mill, via the Walford Sawmill, Bulls Hill and Sharman Hill also meets this description. The long distance footpath was first proposed in 1973 and the route in the parish was designated around 1980. The Walk is planned to reach the source of the river Wye at Plynlimon in the year 2002.

There is a local tradition that a much older road existed from Ross further up the hillside than the line of the present B4234. Certainly some of the present Wye Valley Walk through the parish was surfaced with stone and used by horse and cart traffic in the past, for example from Bulls Hill through to the Walford saw mills. Further sections may be Whitings Lane from the saw mills across to Leys Hill and then straight across the present road to the 'public highway' closed by Edward Partridge in 1855 and referred to later. This pathway eventually comes out at the present road level again at Drybrook via Bakers Lane. The earliest map of the area with sufficient detail (that of Henry Price in 1817) shows the existence of the present B4234 route. Many paths have a solid base of stone, often somewhat buried under mud these days, and they may well have been part of tracks used by packhorses or oxen, moving lime in particular from the kilns that were dotted around the sides of the hills at around the 150 metre height.

Even the footpaths mapped as public rights of way in the current definitive map of 1989 (*see footnote below) are not all the paths that exist and are used, still less all that *did* exist. The Tithe Map of 1840 shows an enormous network

---

*Up until the Second World War, footpaths were just locally accepted but since then there have been several Parliamentary Acts (National Parks and Access to the Countryside in 1949, the Countryside Act in 1968 and the Wildlife and Countryside Act in 1981) designed to put the network on a more formal basis and transferring responsibility of the paths to county councils.

In the 1950s parish councils submitted maps and schedules of information of the rights of way in their area, sometimes together with supporting evidence, either of accustomed usage over the years or actual documentary evidence. The county councils reviewed and published a draft definitive map and then a provisional map, with opportunities for consultation and objections by the general public in the case of the former, and landowners and tenants only in the case of the latter. The results were then published as a definitive map in the 1960s.

On-going review every five years was intended, but this was overtaken by the 1981 legislation. This required reclassification from the category of 'Roads used as Public Paths' (RUPPs) to decide which should become 'Byways Open to All Traffic' (BOATs).

The most up to date local definitive map is that of 1989, but it is intended by Herefordshire Council that a continuous review process shall be operated and updated maps published 'at intervals'.

of these tracks, and papers from the Trinity Session of the Quarter Sessions in 1855 give details of the quite complicated procedures which had to be followed by Edward Otto Partridge when he wanted to close the track past Hazelhurst from near the Drybrook corner of the Lydbrook road across to Leys Hill, presumably to give more privacy to his house.

Other paths simply died of disuse, quickly becoming overgrown and blocked with scrub and brambles. Over the last seven or eight years, however, there has been a concerted effort by parish councils, parishioners and the county councils (Hereford & Worcester to 1998, Herefordshire Council since then) to ensure that any path on the definitive map is kept open and in good order. Many new stiles have been provided and fingerposts and 'yellow arrow' signing put up.

Similar fingerposts and blue signing denote bridleways although there are only around six miles of these in the parish. The Bakers Lane bridleway from Leys Hill to Drybrook on the Bishopswood road has actually been added to the local definitive map quite recently after a lot of public effort, and revision of the definitive maps is now reported to be on-going. Meanwhile the network of paths continues to provide the means of communication that was its original purpose, as well as the valuable leisure facility which is its main use today.

The railway was opened through Walford on 4 August 1873, some 20 years after the opening of the Hereford, Ross and Gloucester Railway (HR & GR) on 1 June 1855. The Ross and Monmouth Railway (R & M) which built the line through the parish, was incorporated by an Act of Parliament on 5 July 1865. However the line that was built was not the first planned route of the railway.

The 1860 plans of the railway show the projected line to run between Upper and Lower Warryfield and across the Wye to the east of Goodrich Castle then through a 70 yard (64m) tunnel near the Dry Arch at Goodrich. The line then crossed the river again at Huntsham Ferry (now Huntsham Bridge) and then continued on to Symonds Yat. The 1864 plans of the projected railway show an even greater deviation from the line that was built, showing the line running immediately to the west of Upper Warryfield, crossing the Wye just to the east of the ferry at Goodrich Boat, and then through a 756 yard (691m) tunnel just to the west of Goodrich. The line continued to the east of Marstow, west of Whitchurch and through Ganarew to Monmouth. While both the 1860 and 1864 routes were more direct, the line that was eventually built was likely to have been chosen as it provided an opportunity to tap the mineral traffic of the Forest of Dean. This was achieved through a connection with the Severn and Wye Railway (S & W) at Lydbrook Junction which the S & W reached in 1875.

The R & M was built as a standard gauge, single line, branch railway. However, had an ambitious railway scheme come to fruition, the R & M could have been part of a main line from the Midlands to South Wales. The plan was for a standard gauge railway extension of the Northampton and Banbury

Junction Railway (N & BJR) through Blockley and Tewkesbury in Gloucestershire to a junction with the R & M in Ross. The 1866 Bill relating to the extension of the N & BJR provided that railway with running powers over the projected R & M to Monmouth and then over the Coleford, Monmouth, Usk and Pontypool Railway (CMU & P) into South Wales.

A petition to the House of Lords from the Mayor, Aldermen and Council of the Borough of Monmouth wholeheartedly supported the N & BJR extension as it would provide a much needed, direct and valuable communication between South Wales and the Midlands, both for goods, in the form of

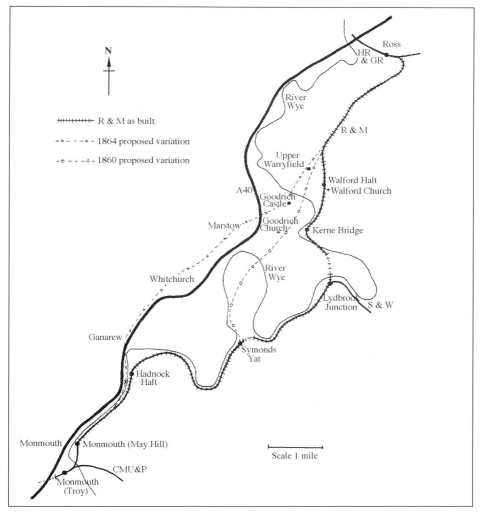

Map showing the line of the Ross and Monmouth railway along with the 1860 and 1864 proposed variations and connecting railways.
(Drawn by David Walshaw)

minerals, livestock and agricultural produce, and also for passengers. The R & M, however, petitioned against the N & BJR extension, in particular objecting not only to the granting of running powers over the R & M but also querying engineering features and project costs.

It soon became obvious that the N & BJR scheme was over-ambitious, and in 1870 the extension plan was dropped and the company reverted to its original name of Northampton and Banbury Railway. Thus the possibility of Walford being on a main line from the Midlands to South Wales had gone and the reality was the rural, single line of the R & M connecting with the HR & GR at Ross and the CMUP at Monmouth.

In 1867 it was suggested to the S & W that the Bishopswood tramroad branch, then moribund or nearly so, be converted to a standard gauge railway and the line extended to join the R & M near Kerne Bridge. However, after visiting the line in the company carriage, the directors were not impressed with the idea and the scheme was never implemented.

It took eight years from obtaining its Act in 1865 for the R & M to complete the building of the line and its opening to Monmouth (May Hill) on the east bank of the river Wye, on 4 August 1873. The contractor who built the line was Joseph Firbank of Newport, Monmouthshire. In common with many other railway schemes, raising the finance was a problem and the R & M tried to persuade Mr. Firbank to accept payment in the form of shares rather than in money, an idea which, not surprisingly, he rejected. In a letter, dated 3 November 1870, he wrote to a Mr. Hewitt as follows: 'Dear Sir, Will you be kind enough to let me know by letter whether I am to continue working or not as if no money is forthcoming I cannot go on with the work. It is no use saying

Railway Bridge over the River Wye at Kerne Bridge, looking north-east.
(Courtesy of Jack Coombes, Ross)

I am to see Mr. Liddle - he cannot give me any money and if you cannot get it, it's best to write and stop the work before I get a debt and then stop ... .'

The building of the railway line necessitated alterations to certain roads in Walford, notably the lowering of the Walford Court to Warryfield road by 5 feet (1.5m) where the line crossed the road to allow the 20 foot (6m) span arch of the bridge carrying the railway to have 15 foot (4.6m) headroom over the road. Rather more major work was required at Kerne Bridge where alterations to the road bridge itself had to be carried out. Buttresses were built at a cost of £276 15s. 3d. (£276.76), the parapets were raised and the toll house rebuilt at a cost of £625 5s. 10d. (£625.29).

When the R & M line was first built, Kerne Bridge station was the first station on the line after leaving Ross and, at that time, the only station in the parish of Walford. The station, with its two platforms and buildings cost £634 18s. 5d. (£634.92) to build. Included in that sum was £66 2s. 1d. (£66.10) for a well in the platform, with a lift pump and cover, to supply the station building with water. Originally, the station had a passing loop with rails serving both platforms, but in 1901 the point at the Ross end of the loop was removed and the line through the platform on the road side of the station became a siding or long headshunt.

Goods facilities were provided on the Monmouth side of the station. However, these did not satisfy the Great Western Railway (GWR), who operated the railway from the start, and in 1885 they requested the provision of a 5 ton crane at Kerne Bridge. Two years later, the GWR further requested a siding and a loading dock for horses and cattle. These improvements were carried out, and in 1904 Kerne Bridge station was listed as having passenger and parcels facilities, a goods station with a 5 ton crane and also facilities for handling livestock and horse boxes. These facilities were still the same in 1956, apart from the loss of the crane.

After leaving Kerne Bridge station in the Monmouth direction, the railway line left the parish of Walford when it crossed the Wye by means of a viaduct. The next station was Lydbrook Junction, where the R & M connected with the S & W and this was followed by a station at Symonds Yat. Originally the line terminated at Monmouth (May Hill) on the east bank of the Wye, a far from satisfactory arrangement. It was left to the GWR to build the viaduct across the river and extend the line to make an end-on connection with the CMU & P at Monmouth (Troy). The CMU & P, in spite of its name, never built the proposed section of line from Monmouth to Coleford.

At Monmouth (Troy), the R & M made a connection with the Wye Valley Railway. This line ran up the Wye Valley to Monmouth (Troy) from a junction near Chepstow and was another railway of benefit to the people of Walford. It opened on 1 November 1876 and provided the opportunity for further scenic trips until it closed on 5 January 1959. Goods traffic continued until January 1964.

Sketch of Walford Halt looking south. (Drawn by Liz Baker)

Although operated by the GWR from the outset, the R & M remained independent until the 1921 Railways Act forced its amalgamation into the GWR in 1922. In its last year, the R & M produced a working profit of £4,362.

In 1931, the GWR made a significant improvement in facilities for the people of Walford with the opening of Walford Halt on 23 February. The *Ross Gazette* of that week carried the front page headline: 'Railway Station for Walford - GWR Enterprise'. The article stated that 'the halt should prove a very useful acquisition to the district, particularly so, perhaps, in view of the industrial developments that are taking place near Lydbrook Junction station'.

GWR notice from Walford Halt displayed at Kidderminster Railway Museum. (Photo David Walshaw)

Walford Halt had a single 120 foot (36.6m) platform on the east side of the line and to the south of the Walford Court to Warryfield road. The platform was of wooden construction of a standard GWR type and was accessed by steps from the aforementioned road, on the east side of the railway bridge. The access path ran alongside the railway at track-level for a short distance, protected on either side by a post and rail fence, with a top wooden rail and galvanised wire beneath. Similar fencing protected the rear of the platform.

The platform waiting shelter was a standard GWR corrugated iron 'pagoda', officially known by the extremely dull name of 'Type A shed'. The 'pagoda' name was given to these shelters because their curving roof gave a somewhat oriental look to the design. The Walford example had a central doorway with a window either side of it. Lighting for the halt was provided by means of oil lamps, of which two were on the platform and one on the access path. Attached to the halt building was a GWR notice giving details of stations served by trains from the halt. As late as 1951, another halt was opened at Hadnock, between Symonds Yat and Monmouth (May Hill).

The opening of the R & M line in August 1873 was not without its problems. On 1 August, Colonel Rich, the Board of Trade Inspector, made a thorough inspection of the line and gave his permission for the line to be opened. Later that day, however, he discovered that there was no turntable at the Monmouth end to allow for the turning of engines. As running tender-first obstructs the driver's view and can therefore be dangerous, the Inspector promptly withdrew his permission for the opening. Following discussions with the railway companies concerned, permission was given for the line to be operated with tank engines, as these do not have tenders and so do not obstruct the driver's view when travelling backwards. The line opened only two days later than intended, on Monday 4 August. Thus one of the most picturesque railway lines in the country was opened for business.

Ex-GWR 0-4-2 Tank Engine 1455 with autotrailer entering Kerne Bridge station from Monmouth shortly before the closure of the line to passengers in 1959. (Courtesy of Eric Rawlins)

In 1871, a locomotive shed was opened in Ross, situated in the fork between the HR & GR and the R & M, the shed being built for the purposes of housing locomotives for the R & M line. The shed still stands, and is now occupied by a retail business.

In the early years the tank engines seem to have been of the 1868 William Dean designed GWR '517' class 0-4-2T engines, which were built over a period of 20 years. Charles B. Collett was appointed Chief Mechanical Engineer of the GWR in 1922 and he improved the '517' class to produce the 48xx class 0-4-2T, later to become the 14xx class introduced in 1932.

The 14xx class seems to have borne the brunt of passenger duties in later years. These engines were adapted for use with special coaches known as auto-trailers in order to save the engine having to run round its train on reaching its destination. When travelling engine-first, both fireman and the engine-driver were on the engine, but when travelling with the engine in the rear, the fireman stayed on the engine, whilst the engine-driver drove from the leading end of the auto-trailer. It was also known for the engine to be sandwiched in the middle, with an auto-trailer on either end. In this case, the driver would again be in the front of the leading auto-trailer with the fireman on the engine. Communication between the two men was by means of bell codes.

Although GWR 0-6-0 pannier tanks of various classes were used for most goods trains, they were not unknown on passenger trains as the photo of an 0-6-0PT and auto-trailer shows.

However tender engines were also used for goods traffic and there is photographic evidence of an ex-GWR Collett '2251' class 0-6-0 entering Ross with a freight (goods train) off the Monmouth branch in 1964. It may be that tender engines were permitted on goods trains once passenger trains had ceased.

A GWR 0-6-0 pannier tank with autotrailer near Walford Sawmills about 1937. (Courtesy of Mary Bevan)

During the Second World War a diesel railcar was used on the line. When the railways became nationalised in 1948, the line became part of the Western Region of British Railways. From the point of view of locomotives and coaching stock, this made little difference, and the line remained very much a GWR branch line in character.

In 1931, there were eight trains on weekdays between Ross and Lydbrook Junction, six of which ran through to Monmouth (Troy). In the reverse direction there were seven weekday trains between Lydbrook Junction and Ross, five of which started at Monmouth (Troy), but the 7.25a.m. from Lydbrook Junction did not stop at Walford Halt. There were slight differences to the timetable on Saturdays.

Bradshaw's 1938 timetable shows a very similar pattern, but indicates that both the 6.40a.m. and the 10.57a.m. departures from Ross ran through to Pontypool Road. In the reverse direction, only the 4.22p.m. arrival at Ross started from Pontypool Road. Two Sunday trains, in each direction, were shown. In the mid-1950s there were still seven passenger trains, each way, per day, in summer and five trains, each way, per day in winter. At this time there were two goods trains each way, per day, which served the Edison Swan cable factory at Lydbrook Junction.

The GWR advertised many 'cheap trips' over the line: from Ross to Kerne Bridge, Lydbrook Junction, Symonds Yat, Monmouth, Tintern, Chepstow and Usk. On Easter Monday in 1931, a 'cheap trip' from Ross to Walford Halt, by any train, was advertised at a cost of 6d. (2$\frac{1}{2}$p.). Also, at this period, cheap return tickets were issued to Ross and Monmouth each week day; to Hereford on Mondays, Wednesdays, Thursdays and Saturdays; and to Gloucester and Cheltenham on Mondays, Thursdays and Saturdays.

During its 86 years as a passenger station, Kerne Bridge appears to have had just nine station masters, as follows: John Mitchell, John Hunt, George Evans, William James Hyatt, William Henry Bunting, George Thorne, Sydney James, Mr. Lane, and Les Rothin who was there at closure. Les Rothin took a great pride in the gardens at Kerne Bridge and for many years the station won the award for the best-kept station on the line.

The opening of the R & M line and Kerne Bridge station in 1873 would appear to have brought almost immediate changes in the neighbourhood, the commercial directory of 1874 listing for the first time the Kerne Bridge Inn. The 1876/77 directory also lists the Albion Inn, Kerne Bridge. Both inns were very close to the station and were probably opened with a view to gaining the patronage of railway passengers. Furthermore, in the 1876/77 directory, William Sillett of the Kerne Bridge Inn is also listed as a coal merchant, and George Davies of the Albion Inn, is listed as a grocer and a coal dealer.

Coal was delivered to Kerne Bridge station from the Forest of Dean pits from an early date. Several other coal merchants are mentioned in the directories up until 1917 but seem to have been small, independent concerns. In contrast, the Phoenix Coal Co (later Phoenix Coal Co [Ross and Monmouth] Ltd) first appears at Kerne Bridge in the 1900 directory. They were still listed in 1937, but not in the 1941 directory. The Kerne Bridge depot was probably closed as a wartime economy.

Extract from Bradshaw's 1938 Railway Guide

In the 1920s and early 1930s, there are memories of people living in the Kerne Bridge neighbourhood collecting coal from the depot at the station in wheelbarrows, or, for those living further away, by pony and trap. A Mr. Sam Woolley would also deliver coal in a horse and cart, and, in the mid-1920s, coal was delivered to a Mrs. Young at the Old Post Office on Howle Hill where $^1/_4$ cwt could be bought for 6d. (2$^1/_2$p.).

When sugar beet began to be grown in the parish, probably after the First World War, this would be hand-loaded into railway wagons at Kerne Bridge goods yard, each wagon taking 10 tons. One farm alone dispatched two wagons per week during the autumn. The sugar beet was then transported by rail to the British Sugar Corporation factory at Foley Park, Kidderminster. Potatoes were also dispatched by rail, with seed potatoes possibly being received by rail from Scotland.

Timber from the Bishopswood estate was also dispatched from Kerne Bridge station. After felling, the timber was loaded on to special wagons and hauled to the station by Shire horses. In later years, probably after the Second World War, diesel lorries took over the haulage to the station. On arrival at the station the timber was stacked in the goods yard and, when sufficient had been stockpiled, the GWR would send a steam operated rail crane to Kerne Bridge station to load the timber on to railway wagons ready for dispatch by rail.

Another commodity arriving by train at Kerne Bridge was a twice weekly delivery of sausages and pies for Jolly's in Goodrich from Harris's of Calne in Wiltshire. This probably took place prior to, and during, the Second World War. As the GWR had requested the provision of a loading dock for horses and cattle in 1887, presumably livestock was also a feature of Kerne Bridge goods yard. Unlike Kerne Bridge station, Walford Halt was purely for passengers.

In the days before many people had telephones in their homes, it was possible to telephone from Kerne Bridge station, and a sign advertising this facility was fixed to the station building above the door leading onto the main platform. Another very useful facility, provided during the summer months at Kerne Bridge station, was the camping coach. Camping coaches were well appointed, having provision for cooking, sitting and sleeping (in bunk beds). They were very popular with holiday-makers who travelled to and from their pre-booked coach by the normal train service. Kerne Bridge must have been a wonderful site. The coach was stabled on the siding opposite the main station building and so was accessed from the second platform. The camping coach was probably in use for many years, with a break during the Second World War.

From the passengers' perspective, the R & M had many and varied uses for the people of the parish, whether boarding the train at Kerne Bridge or at Walford Halt. The trains carried children to school, both in Ross and Monmouth, workers to the Edison Swan works at Lydbrook Junction and, no doubt, to work in Ross as well. The railway was used for shopping trips to Ross and, immediately after the Second World War, carriages could be seen full of mothers, with their babies and prams, *en route* to the clinic in Ross.

The train was also used for visiting relatives as far away as South Wales, and for going away on holidays and for showing visitors the beauty of the Wye Valley. The Howle Hill Gospel Chapel was known to use the train for its Sunday School outings and, in the 1930s, the Edison Swan management even hired a special train to take its workers and families to a pantomime in Hereford, picking up passengers at Kerne Bridge *en route*.

Incoming passengers included those alighting at Kerne Bridge in order to visit Goodrich Castle; the name Goodrich Castle appeared below Kerne Bridge on the station nameboard. On Good Fridays, crowds would come out from Ross for the special celebrations at Leys Hill Baptist chapel. During the Second World War, King George VI travelled on the R & M in the royal train.

The railway played a very useful and important part in the life of the parish for many years but, with the increased use of road transport and the consequent decline in passenger numbers using the trains, the line was closed, throughout, to passengers on 5 January, 1959. The last passenger train over the line was a Stephenson Locomotive Society 'special' on Sunday 4 January, when 300 people made the journey over the Wye Valley Railway from Chepstow to Monmouth and then via the R & M to Ross; a distance of 26 miles.

The line was kept open for goods traffic, from Lydbrook Junction to Ross, but this ceased on 2 November 1964, with the closure of the Ross to Gloucester section of the HR & GR on the same date. All goods traffic for Lydbrook Junction, including private sidings, closed on 1 November 1965. The section from Ross to Hereford had closed 12 months previously.

At the time of writing the nearest railway stations to the parish of Walford are at Hereford, Gloucester, Ledbury and Lydney. Some sections of the R & M track bed now form parts of the route of the Wye Valley Walk.

A mixed train departing from Kerne Bridge to Monmouth around 1901.
(From a postcard by Mr. G.W. Young, Ross)

CHAPTER VI
Agriculture

Agriculture has always been central to life in this rural parish. In general the lowlands are fertile and a rich loam, with gentle slopes to the banks of the Wye. The higher land, while not as fertile (either clayey or sandy), nevertheless provides good pasture for sheep and, in the past, a subsistence living for the many smaller farmers and cottagers.

As there is no specific history of early farming practice in Walford and Bishopswood, it has been necessary to study the accounts of Herefordshire's agriculture in general to indicate local practice.

In the Middle Ages (from the death of Edward I in 1307 to the accession of Henry VII in 1485) the 'open field' system was common in Herefordshire, as in the rest of England. This was very wasteful as the land could not be cross-ploughed because fields were divided into individual strips, and improved drainage was not possible. Another disadvantage of the communal farming system was that stock grazed together on common land could not be improved by selective breeding. Also, 'owing to the absence of turnips and clover, and the scarcity of manure', the only way to rest the land was to let it stay fallow one in every three years. Even so, by the end of the 15th century, arable land was becoming worn-out. An average crop of wheat was only five to six bushels per acre. Arable land in Herefordshire, in 1338, was let at from 4d. to 8d. per acre, and meadow-land at 12d. to 18d. The former rate was in line with the rest of the country, the latter was lower—in the 14th century Herefordshire was the fourth poorest county in England. Labour was the chief resource on the land and agricultural implements were minimal. At Kingstone Manor, Herefordshire, in the early 14th century, there were only three carts, two ploughs, a fork, a spade, a few mattocks and corn sieves, a winnowing fan and some smaller miscellaneous items.

In the 15th century wool gave the best return, with the Leominster mart in north Herefordshire obtaining the peak prices. As a result enclosures became more frequent in the late 1500s and in the succeeding century. The area around

Ross was known as the Ryelands, and the native sheep of the same name were popular because of their fine wool; the breed goes back about six centuries. It was thought that this region was 'particularly favourable to them from the dryness of the soil and the sweetness of the herbage'. However, the animals were very small, with their fleeces only weighing between one and two pounds each—less than a kilogram. The shearing was generally done by women, and the sheep were kept in at night—cotting—as it was thought that this made the wool finer.

Rye was grown in the light lands in the vicinity of Ross, and this was in demand before the dissolution of the monasteries as, mixed with an equal proportion of wheat, it made up the bread-corn, or 'monk corn', used in religious houses. More recently wheat became the predominant cereal crop in this area.

In 1627 a noted writer on agriculture, Speed, enthused about the area in these words: 'the soyle of the county was so fertile for corne and cattle that no place in England yieldeth more or better conditioned.' Stock rearing was soon to take a great step forward with the introduction of turnips c.1750 as they provided winter feed for sheep and cattle. They were also soon thought to be a necessary preparation of the soil for producing any corn. On the hills sheep were folded with hurdles so that they gained access to a limited part of the crop each day. The partly buried shells that were left were removed by hand with a turnip peck or lifter, and 'placed before the sheep again'. This method was changed when a slicing machine was used to cut the turnip bulbs into strips (the sheep having first been fed the tops in their folds) and the results fed with chaff as feed. One ton of hay was usually allocated as fodder with every acre of turnips. Elsewhere in the County, as on the Ryelands, turnips were often sown in June for the market and the ground was cleared for wheat before Christmas. The practice of grazing sheep on root crops systematically can still be seen in both this parish and the neighbouring one of Goodrich.

Clover leys had been introduced into England as early as 1651; clover was used as winter feed for sheep, where the land was too soft for turnips, as this rested the wheat land. Credit for its innovation locally probably goes to a member of the Clarke family of Hill Court, as the Revd. Fosbroke asserted (in his book *The Wye Tour*) that the Clarkes made their fortune trading in clover seed; there was an agent in Ross as early as 1662. The crest of the Clarkes, with the Arms granted to Richard Clarke in 1663, displays three green trefoils, possibly a link with the clover-plant, and this is incorporated in the Evans coat of arms.

A glance at the Probate Inventory of Edmond Bond of Cobrey shows that, in May 1710, his goods included part of a 'reck' (rick) of clover, as well as over 27 acres of 'pease' and 5 acres of beans. Probate inventories were made up by two local men who testified, as 'appraisers', as to the extent and value of the possessions of the deceased in the distribution of the assets to beneficiaries.

The Evans coat of arms incorporates the Clarke arms in the top right quarter

Another farmer, Thomas Chinn, owned unthrashed clover feed worth £2 at his death in February 1713, as well as '5 bushels of small beans [£1] and 2 of great [2 shillings]'. Five years later the appraisers noted that Edmund Harris had owned £3 worth of hay and clover. It is evident that the beneficial effects of these leguminous crops were appreciated.

Hops were also grown, with cabbages, turnips and potatoes grown as 'catch crops' between the rows in the hop-yards. Potatoes were grown by cottagers, together with other vegetables, and cider apples were used for local consumption.

In the past the farmers of Herefordshire were notorious for lack of weed control; one 18th century writer notes: 'weeds, those overseers to watch and punish the sluggard, were rampant.'

Marl, a variety of mixtures of chalk and clay, was used from Roman times to control soil acidity and improve fertility. A property on Howle Hill with the name Marling Pitts has a quarry-like hollow in one field indicating the site of former marl excavation.

Dung from fold-animals and ox-stalls was distributed from the rear of horse-drawn carts, with lime as the most popular alternative fertiliser. The respected agriculturist, John Duncumb, writing in 1805, stated that 'the culture of rye, hemp, flax, turnips and parsnips is much improved with lime as a manure.'

Other fertilisers were also used. 'Of other manures used in Herefordshire, the sweepings of towns is very valuable in those situations which, by their proximity, will admit of its use. Common ashes and those from the soap-boiler's furnace are applied to pastures with great effect. Night-soil is also mixed with earth and other ingredients, and forms a very forcing compost. The shovellings of roads, scouring of ditches, mud from ponds, and other resources of the active farmer, are occasionally resorted to, but not so often as they might be with profit.' Guano (sea-bird droppings) was imported in large quantities from South America but from 1850 artificial manures became the most popular general crop fertiliser.

Extract from Edmond Bond's Probate Inventory
listing some of the stock on the farm in May 1710. (HRO)

Herefordshire was a county of mixed farming, an economic 'cushion' in times of depression. During the Revolutionary and Napoleonic Wars agricultural produce prices rose steeply, with wheat selling at one guinea (21 shillings) a bushel; as a result even poor land was converted to corn-growing and rents were raised. With peace, after the battle of Waterloo (1815), prices collapsed. Although local landlords reduced their rentals, many tenants could not pay. Tithes became increasingly unpopular and the churches were deserted. The larger landowners were the only farmers who could afford to invest in the range of innovative agricultural implements.

Wages on farms were lower in this county than in many others and the farm labourer suffered most, being on the lowest rung of the farming ladder. Above him was the shepherd, then the cowman and at the top the waggoner. In 1805 the average labourer's weekly wage was six shillings in the winter and seven shillings in the summer, with 'liquor and two dinners'. There were extra payments at hay-making and harvest time, with other 'perks' and allowances. 'Lamb-money', a sum for each lamb reared, was awarded to some shepherds.

As late as 1919 cider was still considered a customary perk on some farms in cider districts, and one comment reads 'the men will not work without it. The farmers object to it, because it causes, they say, a waste of time. The men in a field will stop working for five or ten minutes to go across the field to the cider and have a drink, and the horn cup of cider is passed round.'

The unrest caused by mechanisation on the farms increased, and in other parts of the country riots were reported. In Herefordshire some ricks were deliberately fired; a 17-year-old boy from Bridstow was convicted of one of these offences, and transported for seven years. In 1833 a threshing machine in the yard of an agricultural implement maker at Staunton-on-Wye was smashed. The usual practice of manual flailing and winnowing of the grain in the barns provided winter wages in the lean, cold months of winter, but the more efficient, powered machines could do the same work in a fifth of the time.

In contrast the period from 1850 to 1870 was a time of prosperity, with a cycle of good harvests. The newly-established railways increased the size of the potential market for produce, whilst wages for farmworkers increased in the face of competition for labour from the self-same railways and from the burgeoning industrial towns. Even so, agricultural wages failed to keep pace with the rise in commodities. There were strikes by agricultural labourers in the 1870s, and consolidation among farm employees in the newly formed Unions. In 1872 Joseph Arch, (the Warwickshire radical founder of the National Agricultural Labourers' Union) addressed a mass meeting at Old Gore. The meetings were always held on Sundays, and many labourers would walk up to 16 miles to attend. They wanted a rise of four shillings per week, meat and better housing; they also complained of long working hours: 7 a.m. to 5 p.m. in winter, and 6 a.m. to 6 p.m. in summer.

The agricultural depression, culminating in the disastrously wet years of 1879 and 1880, took its toll among arable farmers; the rainfall was one-fourth above the average in this and neighbouring counties. As a result the grass was tough and of poor quality; fodder and grain did not mature properly. On the wet soils 'liver-rot' (caused by a parasitic worm or 'fluke') afflicted sheep and cattle, and even horses, pigs, hares and rabbits were affected. One antidote proved to be dry feed for the stock together with liberal amounts of salt. Even so, in 1867 there had been nearly 350,000 sheep in Herefordshire, but by 1880 these were reduced to 260,000, a disproportionately large decrease in the total reduction of 1,600,000 across England.

On the subject of stock, the famous white-faced Hereford Cattle were not bred, as now, as beef animals. Cows provided both meat and milk, and the oxen were useful draught animals on the farms. In 1805 John Duncumb observed: 'The rearing of oxen for the purposes of agriculture prevails universally; nearly half the ploughing is performed by them, and they take an equal share in the labours of the harvest. They are shod with iron in situations which frequently require their exertions on hard roads.' They were generally sold at the Hereford Michaelmas Fair to graziers from the counties near

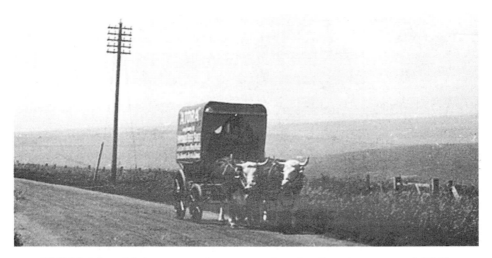

Phil Wright with is oxen and cart crossing the Pennines around 1942.
(Courtesy of Margaret Wilce, Ross)

London, and 'there perfected for the London markets'. The size of the oxen increased alongside their value 'in at least a six-fold proportion. It may here be remarked that there is an extraordinary difference between the weight of a Herefordshire cow and the ox bred from her; it is a fact that a Herefordshire cow will not infrequently be the mother of an ox of nearly three times her own weight.' Oxen were used as draught animals to up to four years of age and then sold to the butcher; until the middle of the 18th century the ox-wain was the only farm carriage.

Over the years horses began to replace oxen on farms, and proved more versatile in the changing conditions. Improvements in horse-drawn machinery then gradually made farms less dependent on manpower, though the waggoner's hours were long; he had to be up by 5.30 in the morning to prepare his team for the day's work, and even on Sundays his charges needed attention. The provision of the horse trough on Bulls Hill (by the parish council) in 1887 indicates the importance of these valuable working horses.

From 1879 there was a strong movement towards emigration to Canada and the

Horse trough on Bulls Hill,
drawn by Mervyn Morgan in 2001

fertile wheat-growing lands across the American border. One historian noted a decrease in the rural population of Herefordshire from 125,000 in 1871 to 108,000 in 1937. Despite several Government Inquiries the wage of the Herefordshire labourer in 1912/3 was still only 13s. 1d. while over the rest of the country the average wage was between 17s. and 20s. A threatened strike was called off because of the national emergency caused by the beginning of the First World War, but a general rise of 2s. per week was granted in August 1914.

An article in the *Hereford Times* in 1932 recalls that, within living memory, stock were sold and farm servants engaged in the streets of Hereford. With the latter the practice was to hire an agricultural worker for 11 months only, so that he would not become a permanent resident and thus a potential burden on parochial rates.

Agricultural implement makers established businesses locally, with the most productive of these in Ross being S.A. and H. Kell between about 1874 and 1913, who also opened another works in Gloucester in 1856. In 1859 they were the biggest exhibitor of agricultural machinery in the Herefordshire Agricultural Show, with eight ploughs, eight sets of harrows, three heavy rollers, two corn drills, three root drills, a manure distributor, two horse-hoes,

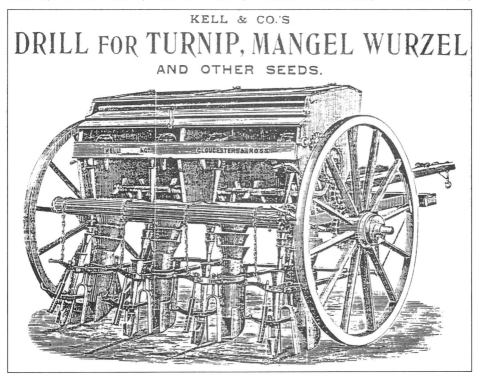

Extract from the Catalogue of Kell & Co. Agricultural Machinery
Manufacturers, around 1890

a tedding machine, two winnowing machines, four chaff-cutters (some horse, some power driven), three turnip cutters, four root pulpers, an oil-cake breaker and a cider mill/press as well as other horse-powered machines. In each class they displayed different designs, and were famous for the varieties of ploughs they made. The firm had a reputation for high standards of engineering and finish. A 5-ton steam tractor was made by a Hereford firm in the late 1800s, and this design was the precursor of the all-purpose, internal combustion engine tractor used on farms today.

The mixed farming tradition of Herefordshire has changed in recent years with landowners growing the same crop year after year, necessitating heavy fertilising to keep up the production targets. Stock practices have also changed, with the introduction of mixed breeds among the sheep, the aim being to produce larger carcases rather than fine wool, as the value of the latter has been much reduced with the introduction of artificial fabrics. Hereford cattle, however, are still bred, with stock-lines documented as far back as 1846, when the first Hereford Herd Book was published. In 1886 this was closed to any animal whose sire or dam had not been previously entered so that, for over 100 years, the purity of the breed has remained intact. At the first Royal Show held at Oxford in 1839, a three-year-old Hereford bull called Cotmore was the Champion; at nine years of age he weighed just under 4000 lbs. or 1.75 tons. From 1839 the renowned cattle were exported to the Americas, Canada, New Zealand and Australia where they thrived. In 1980 a prize Hereford bull, Haven Reign On, was sold for the record price of 27,000 guineas to a Canadian buyer.

Farming in Walford Parish
The history of farming in this parish is not very well recorded, although exten-sive accounts and correspondence exist for the Hill Court Estate, and these are archived in the Herefordshire Record Office. Historical accounts indicate that the oldest settlement in the area was around Hom Green, with the occupier of Homme Farm, Robert Ceorl or Curl, bailiff of the Manor in 1289. In 1303 he bought his freedom from serfdom for himself and his descendants by paying the customary fine of 40 marks, the manumission fee.

Recent research in the English Heritage National Monuments archive has shown that there was a deserted medieval village in the vicinity of Homme Farm, now owned by Eric Drummond. There are also undisturbed peat layers in the soil to the south-east of this farm, near the entrance to the Charity Field which is now in the ownership of the Herefordshire Nature Trust; peat is laid down at a rate of about 1 inch (2.5 centimetres) per 1,000 years and indicates a long undisturbed environment and a valuable area of archaeological investigation. Until 1931 Hom and the surrounding area to the north-east were in Ross parish.

The Walford Tithe Map (drawn in 1840) and its accompanying Apportionment (1843) respectively show and list the use of all the land in the

Parish. This large scale tithe map, showing every building, field boundary and road in this area, was prepared for taxation purposes. David Walshaw, of Walford, has painstakingly coloured in an enlargement of the map which was reproduced by Geoff Gwatkin for the Field Names Project and a copy is included as a pull out at the end of the book. David and his wife, Sheila, have also walked over the parish to ascertain current land use and the changes that have occurred. The most significant are the loss in orchards, particularly in the Castle Brook valley, the reduction of pasture, mainly to arable, and also the significant loss of the water meadows now converted to arable. Additionally some of the woodlands in the south-east of the parish have gone, to be replaced with cultivated land, whilst Suff Wood has been considerably reduced in extent.

In the Parish Council Newsletters of 1980 Jonathan Claxton provided several facts derived from the 1840 Tithe Map. There were 1,878 acres of arable land, 1,159 acres of meadow or pasture and 985 acres of woodland, all subject to a 'rent' charge. In addition there were 47 acres of common, 90 of roads and 40 of 'rectorial' glebe with one acre of 'vicarial' glebe land but none of this land was subject to such charge. The total area was 4,200 acres.

At that time there were 195 landowners, the majority living in the parish, and 171 tenants. Of the latter several were themselves small landowners. The land was good, agriculturally, and the woods were also profitable, providing hop poles, fencing material and fuel. There were 22 farms of over 40 acres, about 150 holdings between 2 and 40 acres, and 144 holdings of less than 2 acres. The three large landowners, Kingsmill Evans of Hill Court, John Stratford Collins of the Wythall and John Partridge of Bishopswood Estate owned, between them, half the total acreage. They all ran their 'home' farm, and let many of their other holdings.

The moderate sized farms were a mixture of owner occupied and tenanted, and the census details reveal the number of employees required in each case. Many of the smaller holdings would have provided land for vegetables and poultry for the families, and, as in the Forest of Dean, many householders could have kept a pig.

In 1840 the rent charge, (the substitute for tithe, which was formerly a deduction of one-tenth of the farmers' produce), totalled £745 17s. 1d. of which only £242 10s. went to the Vicar and the remainder, £503 7s. 1d., to the 'Appropriator or his Lessee'; in other words the ecclesiastical body in charge of the parish church. The distinction is similar when previous references to 'little and great tythes' are made, the former to the vicar and the latter to the Dean and Chapter of Hereford Cathedral, or their lessee.

As the saying goes 'only two things in life are certain — death and taxes', and in the early 1800s much of the farmer's income went on taxes. All the money spent by the parish came out of the Poor Rate, and this was assessed on the value of the land, and levied on the occupiers, whether they were the tenants or the owners. As a result the wealthier landowners paid very little because their tenants were paying the rates. County Rates, another liability, were used to repair bridges, transport convicts, administer the county gaol and pay the families of the militia. Window Tax and Land Tax were payable to central government. A Land Tax assessment for the year 1795 lists 43 different landowners, some occupying their own land, but in many cases their tenants are listed, together with the tax payable on each property or parcel of land. The total tax payable was £204 6s. 4d., at a rate of 4s. in the £. In addition there were sundry other taxes on carthorses, saddle horses and gigs, as well as 'malt' duty, all to be added to the ongoing costs of maintenance, repairs and, in the case of tenants, rent for the landlord. After all these outgoings the parishioner had to provide a living for himself and his family! In the really lean years the landowners lost out as their tenants could not afford to pay the rents.

Kelly's Directory of 1879 notes that the chief crops grown in this region were wheat, roots and barley. The population in 1871 in Walford ecclesiastical parish was 1,303, and in that of Bishopswood it was 446.

The *Walford Women's Institute Local History* of 1954/55 has a valuable section on local agriculture 'within living memory', and this includes official returns showing crops grown in the month of June in 1867, 1914 and 1954. The table on page 98 shows that, while wheat crops had declined, the acreages of barley and oats had increased.

The decrease in wheat growing could be explained by the drop in prices in home-produced wheat which followed the large-scale importation of cheaper grain from the prairie lands of America. This was possible as large quantities of grain could be stored in specially constructed steel holds in the large steam-powered ships crossing the Atlantic. The market for home-produced wheat was worsened by the repeal of the Corn Laws from 1846. However, barley suitable for malting could be grown locally and the good prices made this a popular crop. Oat-straw was more nutritious animal feed than wheat-straw and an increasing tendency to over-winter cattle in fold-yards also led to an increased acreage of oats. Burgeoning stock numbers required more land for grazing, using yet more of the land released from growing wheat. Until the decline in the use of horses, both in the country and in the towns, oats remained an important crop.

Around 1920 the tenant of Walford Court farm, Ralph Wilson, owned a Moline-universal two wheel tractor. This machine was designed and built in the U.S.A. and Richard Yemm was given Ralph Wilson's handbook many years ago. This describes the working of the 'gas engine' which was replacing the former steam engine as motive power. The tractor had specially designed implements, which made the assembly an integrated unit, and was driven by Con Lewis, later the postmaster in Coughton. The handbook advises the user to 'give this tractor the same degree of consideration and attention you would a

Moline Universal Tractor with Grain Drill fitted, from the
Moline Tractor Handbook 1918. (Courtesy of Richard Yemm)

team of horses costing as much'. In 1932 a rubber-tyred Fordson tractor was to take its place.

With the formation of the Milk Marketing Board in 1928, dairy-farming became popular, and crops of oats and barley, with peas or beans, increased. Potato crops rarely exceeded 20 acres, until subsidies were introduced in the Second World War; a very different situation from the present. The considerable fall in the popularity of turnips and swedes for stock-feeding can be explained by the loss of cheap labour over the period, although mangold growing was a partial substitute.

Sugar beet cultivation was introduced locally in 1927 and advice notes exist listing the loads of up to 6 tons collected at Kerne Bridge Station from October to December 1929 for delivery to the processing plant at Kidderminster. In 2001 this is still a substantial crop locally, but from 2002 the beet will be processed at Alscott, near Telford (Shropshire).

It seems surprising that there was such a small acreage of hops listed in 1867. In 1843 field tithe-numbers 715 and 720 were described as 'Hop Field' (14 acres in all) and they are situated below the woodland still called Hopes Wood, (probably originally Hops Wood), lying above Daycroft Farm. Hops were grown near the Hunt Kennels near Castlebrook and a local farmer recalls being told that the hop-yards were dismantled *c*.1892 when Mr. Eveley took his horses and wagons up there to haul away the poles.

The acreage under orchards, mainly of cider apples and perry pears, was much reduced by the middle of the 1900s. Many parishioners will remember

Crop	Acreage		
	1867	**1914**	**1954**
Wheat	596.75	191.5	154.5
Barley	114	208.75	210.5
Oats	8	153.25	58
Mixed Corn	N.R.	N.R.	67.25
Beans for stockfeeding	13.75	0.75	—
Peas for stockfeeding	47	1.75	3
Potatoes	22.5	12.75	86.75
Turnips & Swedes (stockfeeding)	338.75	88.75	75.25
Mangolds	8.75	65.75	49.5
Sugar beet	—	—	23.5
Hops	10	—	—
Vetches & other Green Crops	29	20	23
bare fallow	35.25	10.5	11.5
Orchards (grass below)	N.R.	97.75	68.5
Small Fruit	—	—	8
Clover & temp. Grass for mowing	283.25	188.25	259.75
Ditto for grazing	—	32	152.5
Permanent Grasses for mowing	1016.75	591.5	380.75
Ditto for Grazing	N.R.	1286	1050
Rough Grazing	N.R.	N.R.	163.75
Total Cattle	270	532	907
Sheep	2956	1629	2453
Pigs	324	297	463
Horses	N.R.	162	29
Poultry	N.R.	N.R.	3692
Labour	N.R.	N.R.	86

Ministry of Agriculture and Fisheries 4 June returns for the Parish of Walford for the years 1867, 1914 and 1954. N.R. = Not Recorded

taking apples to their nearest cider mill, and, much later, collecting the cider in a jug to carry home.

The commercial cultivation of soft fruit is a recent innovation, with 20 acres of raspberries plus 100 acres of strawberries at Homme Farm. Blackcurrants have taken the place of a dairy herd at Arbour Hill Farm and the farmer, Martin Boynton, aims at a total of 110 acres on his three farms (Hildersley, the Vine Tree and Arbour Hill).

Older residents have said that they thought there used to be vineyards on the slopes above Walford village, and there are three place names in the parish which indicate this: Vineyards, near Bishopswood, Vineyard Villa where Manley Bodenham lived in 1910, near Leys Hill Baptist Chapel and the

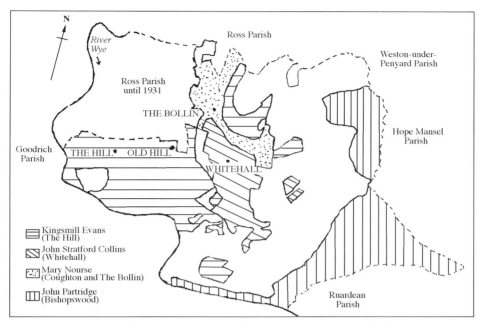

Map of Parish estate holdings c.1840, drawn by Virginia Morgan

Vineyard, near World's End, Howle Hill. The Vine Tree Farm, on the northern parish boundary with Ross, has land strips arranged in a herring-bone pattern indicating that grape vines were planted there.

Over the centuries the principal landowners have been the owners of two large estates at the Wythall and Hill Court along with, from the early part of the 19th century, the industrialist owners of the Bishopswood Estate. These estates merit further description.

Bishopswood Estate

This large estate in the southern part of the parish was acquired by William Partridge, of Monmouth, in 1801; the vendor was the 2nd Marquis of Bath, and the purchase price was £11,500. Included was a furnace with adjoining foundry, coppices and several farms, namely Labour in Vain, Hill or Furnace, Coppice with Caldicots and Lodge Farm. Eight years later a further purchase was made of other land and woods from the beneficiaries of Miss Jane Clarke of Hill Court.

William Partridge's son, John, erected a mansion near the iron-works site around 1824 but a disastrous fire in 1873 reduced it to a shell. In the following year John Partridge, then aged 79, decided to sell; the estate was described as a 'Freehold Residential Renowned Shooting Property' comprising 1,328 acres, for sale 'by direction of the Owner, who, at his advanced period of life, shuns the anxiety of rebuilding the Mansion recently destroyed by fire'.

The purchaser was Jacob Chivers of Hawkwell Tinplate Works. In 1878 the estate was again on the market, with interesting remarks added to the essential details. Among the 600 acres of woodland 'there are many anthills (indigenous to the soil) which afford excellent and special Food for the Pheasants'. The Home Farm was in hand (36 acres) but Upper and Lower Coppice Farms had

---

BETWEEN ROSS AND MONMOUTH.

In this lovely part of the country, far-famed for its

GRAND SCENERY, SHOOTING, FISHING AND RESIDENTIAL ADVANTAGES;

Four and a half miles by a good road from Ross with its station on the Great Western Railway, whence London, the Midlands, Manchester, Liverpool and the North are easily accessible, 1 mile from Kerne Bridge Railway Station, 5 miles from Coleford, 7 miles from Newnham, 7½ miles from Monmouth, and 15 and 18 miles respectively from the Cathedral Cities of Gloucester and Hereford.

PARTICULARS, PLAN, VIEWS AND CONDITIONS OF SALE,

OF THE EXCEEDINGLY ATTRACTIVE FREEHOLD (SMALL PART COPYHOLD)

Residential and Sporting Estate,

DISTINGUISHED AS

"BISHOPSWOOD,"

COMPRISING

A PICTURESQUE MANSION,

On a moderate scale, occupying a CHARMING POSITION, overlooking the River, with CAPITAL STABLING and BEAUTIFUL PLEASURE GROUNDS,

Well-Timbered and Boldly Undulating Park-Lands.

AN

EXCELLENT GENTLEMAN'S RESIDENCE,

KNOWN AS

"THE COPPICE,"

With FIRST-CLASS STABLING, and GARDENS with GLASS HOUSES,

AGENT'S HOUSE WITH STABLING,

ALSO

SEVERAL GOOD FARMS,

With NECESSARY HOUSES, BUILDINGS and COTTAGES, including the

VERY SUPERIOR MODEL BUILDINGS

Attached to the HOME or STUD and JERSEY FARMS; FIVE ENTRANCE LODGES, KEEPERS' and other COTTAGES, SMALL HOLDINGS, &c.; in all about

2,015 ACRES,

Of which about 600 Acres are Wood well distributed over the Estate, and affording

SHOOTING OF THE HIGHEST-CLASS;

the Total actual and estimated Rental amounting to over

£3,000 PER ANNUM,

Together with the Advowson and Right of Presentation to the Vicarage of All Saints, Bishopswood, the Church being on the Estate and near the Mansion:

WHICH WILL BE SOLD BY AUCTION,

AT THE MART, TOKENHOUSE YARD, NEAR THE BANK OF ENGLAND, LONDON, E.C.,

On THURSDAY, the 23rd day of JUNE, 1898,

AT TWO O'CLOCK PRECISELY

(UNLESS PREVIOUSLY DISPOSED OF BY PRIVATE CONTRACT

IN ONE LOT.

Particulars, with Views, Plan and Conditions of Sale may be obtained of Messrs. ROOPER & WHATELY, Solicitors, No. 17, Lincoln's Inn Fields, London, W.C.; and, with Orders to View, of

Messrs. TROLLOPE,

Estate Agents, Surveyors and Auctioneers,

14, MOUNT STREET, GROSVENOR SQUARE;
7, HOBART PLACE, EATON SQUARE;
WEST HALKIN STREET, BELGRAVE SQUARE; and LONDON.
5, VICTORIA STREET, WESTMINSTER:

Bishopswood Estate sale particulars in 1898 (HRO)

been combined to make up nearly 187 acres which were leased to William Morgan for a 14-year term from February 1877. The landlord would have 'an exclusive right of shooting, sporting and fishing' over the entire property, and he would continue to support All Saints Church where 'there is a large Pew, with Fireplace, used by the Owner of the Property'.

The next owner was Colonel Harry L.B. McCalmont who carried out considerable improvements, including routing the new road past the church and school. It was during this work in 1895 that his workmen found the famous hoard of Roman coins described in chapter one. An article in the local paper described Col. McCalmont's generosity to his 50 or more employees: 'On at least one occasion many of them were treated to a champagne dinner of many wines put on by a London caterer in first class style'.

He sold up in 1898. Over the years more land had been added and by that time the estate totalled 2,015 acres.

There had always been a great deal of woodland (608 acres in 1898) which would have been a considerable attraction to the iron-master owners in the early days. There were also six acres of quarries and lime-kilns. Salmon, trout and other fishing was available. An earlier sale describes a valuable resource underground 'there is an abundant supply of limestone under the surface of the estate well sited for agriculture or building purposes and, if worked, could be made a source of considerable income. There is also sandstone suitable for building'.

Land in the adjoining parishes of Hope Mansell and Ruardean was included in the estate, and detailed in the various sale particulars, but for the purposes of this account only the farms within Walford Parish as defined at the start of the new millennium will be described.

In 1898 the Home Farm, (166 acres) and Howle (now Great Howle, approximately 232 acres) were both farmed 'in hand' (i.e. by the estate owner), as were Atlas (22 acres), Howle Green (29 acres) and Oxlips (Oxlet) nearly 30 acres. Several other holdings were let, and these included: Vain Farm (tenant E.J. Meredith, 31 acres), Hill Farm (tenant Henry Bodenham, 35 acres), Lodge Farm (tenant J. Meredith, 28 acres), Hawker's Green Farm (now The Chadwyns, tenant John Gwatkin, 9 acres), Dunderhole Farm (tenant John Gwatkin, 12 acres), Warren Farm (tenant Mr. Roberts, 15 acres), and Forest Green Farm (tenant G. Counley, 8 acres).

In 1913 180 acres of the outlying portions of the estate were sold, which included Hazelhurst Farm with nearly 23 acres, (tenant Frederick Matthews) Hill Farm (24 acres let to Frank Gwatkin) and Warren Farm (14 acres let to J. Roberts). Several pieces of accommodation land and cottages were available.

In 1921 Robert Holme Storey sold more of the outlying portions of the estate, totalling 1,224 acres and including Great Howle Farm (318 acres), Paddock Farm (96 acres), Vain Farm (46 acres), six smallholdings (67 acres), accommodation land (76 acres), woodland (292 acres), 14 cottages and the

At Lodge Farm, Deep Farm, in 1882. On the left is William Smith,
on the right George Collier, then aged 5. (Courtesy of Nancy Roberts)

'charmingly situate residence known as The Queach'. Several of the tenants took the opportunity to purchase the properties they farmed, including E.J. Meredith of Vain Farm, and L.J. and J.W. Gwatkin of the 9-acre Coldharbour. Little Howle Farm (45 acres) went to A. Cotton, Yatton and Forest Green Farm (7 acres) to G. Perkins, Cinderford. Woodland, arable fields and grass accommodation land were sold to various purchasers.

The farm now known as the Paddocks is noted on the 1898 Sale map but by 1921 it appears to have been combined with the nearby Lodge Farm, previously called Walford Lodge Farm. In earlier times it was the freehold property of the Croose family; both Richard Croose, who died in 1668 and John Croose of Castlebrook, who died in 1716, left substantial estates. The latter gave away 10 hogsheads of cider in his will. In 1844 James Edwards was the tenant of Lodge Farm, with 27 acres of grass and arable land, and in 1874 Samuel Smith was the tenant with the same acreage. At the time of the 1921 sale Paddock Farm comprised 96 acres, farmed by three different tenants and some of the field numbers align with those of Lodge Farm.

The Home Farm, (previously called Upper Coppice, or Coppice Farm), was described in the sale details of 1898 as being 'in immediate proximity to the Agent's House with Very Superior Model Buildings'. These included the Jersey Herd Farm and the Stud buildings as well as many stone and wood-built loose-boxes beneath the Clock Tower. From this stable came the famous racehorse

Isinglass who not only won the Derby in 1893, but also the 2,000 Guineas and the St. Leger in that year, thus winning the Triple Crown. On a later occasion he won the Ascot Gold Cup. He had been bred on the estate, and his mother was a brood mare 'brought out of the shafts of a cab for £19'. He was broken in and schooled by Fred Banks of Hangerberry who used to exercise the young horse between the estate and Hangerberry (Lydbrook) stabling him near his parents' house while having his mid-day meal. The amazing horse's winnings amounted to over £57,000.

In addition to the Newmarket style stables, a fine pure-bred herd of Jersey cattle was kept, with systematic milk-recording. Huge pheasant shoots were organized with some 4,000 birds reared for the sport. From daylight to dark two keepers had to patrol outside the wood above Bishopswood Post Office to stop the birds crossing the river to the Courtfield Estate.

In 1910, under the ownership of Sir George Bullough, Coppice Farm (169 acres) appears to have been managed by Harry Campbell, who lived in the house. The coat of arms of Sir George Bullough can be seen on four of the five Lodges on the former estate; the odd one out is Grove Lodge.

Gamekeeper's Cottage on Bishopswood Estate, c.1940.
(Courtesy of Basil Brown, Mitcheldean)

In 1949 788 acres of the remaining estate were put on the market and the owners, Mr. and Mrs. R.H. Storey, retired to the Home Farm. On Mrs. Storey's death in 1976 that property was purchased by Mervyn Freeman.

The larger farms on the estate were:

Great Howle Farm

The name is said to come either from the Welsh 'hywel', meaning conspicuous, or the old English word 'hyll', a hill. This farm is of great antiquity and was once the property of Flaxley Abbey, Gloucestershire. It formed part of the Howle Estate in the 15th century when it belonged to the Walwyns of Hellens, near Dymock. Richard Wallwyn's grandson, Foulke, gave Howle to his second wife and in turn it was inherited by her son Alexander. A legal tangle was settled with possession in the hands of his two-year old son, Thomas. When Thomas died unmarried, Howle then belonged to his sister who married William Stratford (owner of the Wythall estate) in the 16th century.

The tenants for many years had been the Yemm family who subsequently purchased the property. Their male line ended in 1707 with the heiress Elizabeth, only child of Edmund Yemm, who was married to Edward Chamberlain, lord of the manor of Dymock. Their son sold the Howle to a Mr. Hardwick who sold on to William Haines c.1840; George Haines was there in 1858. In 1881 Samuel Phelps was manager and bailiff of the farm, in charge of 236 acres and 'employing 5 labourers, 2 boys and 2 women'. In 1890 Col. Harry McCalmont incorporated the farm into his Bishopswood Estate and rebuilt the farm buildings, which remain generally unchanged, a good example of Victorian farm buildings. The house was empty and became derelict. Sir George Bullough, a subsequent owner of the Bishopswood Estate, refurbished the farmhouse and added a south-west wing at right angles to the original building.

Great Howle Farm around 1905. (Courtesy of George Jones)

In 1910 the farm included 218 acres; Arthur Harris farmed them, and rented the house and buildings, Vineyard House and Moors Farm (7 acres). When the Storey family bought the estate in 1911 one of the joint tenants was Arthur Harris, who together with Mr. Little and C.H. Bundy farmed just over 317 acres at Great Howle until the outlying parts of Bishopswood Estate were sold in 1921. Before the First World War the Massey-Lynch family lived at Great Howle and then in 1921 George William Bennett Jones bought the farm which is now owned by his grandson, George Jones.

Vain Farm, also called **Labour-in-Vain Farm**
Situated in the most distant south-east corner of the parish, this farm was part of the large Bishopswood Estate from 1801 until the sale in 1921 when there were 46 acres. The earliest tenant was James Philips, and the fields included Thistley Fallow and Gorsty Piece, indicating poor ground. More recent tenants were John Burraston in 1858, and Charles Bullock from 1861 until 1874 at least, when he farmed 158 acres. Cornelius Brain was there from 1875, with a 14-year tenancy; he had 170 acres, employing two men and one boy, the land being described as 'useful grass and barley land'. In 1910 Henry John Meredith was the tenant, with 150 acres. At the time of the sale in 1921 E.J. Meredith was the tenant, (46 acres), and became the owner. The farm now belongs to the Freeman family.

Smaller farms in the estate varied from 45 to 8 acres in size in 1910, and included Howle Green (45 acres), Paddock, Hazelhurst, Prospect, Lodge, Atlas, Queach, Warren, Little Howle, Hawkers Green (now The Chadwyns), Coldharbour and Dunderhole (8 acres). Twelve acres of river meadow land, near the Wye, were farmed by A.W. Latham, and a further 18 acres by William and James Dawe. In 1913 Hill Farm (nearly 25 acres) was let to Frank Gwatkin, together with two nearby parcels of accommodation land. He evidently bought the farm, as well as a small field known as Bonnor's Meadow, because, after his death in 1949, these were conveyed to his son, John Wallace Gwatkin. Under his will John left the whole property to the National Trust when he died in 1974, but in 1995 it was auctioned and split up.

Hill Court Estate
The account of the sequence of ownership of this estate can be found in chapter nine. In the 1873 'Return for Owners of Land' Kingsmill Manley Power is listed as owning 1,493 acres. On his death in 1888 the estate was put on the market. At that time it totalled 1,270 acres, comprising most of the lowland in west Walford, (with the exception of the Charity Field), two fields to the west of Old Hill Court, the meadows to the north and south of Walford Mill and land to the north of the Spread Eagle (now the Mill Race), the Old

Bakery in Walford village and also a parcel of land immediately opposite Newall Cottage.

The larger farms on the estate then included the Home Farm of 189 acres which was in the hands of the estate owner, Hom Farm (233 acres), Walford Court and Brook Farms (212 acres), The Callow (192 acres), Old Hill Farm (151 acres) and Warryfield (124 acres), all tenanted. The other tenanted farms were Arbour Hill (74 acres) and Balls Farm (40 acres). (There was a change in the boundary between Ross and Walford Parishes in 1931, under the Herefordshire [Ross Urban, Ross Rural and Whitchurch Rural] Order which created the current boundary. Before that date the dividing line ran through the Hill Court grounds, to the north of the main drive, and zigzagged around Old Hill Farm, with Hom Farm, Balls Farm and Arbour Hill Farm forming part of Ross Parish.) Ten acres of land surrounded the Mansion House together with gardens and buildings.

The purchaser was Major Lionel Trafford, who owned Hill Court and the land, but not the title of Lord of the Manor which remained with the Manley Power family (see also chapter nine). When Dorothy Trafford died in 1954 she was succeeded by her younger son, John, as the elder son, Guy, had been killed in a car accident in October, 1933, aged only 23. On John Trafford's death in 1978 the estate tenants were given the opportunity to buy their farms.

In 1890 the estate included just over 34 acres of woodland and an osier bed. There were three miles of frontage to the River Wye, with the valuable salmon fishery; additional sport was available with shooting and hunting. In 1910 the estate, within this parish, contained some woodland (Hopes, Grove Lodge Wood and also near the Bollin) and there were still five large farms. In order of size these were: Walford Court, Callow, Hill Court (Home farm), Warryfield and Old Hill Farm. Guy Trafford, senior, also owned Brook Cottage, one acre of Coughton Marsh, four further acres of marsh, and William Howls' blacksmith's shop with one acre of land.

Walford Court

The earliest leaseholder-farmer traced was John Elton, the only son of Samuel Elton of the Twisling, Hope Mansel. John's eldest son, another John, died in 1798 and left the residue of his lease to his brother-in-law Richard Green, 'husbandman' of Little Dewchurch. Richard's wife, Sarah, was John Elton's sister. He also left his 'without and within implements in husbandry' together with 'such parts of my horses Cattle Sheep Piggs and living and dead Stock' that Richard Green was willing to retain at a fair valuation, paying interest at 'five pounds per cent per annum' for these. John's younger brother, William, was born at the Court in 1740, but only inherited the Hope Mansel property which he sold, investing the proceeds in his Bristol firm; he was a West India merchant. His son, John, was to be the great-grandfather of the first Baron Elton.

In 1835 John Smith was the occupier, and from 1840 to 1861 William Terrett lived at the Homestead. In 1851 the latter is described as 'farmer and tax collector'. He was succeeded by Isaac Theyer from at least 1868, who is shown on the 1881 census as farming 350 acres, employing eight men and one boy. At this time Brook Farm was probably incorporated in the holding.

Subsequent leaseholders of Walford Court were John Leonard Bennett (in the early 1900s, with a total of 216 acres), followed by Ralph Wilson, who was killed on the road near the Bollin in January 1921 when he was thrown from his horse. The next tenant was John Stephen Roberts. The latter's much-respected son, Jack, took over the house and farm after his father's death and he and his wife Mary were there until Jack died in 1974. William Chinn then went into partnership with John Trafford to farm the land, and in 1976 moved into Walford Court. Sadly Mrs. Mary Roberts died during 2001 after many years of illness. The old farmhouse has been sold recently (2001) and the buildings have been advertised for sale as industrial premises.

Callow

In the resolution of the dispute between the freeholders of Walford and the owners of the Manor of Ross Foreign in 1614, Sir John Scudamore of Holme Lacy was named as one of the freeholders; he owned both this farm and Hope Farm (probably Daycroft Farm). They descended to John Higford and were purchased by Mr. Evans and Mr. Collins respectively. Callow formed part of the Hill Court estate until 1982. The fine farmhouse dates from the 17th century and is a listed dwelling together with the outbuildings. In 1840 Richard Messenger was the occupier, Richard Loveridge was farming it in 1858 and 1862, and he was followed by his widow Elizabeth in charge of 315 acres. In 1890 and 1895 Henry Phillips Gatfield was there, with Robert Newbury Dampier farming the 189 acres in 1910. John Harper was the farmer, with his sons, for many years until his death in 1977. Mrs. Dinah Moore is the present owner of the house and land.

Warryfield

This farm is mentioned in the record of Historical Monuments as the partly timber-framed farmhouse is a listed building: 'some timber-framing is exposed on the north side, and there is an original window of four lights with diamond shaped mullions'. The west part is the oldest, (built c.1600) and the house was extended towards the east c.1700. A document of 1690 cites Lydia Markey, 'relict' (widow) of William Markey of Alton Court, Ross, as the owner when the occupier was John Fletcher. The other party to the document is Richard Clark of Hill Court. In 1843 the Tithe map details note that Kingsmill Evans owned both the Warryfield properties, that is Little Warrifield Homestead (now Upper Warryfield) and land (tenant Joseph Cross), with Great Warryfield

Homestead (now **Lower Warryfield**) and land (tenant Thomas Wood who was still there in 1868). The former is the large barn now housing the double-glazing and pine furniture businesses with the farmhouse set back, whilst the latter forms part of a complex of very old, half-timbered houses just beyond Walford Court on the north side of the road to Hom Green. The 1910 Land Valuation details list Alfred William Griffin in charge of 126 acres of agricultural land, together with the buildings, a cottage and garden. Malcolm Harper lived with his mother at the Lower Warryfield farmhouse until they moved out of the parish recently.

Old Hill Farm

The farm lay in Ross Parish until 1931. The land was purchased by Captain Kingsmill Evans around 1816 and was once the property of the Markeys. In 1888 there were 151 acres; in 1910 the land was farmed by Thomas Jenkins, (114 acres) and the house, Old Hill Court, was the residence of Edward Keene. As described on p.160, this is a listed building of great interest.

Arbour Hill and Balls Farm were also in Ross Parish until 1931 but there is mention of the latter as early as 1654 when by a Deed of Exchange Richard Clark paid John Ball and Thomas White £41 in exchange for 5 acres of land and a house near 'Mr. Pearse's Land and 2 acres near Mr. Chin's land'. Frederick Griffin purchased the farm from the Trafford family in 1921, and later Martin Boynton bought Arbour Hill (in 1978). Balls Farm passed into the hands of the Misses Griffin in 1953, then came into Eric Drummond's ownership; in 1984 the house and some of the land was sold to Maurice Reeves.

Hopes Farm is believed to form the land now called Daycroft, as it lies under Hopes Wood. The 1874 sales particulars of Daycroft describe it as freehold 39 acres of arable, meadow and orchard lands with a farmhouse, farm buildings, cottage and garden. Miss M. Whittingham lived there and Thomas Wheeler farmed 29 acres in 1891 with his son William Henry adding another 50 acres. The younger Wheeler is noted as 'farmer and timber haulier' up to 1902, and Evan Jones was farming there from 1927 until his death in 1972. Subsequently his daughter, Nancy, and her husband, John Phillips, came from The Model Farm, Hildersley, to farm there, and their son Michael is the present farmer.

The Brook Estate belonged to the Harris family for several generations, and it is believed that the allusion then was to 'Harris's farm'. They intermarried with the Kyrles and the Clarkes. In 1718 Edmund Harris left a respectable £62 worth of goods, of which £46 was husbandry-related. In 1816 Kingsmill Evans bought the farm and added it to the Hill Court holdings. The farmhouse is listed in the County Sites and Monuments Records and dates from the mid to late 18th century.

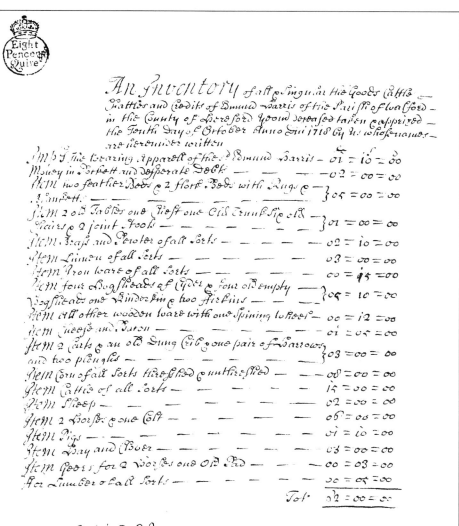

Copy of the probate inventory of Edmund Harris of Walford, 1718 (HRO)

The Wythall Estate

As described in chapter nine, this estate has a very long history and the descendants of the Collins family have been the owners since the 16th century. In 1611 Ferdinando Stratford died, leaving Upper Wythall and land at Howle,

Ruardean, Alton and two other areas. He had sold Lower Wythall (the farm-house) and the Dew family lived there from 1609 to 1823 when John Stratford Collins bought it back into the family's ownership. In 1813 there were 100 'customary' acres of land along with the mansion called Upper Wythall as well as five acres of woodland. Of this only 16 acres were arable, and the rest good meadow and fine orchards 'planted with choice fruits and capable of producing One Hundred Hogsheads of Cider in a fruitful year' (a hogshead held just over 52 imperial gallons). In 1841 the estate still belonged to John Stratford Collins and, with the addition of the 107 parcels of land noted in the Tithe Map Apportionment of 1843, came to approximately 180 acres. Seventy of these pieces of land were farmed 'in hand', and the remainder let to seven different tenants, each with a small amount of land. In his history of the county published in 1882, W.H. Cooke notes that the estate contained 250 acres.

Lower Whitehall, the farmhouse, is rumoured to pre-date the Upper Wythall main house and is also noted in the County Sites and Monuments record. It was occupied by William Whittingham in 1841, Thomas Haines in 1862 (farming 70 acres and employing one man), Ann Harris in 1881 (a widow aged 75 farming 80 acres) and Joseph Stephens in 1891 and up to at least 1910. The farm, in 1910, comprised 99 acres. At this date the Wythall mansion had only 9 acres of grounds, with 19 acres of woodland, in addition to the farmland; other tenanted parcels comprised 87 acres approximately, plus 16 acres of

Lower Wythall in 1986 from estate agent's sale particulars.
(Courtesy of Barrie Davies, Newlands)

meadowland occupied by W.H. Phillips. Most of this tenanted land was on the slopes of Bulls Hill and the valley between Howle and Bulls hills at Coughton.

By 1919 only about 65 acres remained in the estate with most of the smaller holdings sold. The last of the male line was John Stratford Collins who was born in 1882 but died, unmarried, in 1912 when he was succeeded by his sister, Sibell Edith Kyrle Stratford Collins. On her death both Upper and Lower Wythall and the land were left to members of the family. In 1970 one of the beneficiaries sold Lower Wythall and, six years later, several parcels of land. This house is now owned by Dr. and Mrs. Wyllie. Upper Wythall and the remainder of the land is still owned and enjoyed by descendants of the Stratford Collins line.

Though not part of the Wythall estate another member of the family, Ferdinando Stratford Collins (born 1850, died 1919) owned a large amount of land in 1910 totalling 709 acres. Ferdinando was a second cousin of John Stratford Collins of the Wythall and a descendant of the second son of the John Stratford Collins who had died in 1809. The 709 acres included 107 acres of woodland at Chase Wood, therefore mainly in Ross Parish. It also included 83 acres at Coughton, tenanted by Thomas Meredith, together with 290 acres at Cobrey and Coleraine farms and 188 acres at the Bollin farm. These farms are detailed below.

Cobrey (sometimes called **Cokebury**, **Cowbry**, **Colbury**, or **Coughbury**; *Chalceburge* in Domesday Book):
John Markey, the second husband of Alice Kyrle, owned the estate but later it was sold by his son who purchased Alton Court in Ross, and in about 1670 it was purchased by Edmond Bond of St. Briavels. He died in 1710, and the probate inventory 'apprized' by John Merrick and John Rudge lists all his goods and chattels. They were worth a total of £980, of which 77 per cent were agricultural assets. The son of his successor, Richard Bond, (another Richard) passed the property in his will, proved in 1733, to his only child and heiress Elizabeth, who married Gabriel Hanger, M.P. of Driffield, Gloucestershire. He was created Lord Coleraine in the Peerage of Ireland in 1762.

An Indenture of 1773 records the efforts of Elizabeth Lady Coleraine, 'relict' (widow) of the Rt. Hon. Gabriel late Lord Coleraine, and her son John, to pay off their debts by selling several properties, including the 'capital messuage called Cowbry' and nearly 300 acres. The properties sold included 'three Water or Corn Mills lying under one Roof late in the tenure or occupation of Richard Evans and the messuage adjoining the said Mills called Mill House ... all in the Parish of Walford'. In addition the 'dwelling-house and Paper Mill called Bill Mills' was sold.

In 1776 Charles Trusted, a Quaker of Ross, was recorded as the new owner of Cobrey, and he left it by will to his son, Immanuel. In December 1812 Henry

Barnett, possibly of 'the Isle of Jamaica', bought the property and rebuilt the mansion 'at an expense of £5000'. The estate was left to his widow and children on his death in 1831. However a newspaper cutting records that in September 1849 the 'freehold estate called Cobrey with a Mansion House, grounds, timber, farm buildings and 324 acres and also a Capital Water Corn Mill (let at the yearly rent of £110. together with 18 acres of land) was to be Peremptorily Sold'. There was a dispute leading to a legal case between members of the family.

On the resolution of this case, in 1851, the mansion, stables and farm buildings with 324 acres of 'most highly fertile land' were for sale; still included were the 'capital water corn mill, with three pairs of French stones and two overshot water wheels'. From 1856 until 1881 Thomas Skinner Bradstock lived there. The 1871 census records that he was farming 500 acres and employing 16 labourers, but in 1881 the acreage had reduced to 315 acres and only five men and one boy were employed on the farm.

In 1864 Miss Mary Stokes bought the property for £19,000. John Leonard Piddocke appears to have been farming it and was a tenant of Castle Brook until his term expired in 1892, the year that Miss Stokes died. It is thought that from 1895 until at least 1908 Ferdinando Stratford Collins lived in the big house; in 1910 his agricultural land at Cobrey totalled 289 acres in the combined farms of Cobrey and Coleraine. Edward Henry Chapman lived at Cobrey Park from 1909 and the farmer was James Humphrey Bromage in 1910. Mr. Pearson, an estate agent in Ross bought the large house and farm, later selling the house to A.E. Rudge from Parkfields, (who sold it to Guy's Hospital), but kept the house as a summer residence. Wilfred Chinn was the tenant farmer of the land from 1925 to 1941. At the beginning of the Second World War the mansion was turned into four or five flats. At this time it was in

View of Cobrey Park Estate around 1938, with Emrys Samuels
on the horse-drawn mower, Reg Price assisting. (Courtesy of Violet Chinn)

the ownership of Mr. Woodward. In 1956 Wilfred's son, William bought the house and in the following year he bought the farm, then totalling 270 acres, from Guy's Hospital. Cobrey Park is still the home of some of the younger members of the Chinn family. It is recorded in the Sites and Monuments Record for Herefordshire.

The Bollin (or Bollen)

This belonged, for some years, to Ferdinando Stratford Collins, but before that it was the property of the Kyrles, followed by the Seymours. A 1747 Quit Claim by Frances Seymour, the widow of Daniel Seymour, mentions her interest in the Bollin. The heiress of this family, Ann Seymour, married William Chinn of Coughton and 'thus carried the estate into the Chinn family'. William Chinn served as Sheriff for Herefordshire in 1733. On his death in 1758 his estates in Coughton and the Bollin passed to Thomas Nourse of Weston and remained in the possession of this family for many years.

In his book *The Wye Tour* published in 1826, the Revd. T.D. Fosbroke describes the farmhouse as 'a respectable old dwelling of delightful situation'. With its unspoilt yard and old sandstone buildings this is still an apt description. In 1858 and 1862 John Hardwick Junior was there and in 1871 the estate totalled 217 acres. This acreage had increased by 1881 when N.J. Hardwick farmed 247 acres, employing five men and two boys, presumably for the proprietor, the Deputy-Lieutenant Edward Nourse Harvey J.P. In 1891 Robert Newbury Dampier, 'auctioneer and farmer', lived there, but in 1910 Francis J. Evans was farming the 188 acres and living in the house. The owner at this time was Ferdinando Stratford Collins. The next farmer was a Mr. Watkins, who was followed in 1938 by Milwyn Davies and his wife, Winifred. The present traditionally-run mixed farm of 130 acres is now in the ownership of their son, John.

Castlebrook and Coleraine

At some stage Coleraine appears to have been a farm in its own right and Castlebrook was always a very small holding, with about 10 acres. Under the ownership of Ferdinando Stratford Collins Cobrey and Coleraine were farmed as one, and around 1908 the house at Castlebrook was converted into the house serving the combined farm. The names of the occupiers of Castlebrook are noted from 1840, when it was an Inn. In 1871 Edward Hartland (aged 73) farmed 8 acres there, followed by Mary Harris, widow, 'left in charge'. In 1885 Bedlington Kirkhouse is noted in a directory; he was followed by George William Jones in 1900, James Humphrey Bromage from1909 until 1917 and Gwynne James Bromage in 1929 with over 150 acres. At this time Edward Henry Chapman lived in Cobrey Park, with 4 acres of garden and shooting rights over the estate. Wilfred Chinn and his family were at Castlebrook from 1925, and took over Coleraine (150 acres) in 1931 from Gwynne James

A break in hay making around 1920. From left to right: Richard Young, Rosalie Young, John Collier, Arthur Young. (Courtesy of Harvey Hemms, Ross)

Bromage. When Wilfred Chinn bought Coughton House in 1949 his older son, William, moved into Castlebrook.

Corn, potatoes and sugar-beet were grown on the combined farms and a dairy herd kept until 1932, when calves were bought in. Other stock included sheep and horses. In 1936 a steel-wheeled tractor was used on the farms, and in 1938 it was followed by a rubber-tyred model.

In 1840 the majority of the parish was in the hands of the three large estate landowners described above. The 1910 Land Valuation Lists indicate the land and property owned by private individuals. Notable among these were the enterprising Gwatkin family, with John at the New Buildings, Forest Green, Wallace at the Stubbs (near Marks Well) and Thomas at the Dam. Miss Eliza Jones owned Sandyway and the Quabbs (the latter with 12 acres), and Alfred Jones owned Daycroft with 43 acres. James Jakeman owned 10 acres at Rose Cottage, together with the Wenslows, and John Gwatkin was his tenant. Hiram Jenkins was at Bristol Castle but no land is mentioned; John Collier owned just over 3 acres at Deepdean. Hazelhurst was the largest small farm, with 44 acres, owned by Mrs. Marian Ashmore. Holcombe comprised 18 acres with George William Butt as the owner, and this land included Rock Farm and Marks Well.

The impression left after studying all the intricacies of the ownership and use of the land is of continuity and hard work over the centuries. The varied land-types and topography required human initiative and energy—and these qualities were not lacking.

CHAPTER VII
Industry

In a large rural parish, such as this, agriculture has always been the primary industry, but the natural resources have provided other means of making a living. These include forestry, iron-smelting with associated charcoal burning, quarrying and lime-burning, coalmining, brick-making, milling and the many skills required to support the farming community. Among the latter were the indispensable wheelwrights, blacksmiths and carpenters, and, in more recent times, the mechanics and engineers who maintained the threshing machines and agricultural implements and, from around 1915, the new 'work-horses', the tractors.

Trade directory entries and census details reveal the variety of other occupations over the years. Many people 'wore two or more hats' in that they carried on multiple occupations. Among these were John Gwatkin, a farmer, haulier and beer retailer around 1900 and William Webb, a haulage contractor, car proprietor and coal dealer from 1929 until at least 1941.

In alphabetical order the trades practised in the parish from the 1830s included: basket-maker, blacksmith, brickmaker, carpenter, coal dealer, cordwainer, corn merchant/factor, engine fitter, haulier, hoop-maker, hurdlemaker, lime-burner, mason, miller, millwright, miner, plasterer, postman, quarryman, shoemaker, spokemaker, stone-breaker, tiler, timber merchant, wheelwright, woodman and woodturner. Associated with the farms there were agricultural labourers, shepherds and the much-valued stockmen and waggoners. Some women worked as dressmakers or laundresses and many of them were domestic servants in the larger households. The occupations associated with the retail trades such as shops, bakeries, public houses etc. are described in chapter eight on Post Office, Shops and Public Houses.

The employers of the industrial workers were the millers, both of corn (or grist) mills and saw mills, together with the iron-works owners, the building firms, the master lime-burners and the quarry owners and, in the late 1800s, the railways. Blacksmiths and wheelwrights were usually self-employed as were the engineers involved in agricultural machinery maintenance. Those involved in tree felling and timber haulage were also independent operators. A few coal-miners are noted in the more recent censuses.

Initially the mills were water-powered, with their locations necessarily near a stream or a leat. In the words of the historian W.G. Cooke (1882) 'a Brook enters this parish from Weston in the east flowing into the Wye near the Kerne Bridge, turning in its course to Bill Mills, Coughton Mill and Walford Mill'.

The southern parish and county boundary of Lodge Grove Brook, (formerly known as Bishop's Brook), provided another source of mill-power. As early as 1336 Richard Talbot obtained permission to construct a mill on this stream, probably that known as Diggins Mill, a grist mill which was worked until 1706; this would have been inside the present parish of Ruardean. Further down-stream, in this parish, stood New Mill, which belonged to Robert Devereux, Earl of Essex, who died in 1646. This could have been the site of a later forge, part of the Bishopswood ironworks, as in 1878 this derelict forge was described as an 'old corn mill'. The Dry Brook, rising in Suff Wood and running below Dunderhole Farmhouse, through the Oxlet to the Wye, could have powered a very early mill, and there is an 1844 reference to 'The Mills' at the Dunderhole just below what is now a wet area, formerly a pond.

The corn mill at Coughton is very old. It is presumed that it was part of the manor of Coughton or Coketon, which was given by Richard I to Richard

Coughton Mill c.1937 taken from the Mill House with Desmond and Violet Samuels in foreground. (Courtesy of Violet Chinn, née Samuels)

Talbot 'for his services' between 1157 and 1199, and and made subordinate to the Manor of Eccleswall and Linton. In 1369 Gilbert, Lord Talbot, authorised Hugh de Monnington and John de Mynors to convey to the priory of Wormesley lands in Coketon, 'that prayers might be made for the souls of himself and of Petronilla his wife', and later this was augmented by the rent accruing from his mill at Coketon. This income, with an additional charge of 10 shillings on the rental of the same mill, was to increase the money needed for the maintenance of the canons. In due course the priory acquired the whole manor, to lose it at the suppression of the religious houses, when it was purchased by George Chaldecote, sold again, and by 1549 it was held by Walter Kyrle, father of Robert.

W.G. Cooke notes that, just before his death, Robert Kyrle held Coughton Manor and a 'water-mill thereto appertaining, [held] of the Crown by the service of a hundredth part of a Knight's fee', in addition to the manor of Walford Court (held of Lord and Lady Clanicarde) and other estates. (A knight's fee was the service due as a return for the grant of sufficient land for a knight and his family to subsist for a year.) The estate was purchased by a Richard Chinn whose ancestors were residents in Walford in the 16th century. When William Chinn died in 1758 Coughton was inherited by William Nourse of Lower Weston, and in 1882 it was part of Edward Nourse Harvey's estate.

The mill is marked on Price's map of 1817, Bryant's map of 1835 and the O.S. map of 1904 refers to it as 'Coughton Mill (disused)'. The building is still in good order, and part of Coughton Farm. There used to be a long pond there, and on the opposite side of the road the house is called The Mill. Millers noted are: William Howell (1835-44); James Matthews (1856, corn factor as well); W.H. Bussell (1862 and 63, miller and corn factor; 'Bussell and Pike' were corn merchants in Ross) although the directory reference gives the initials as H.T.; H.T. Bussell (1867, miller at Ross and Coughton with James Hope manager at Coughton); William Smith (1885); and Clement Hall (1895 until the mill went out of use in the early 1900s). From 1931 the mill, along with the farm, was occupied by Emrys Samuels. He later purchased it but then sold the Mill House to Wilfred Chinn in 1951. Wilfred's son, Robert, and his wife Violet, Emrys' daughter, own the old mill building and the farm where they live now. All the mill machinery was removed during the Second World War.

Walford Mill is located at S0 586 198. It is believed to be about 250 years old and the wood-working machinery was installed in 1870. The mill was in continuous use until 1930, and it was acquired by the present owner's father, Herbert Worgan Smith, in 1939. Corn was ground for animal feed there until the early 1950s. During its lifetime the original waterwheel was replaced by an overshot iron one, measuring 12 feet by 4 feet, driving three pairs of stones. The iron axle was 6 inches square, and said to have been made at Bishopswood

Part of the mill building at Walford Sawmills in 1969. The waterwheel was to the right of the building. (Photo by Harry Paar, courtesy of Gerald Smith)

in the late 1800s. In 1969 Harry Paar, with the permission of the owner, took photographs of the Mill House and the remnants of the 'newly dismantled' waterwheel, and he was particularly interested to see the faint mark of a bird, possibly a partridge, embedded in the ironwork.

The Walford millers traced from the directories and the censuses are: Charles and Henry Cuddener (1841); Charles Morgan (1851); Henry Phelps (from 1856 to 1858, miller and shopkeeper); Mrs. Taylor (1860, miller, shop-keeper and beer retailer); Joseph Stephens (from 1876 to 1881, Master Miller, employing two men and one boy); Charles Frederick Sims, (1885, miller, wood turner and timber dealer); William Phillips junior (1890); Richard Jones (1900); Richard Jones & Yemm (from 1905 to 1913); Richard Jones (from 1914 to 1917); Richard Jones & Sons (from 1922 to 1926); Daniel Walkley (from 1929 to 1934); Park End Saw Mills (1937). In 1939 Herbert Smith bought the site, and production restarted in 1945. The busy saw-mill is now in the hands of his son, Gerald, but the Mill House was sold in 2001 as a private residence.

The *Walford Women's Institute Local History* written in 1954/55 notes 'the water wheel also drives a variety of wood-working machinery such as saws, lathes and planes. It turns out quite a lot of timber for the Coal Board and others; also a very considerable quantity of worked wood for furniture-makers'. There was an alternative drive to six wood-turning lathes.

Due to the considerable increase in output, a large diesel engine was introduced in the mid 1900s to power most of the timber sawing. The writer of the W.I. account had access to a ledger of 1870 detailing item prices:

1 broom handle	2d
6 dozen ladder rounds	6s 0d
Turning a set of croquet balls	1s 6d

Also noted is the large quantity of timber ordered by the firm of Richard Thomas & Co. of Lydbrook, (now Richard Thomas and Baldwin of South Wales), and the requirements of the local wheelwrights for turned wood.

A house near the bottom of Leys Hill, Glen Kerne, the property of Joan Joseph, was in 1873, occupied by the Walford Saw Mills and Turnery Company. Around that date the company had gone into bankruptcy and an inventory describes the varnishing room in a barn. In earlier years the engines and horses had been sold and by 1882 there were two cottages on the site, later converted into one.

Waggon built at Walford Sawmills in 1923 for Walford Court.
From left to right: Arthur Jones, Trevor Collier aged 16 (sitting in the waggon), Harry Scarisbrooke, Harold Jones, Chesney Jones.
(Photo by George W. Young, courtesy of Nancy Roberts)

Iron-working was another early industry with the trees in Bishopswood a ready source of charcoal, the fuel first used for firing the furnaces. In Britain iron-working began around 200 BC but with the arrival of the Romans the output increased, mainly for their military purposes. The intriguing reference to a Roman camp in Lodge Grove Wood, and, of course, the coin hoard found near Bishopswood Church (mentioned in chapter one), indicate a Roman presence. Their *Ariconium* industrial complex was not far away.

Bloomeries were the earliest means of extracting the ore from ironstone, and the product of these early furnaces is called a bloom. A local expert explains early iron-working thus: 'the two main methods of smelting both used charcoal: the bowl furnace and the shaft furnace (bloomery)—the latter probably having been introduced by the Romans. Roasting of the ore was an essential preliminary. The bloom was probably an agglomeration of reduced metal, slag and charcoal, and the bloom would have been finally consolidated by heating to a red heat and hammering to shape'. The bowl surface left a shiny surface on the cooled 'bloom'. However, the process was inefficient as indicated by the high iron content in the cinders left at the many sites in Gloucestershire, Monmouthshire and Herefordshire. The cinders were resmelted in more recent times, and the field names Cinder Pits, Cinderbees (or Sinderbees) and Cinder Hill may be clues, in this parish, as to where they were found. These early iron-extraction works did not need waterpower, but with the introduction of blast-furnaces in the 16th century proximity to a water supply was essential—the water falling over (or sometimes under) the waterwheel then powered the bellows.

Charcoal burners worked in the neighbouring Forest of Dean and in this parish from the 13th century, their work requiring experience and skill. In his book *The Industrial History of Dean* Cyril Hart describes the iron industry in the Forest of Dean and environs from the early 16th century. There was often a forge associated with the furnace where the crude ore tapped from the furnace was beaten, refined and shaped. With the increasing numbers of furnaces and forges, charcoal was in high demand and the ironmasters realised they would have to plant regenerative trees to provide coppice wood for future years. Coal was sometimes used but produced adverse sulphur in the molten mix which resulted in brittle wrought iron.

The whole technology changed with the introduction of coke as the fuel, as then it was proximity to the coal-fields, rather than woodlands, that became the priority. In the Forest the earliest coke-burning blast-furnaces are recorded in 1773 at Lydney and in 1795 at Cinderford but it appears that the Bishopswood works continued to use charcoal and cinders as fuel until 1805, with some ore imported from Lancashire.

In 1810 an extension to the tramroad supplying the ironworks was authorised by the Severn and Wye Railway Company, as this was needed to bring in

Old cottage at the Oxlet in 1969.
(Photo by Harry Paar, courtesy of John Daniels)

coke and coal and take out bar-iron. By 1814 bar-iron was being imported to the forge from Lydney, which suggests that the furnace was, by then, out of use. Around 1821 William Partridge, the local ironmaster, built his mansion at Bishopswood very near the site of the furnace, which also indicates that the noisy and noxious process had ceased.

Harry Paar, a respected writer on the Forest railways and tramroads, has long puzzled over what he calls the 'Drybrook Mystery'; he used to be convinced that there were furnaces and possibly a forge in the Oxlet area. Mr. H.B. Storey of Home Farm, Bishopswood, first put this possibility to him, and Mr. Paar examined early maps and walked the ground to find clues. The field names on the 1840 tithe map seem significant—Furnace Wood and Furnace Grove are marked east of the Dry Brook. The 1887 O.S. 6 inch map shows The Dam and Dam Wood, but does not show the actual pond noted near Dunderhole Farm. The conclusion was that it was an amenity for wildlife in connection with Bishopswood House (formerly known as The Coppice). The Oxlet has kept its secret; the few old houses on the west side of the footpath WA 90 are the only tangible evidence of activity in that secluded valley.

From the early 1590s Robert Devereux, the second Earl of Essex, had two furnaces at Bishopswood and a forge at Lydbrook. Between the 1590s and 1612 J. Challoner and partners were tenants of the Essex family, and in 1617 two ruined furnaces were let to James Hawkins with permission to build one furnace. In 1663 Sir John Kirle leased, (from the owner Benedict Hall), a furnace at Furnace Pool, which was probably at Bishopswood, in addition to a forge at Lydbrook (Upper Hangerbury). Benedict Hall appears to have disposed of the property before 1650, and, according to Cyril Hart's account, 'the furnace was supposedly demolished by the Preservators of Dean on 30 January 1650'. Shortly after this the Foley dynasty took over.

Starting with Richard Foley (1588 to 1657) a network of Foley ironwork enterprises was set up. In the late 17th century their 'Ironworks in Partnership' controlled four furnaces, 13 forges, four slitting mills and a warehouse. These works were situated in the Forest of Dean, the Stour Valley and as far afield as Pembrokeshire. Pig iron made at the furnaces was converted into wrought- (bar-) iron at the forges (the 'pigs' were the runnels of melted iron that ran out from the bottom of the furnaces after heating). With their network of forges the Foley entrepreneurs 'mixed and matched' the furnace products to achieve the differing end-products required by the consumers. As the industry burgeoned pig-iron became scarce and some of the forges had to be 'fed' from sources as distant as America from 1728 until 1763; other sources were iron ballast squares from wrecked ships.

Another prominent member of the ironmaster hierarchy was Richard Knight (1659-1745) who became a partner in the Foley business at the beginning of the 18th century. By this time it seems that the furnace on Lodge Grove Brook had ceased production. The 1840 Tithe Map shows field number 1508 as Forge Meadow with the owner and occupier John Partridge, but by that time the usage was 'meadow'.

Masons feature prominently in the record of occupations in the parish, with 20 of these craftsmen listed in the census and directory details between 1840 and 1929. The longest-lived family name of masons are the Whittakers, with Thomas, of Bulls Hill and Queachent Tree Cottage from 1840 to 1877 and George (Belle Vue Cottage, Bulls Hill) from 1851 to 1877. William Whittaker was at Marks Well Cottage No. 2 in 1861 and 1867. Other family surnames recur, with John, Thomas and William Baker from 1841, and the Webbs (James and Benjamin, the former a stone mason at 'Kerne'), in addition to the versatile Gwatkins at the New Buildings, Forest Green from 1876 to 1929. John Gwatkin (senior and junior) were masons, hauliers, quarry proprietors, carpenters and builders and from 1898 John Gwatkin was also the licensee of the public house there.

A stonemason, James Symonds, helped in the construction of St. John's Church on Howle Hill. His three sons, William, George and Andrew, followed his profession and during the First World War William and Andrew founded the building firm called Symonds & Co. Among their many achievements is the house now called Red Hall (formerly Four Winds and before that Hill View) which was built, in 1915, for Laura Isabella Gwatkin and her sister Lucinda

The Symonds family—father and three sons—in 1962. Standing, left to right: Leslie ('Chappie'), Gordon and Derrick, with Andrew (father) seated. (Photo by and courtesy of Jack Coombes, Ross)

Emmeline. In the 1941 trade directory the entry reads: 'builders, painters and house decorators'; for many years the firm were also undertakers. Andrew's sons, Leslie and Gordon, continued the family connection for over 50 years until their retirement in 1972, but the business carried on under Cyril and Pauline Powell for a further 20 years. As noted in chapter nine, the builders' yard is now the site of a small housing development opposite Walford School.

Trevor Collier was a builder of some status in the Ross area; he was the last of his family at Deep Dean, where he was born and reared. He became a wheelwright and joined the firm of Symonds & Co. as a carpenter and joiner. In 1934 he married Dorothy Jane Symonds and built their home at Coughton. A few years later he formed a partnership with John Brain and together they founded the builders' business, Collier & Brain, of Drybrook. Trevor Collier carried on in the firm until his 90th birthday and died aged 93, in 2000.

Many carpenters are listed, often also described as wheelwrights or joiners, and in 1909 one, Charles Smith, is noted as wheelwright, carpenter, undertaker, general merchant and engineer. The Davis family were carpenters in an old house, now demolished, associated with Rock Farm (Holcombe Lodge) as was Henry Webb, who lived first at No. 1 Marks Well House, (where there is a stone inscription) and later at Glebe Cottage between 1856 and 1890. He was for many years the Parish Clerk and Assistant Parish Overseer.

Between 1890 and 1902 Thomas Cawthorn was a carpenter and a farmer at Coughton. More recently the wheelwright's shop belonging to Arthur Jones was situated to the north of Chestnut and Newall Cottages (in Walford village) and in due course Chestnut Cottage came into the Cawthorn family through the marriage of Arthur Jones' grand-daughter, Barbara Webb, to John Cawthorn.

In 1881 Robert Smith of the Spread Eagle (now the Mill Race) was a wood turner and master millwright, and a few doors away William Smith, of Sandiway Cottage, was a wheelwright. From 1891 Charles Edward Yemm is recorded as a wheelwright and farmer at Coughton Mill, and from 1905 until his death in 1914 he was associated with Richard Jones at Walford Mill; they were described as wood turners and timber dealers. Frederick Yemm was, in 1926, a wheelwright living at Porter's Lodge, (then called Jesemine Cottage) moving later to Parbrook.

Only a few brickmakers are mentioned including Joseph Edwards at The Dam in 1858 and two Jacksons, John and Ephraim, from1856 to 1863. In 1871 William Symonds was both a brickyard proprietor and brickmaker, as well as a boot and shoemaker, living at Brickyard Cottage, Forest Green. Later he was a shopkeeper at Forest Green and in 1881 he lodged, still a brickmaker, at Coldharbour (now Peacehaven). The 'brick manufacturer', John Bussell Kemp (living in Ross) owned the brickworks near Forest Green in 1890 and 1902, but by 1922 they were described as 'disused'. In 1965 John Stafford Kemp conveyed to his company (presumably Kemps of Ross) Brick House Cottage with three acres of land 'more or less' which, it is presumed, would have included the brickworks site. The clay-pool remained until the mid-1970s, near Pear Tree Cottage, providing a useful rubbish tip. There was a brickworks at Hom Green, with the Brickyard Cottages Nos. 1 to 4 as the only reminder. Victor Loveridge has lived in two of these (converted to one dwelling) for nearly 50 years and has been told that there was a brick kiln nearby. There is a pond in the garden of the adjoining cottages, now called Rose Cottage, which dries up in hot summers, leaving a cracked surface. Additionally there is a curved, low brick structure on the property which could be the remnants of the brickworks.

Among the local tradesmen serving the building industry were the plasterers and tilers. As early as 1840 John Hall (plasterer and tiler) was living at 'Chusnut Cottage' in the centre of Walford village, adjoining the housing development called Nelson's Place. In 1871 John Carpenter, another plasterer, was at Spring Meadow Cottage, then Tan House, Coughton in 1876/77 and in 1895 at Forest Green. Charles Mills, or Miles, of Bishopswood is noted as a tiler from 1895 to 1902.

Lime-burning was an important part of the local economy from around 1810 with most of the activity near the top of Howle Hill. Quarrying for stone was often associated with lime-burning and the censuses reveal that many of the master lime-burners were also quarry owners. The Whittingham family, initially at the Slad (now Craig Farm) and later at Fir Tree House, Coughton, were farmers, lime-merchants, quarry owners and stone hauliers for many years, and are recorded in every census from 1841 until 1881. The Youngs were also lime-burners, with Amos and Levi in 1861, Richard in 1871 through to 1900, and James Young (aged 73) a labourer at Lime Kiln in 1881. Richard Young was a Master Lime-burner, living at Whittingham's Cottage and later moving to Marling Pitts in 1881. 'Young's Kilns' can still be seen near the top of Sharman, Howle Hill, although rather obscured by brushwood. The charge-hole above the kilns has been filled in.

The opening of the railway in 1873 provided jobs both to staff the station at Kerne Bridge and with the line itself. William Dew was a plate-layer in 1881, while others are described as 'railway labourers'. In the same year George Windridge, aged 25, was a 'local engine driver' and George Richardson an 'engine fitter'.

Blacksmiths were always an integral part of a village economy and in this parish the Howells, or Howls, family were among those who took this role. Thomas Howls was the Walford blacksmith until his death in 1770. In 1840 Gilbert Howells owned the smith's shop, with house and garden, near the centre of Walford village but in 1881 he was a 'master blacksmith' at Coughton. His son William, born 1849, worked as a blacksmith for many years. He was also the sexton and for some years c.1900 the Parish Clerk.

At the other end of Walford, in Coughton Street, Amos Penn had his smithy from 1840 until 1867, and his house-name has reverted to its earliest description, Coughton Forge, formerly called Hazebrook. At Bishopswood the smith

Bishopswood Toll House with the Forge behind, c.1920

operated on the main road, near the border with Gloucestershire, in a building behind a house still called the Forge. A parishioner remembers taking her father's horse down the slope to the forge for shoeing; she was so small that she had to be helped onto the horse's back to ride him back to the farm. Jim Lewis followed in the footsteps of his father as the blacksmith there; he also ran the Albion pub until he took over the Queen's Head in Ross in the 1950s. The house in front of the forge served as the toll house on the exit from the parish.

Blacksmiths and wheelwrights were the innovators who were to evolve into the engineers and mechanics needed in the machinery revolution of the 19th century. As far back as 1867 John Price was a threshing-machine proprietor and the first agricultural mowing machine to be used in the parish was assembled in the Coughton blacksmith's shop and used by William Onions of Deep Dean in 1880. In the 1881 census John Price 'threshing machine proprietor' was living at Whitings Lane. More recently Charlie Price and his brother Bill continued as threshing contractors, the former living at the house now re-named Coughton Forge before moving into Ross; Bill lived at Marling Pitts and later at Lodge Farm.

The *Walford Women's Institute History* (1954/55) has interesting detail of the introduction of farm machinery locally. In 1890 two reapers and self-binders arrived, one at Walford Court and the other at Great Howle. Andrew Symonds had recalled a 'great crowd of people gathering to see one of these binders in operation'. Hay-making machinery followed, with swath turners and side-delivery horse-rakes; also elevators. The arrival of the tractor between

Threshing machine at the Bollin Farm, early 20th century
(Courtesy of Fred Druce, Ross)

Group of woodcutters at Deep Dean c.1895.
Standing, left to right: ?, ?, William Jones, ?
Seated: Edwin Richardson, 'Old' John Collier, 'Bouncer', Charlie Green,
George Collier, William Gardiner, ?, Ambrose Jones
(Courtesy of Nancy Roberts)

1914-18 was followed by more sophisticated models with hydraulic lift and depth control from 1937. All these labour-saving devices depended on the skill and ingenuity of the engineers; even today a crop can be lost if the combine-harvester breaks down and cannot be repaired immediately.

Tree-felling and haulage were the occupations of skilled independent operators, and Joe Lewis of Pontshill, himself a skilful woodman, recounts the exploits of some of these renowned axemen. A team of woodcutters felled a large oak near Sharman in the 1930s. Having stripped the bark (for tanning) they paused for a break during which a number of gentlemen came along. One of the gang decided on a means of gaining some cider for their refreshment and, for a wager, told one of the gentlemen that the team-leader could split a match-head with one blow of his axe—if he was successful there should be cider for the whole team. The wager was accepted. A match was placed on the bole of the felled tree. The woodcutter raised his 9 lb. axe above his head, and brought it down on the match-head. The feat was repeated twice more. Amazed and impressed the gentlemen paid up and the cider was awarded.

In 1841 James Watkins was described as a Timber Hewer and over the years several farmers were also hauliers. These included Thomas Meredith and James Young in 1858, Thomas Broben of Atlas Cottage and William Phillips of Shop Farm in 1881. William Henry Wheeler of Daycroft Farm was a timber haulier from 1881 until 1902 and others included Richard Joel Tummey of Stoney Way from 1913 for some years. In 1881 Charles Sims was a timber merchant living at Brook Cottage. Huge loads of timber were conveyed by a team of horses as illustrated below.

Arthur Young of Howle Hill was another entrepreneur. For 53 years he was a road contractor and helped lay down most of the roads in this area. One of his grandsons, Harvey Hemms, currently delivers mail in the parish. William Webb of Forest Green has been mentioned, with his many interests—haulage contractor, car proprietor and coal dealer from 1929 to 1941. In 1900 John Henry Hall was a coal merchant at Bishopswood and the firm later moved to Ross under the name of Webb, Hall and Webb. From around 1874 William Sillott owned the Kerne Bridge Inn and had a coalyard there, as well as on the opposite side of the road. He died in 1887; the coal business was sold to the

Horses hauling timber load at Walford around 1920,
with Chesney Jones at the reins. (Courtesy of Nancy Roberts)

Road contractor, Arthur Young (far right), and his team at Starve Beech around 1920. (From Ross on Wye Advertiser, *3 June 1970)*

Porters of Yorkley in 1939 (the Phoenix Coal Company) and subsequently moved to Ross. Several coalminers are named but they would probably have been employed out of the parish, as would the tin-plate workers. As recently as 1881 a charcoal-burner, George Griffiths of Boweries Place was listed in the trade directories; another unusual trade was that of Francis Dawes—he was a hoop-maker.

Basket and hurdle-making were other employments and James Baldwin of The Rock, Thomas Pritchard of Thorn Tree House, Thomas Pritchard of Yew Tree and James Pritchard of Leys Hill are all first recorded in these occupations in 1841. James Pritchard (1851) was also a fisherman at the Kerne. In the 1851 census James Welling was described as a 'journeyman basket-maker' at the Kerne; by 1862 he appears to have graduated as he was simply a basket-maker. As recently as 1917 William Jones of Myrtle Cottage is listed as a hurdle-maker. In the early years of the 20th century there was a besom (broom) factory in the woods between Howle Hill and Deep Dean. One of the bombs that was dropped in the Second World War landed here, leaving a huge crater which obliterated the remains of this unusual enterprise.

Great Howle Farm, at the top of Howle Hill, was the centre of open-cast coalmining between 1972 and 1977. Old coal mines had been worked for about 200 years but closed around 1900. After nationalisation in 1947/8 the mineral mining rights belonged to the National Coal Board. In the early 1970s it proved economic to mine about 50 acres on four sites: between Little Howle towards

Great Howle, on the east side of the road; on the west side of the same stretch of road; between Great Howle and Howle Green; and part of Suff Wood. Approximately 100,000 tons of coal was extracted and taken away by lorry down Sharman (Howle Hill). The first consignment went to the Parkend railhead and on to a power stattion on the Severn estuary, with subsequent tonnages going to a power station near Bewdley; some was exported to Belgium. The Howle Hill coal was good quality and burned with a low ash content. After economic extraction was completed, the topsoil was restored and the area is now good quality agricultural land.

The industry of the parish today is very different these days. The saw-mills at Walford employ 28 men and no longer saw timber but make wood products. The railway closed long ago, the garage more recently and the building business in 1992. Many people commute to work or use home computers to earn a living. Wood-cutters have been replaced with chain-saw users; laundresses with washing machines. Engineering skills are still a valuable asset on the highly mechanised farms but the industry of the parish in the present is very different from that of the past.

CHAPTER VIII
Post Offices, Shops and Public Houses

The first mention in the local trade directories of a postal service in the area is in the 1856 Post Office Directory of Gloucestershire with Bath, Bristol and Herefordshire where a John Hall is mentioned as 'Receiver' at Walford. Letters were routed through Ross, and arrived at 10 a.m. with dispatch at '20 min. past 5 p.m.'. The nearest money order office was given as Ross. John Hall is also mentioned in the trade section of the same directory as 'plasterer and post-master'. In the 1851 census there is a John Hall, aged 50, residing at Chestnut Cottage in Walford village, who was a plasterer and who would appear to be the same person.

By 1862 his widow, Mary Hall, was the sub-postmistress and receiver, and is mentioned as such until the 1876-77 *Littlebury* directory, by which time Henry Holder had taken over the job. By then letters at this time were brought by messenger from Ross and post-boxes had been installed at Coughton, Kerne Bridge, Howle Hill and Forest Green, with the one at Coughton the earliest, first noted in the directory in 1867.

Post offices were usually established in the house of the person who was the sub-postmaster or mistress at the time. Henry Holder and, after his death in 1907 at the age of 85, his daughter, Miss Sarah Jane Holder, lived in the house that is now called Laburnum Cottage, next but one to the Mill Race public house. Mr. Holder had the cottage built, and the remains of the letterbox were left in the wall when the post office transferred to the house across the road. The post office facilities available at Walford gradually expanded and by 1879 it was described as a 'Post Office and Money Order Office and Savings Bank'; in 1909 'Insurance' was added. Goodrich, at this time, was the nearest telegraph office.

The last entry for Miss Sarah Jane Holder as sub-postmistress occurs in 1917, and the next directory available (for 1922) gives Miss Dorice Bertha Phillips as sub-postmistress. Her father, William Henry Phillips, was the shop-keeper in Walford village, and lived in the house now known as Witsend. William Phillips died in 1932 and the post office and shop continued under the management of his daughters, Dorice and Gladys, at least until 1941, which is the date of the last available directory for the area. Gladys married Jack Owen Rogers and they continued the business. Jack is remembered as delivering groceries around Leys Hill, Sharman and Bulls Hill after the Second World War. There was also a bakery associated with the Phillips' shop, from which bread was delivered by horse and cart; the present occupants, Mr. and Mrs. Eachus, found the oven still there when they moved in.

From the Phillips' day the shop and post office in Walford was run as an entity, with the income from the post office helping to keep the enterprise going. Later the shop and post office were run successively by Mr. and Mrs. Austin (who were the owners in 1955), Frank Kirby and his wife, Mr. and Mrs. Hockley, Mr. Foreman and, finally, Mr. and Mrs. Eachus who still live in the house. When the post office was taken over in 1988 by the latter they were told that the level of use was only appropriate to a 'community post office' and that they would only be paid for opening from 9 a.m. to 12 noon, six days a week, with an extra hour on Saturdays for the bookwork. In spite of increased usage, this arrangement remained unchanged and helped to precipitate its closure in 1996.

Separate sub-post offices for the Bishopswood, Coughton and Howle Hill areas were not established until much later than Walford, all being first noted in the directories between 1885 and 1890. Much earlier, however, (in the 1841 census), Andrew Pool is described as 'postman' of Bishopswood.

In 1890 Mrs. Rodman is the first-mentioned sub-postmistress for Bishopswood, and in 1895 the post was held by Miss (Sarah) Jane Rodman, (who was aged 18 in the 1891 census). By 1900 Miss Mary Lewis had become the sub-postmistress, and she continued in office at least until 1934, while Mrs. Mary Paulfrey is listed in 1937 and 1941. A shop seems to have been added to the business by 1929 and this has continued to the present day. However, these listings do not appear to be entirely accurate as Mr. James ('Chappie') Webb recalls that he took over the business in 1937 when there was no shop, starting that part of the enterprise himself. James Webb rented the site of the old Bishopswood Mansion gardens, together with the business, and at one time the shop and post office were located in the house opposite the bottom of Bishopswood Hill, which had previously been the laundry belonging to the Mansion. He bought the whole site in 1949 when the Bishopswood Estate was up for sale, retaining the garden part for use as a caravan site; it had been used as a market garden during the War.

In 1952 the post office and shop was sold to a Mr. Turner who, in turn, sold it two years later to Mr. Powell. Mrs. Walkley was the next owner and, on her marriage to Jack Gwatkin of Hill Farm, James Webb bought the business back (in 1962) and moved it across to the adjacent filling station site. Here it has remained since, with Mr. Webb's daughter, Mrs. Monica Edmunds, taking over officially as sub-postmistress around 1973, a post she still holds.

Coughton post office was under the care of Thomas Hargest for over 30 years, from its beginning in 1890 until 1922, in the house now known as The Old Letter Box. Both this office and the one on Howle Hill seem always to have been smaller and to have offered fewer services than either Walford or Bishopswood; neither now exist. In 1936 the Coughton sub-postmistress was Mrs. Kate Davies at the house now called Lamorran, earlier known as Greensleeves, but thereafter no names are given in the directories which are available.

Con Lewis is remembered by many people as the Coughton postmaster and postman. Originally named Conrad Hubert Baumgarte, he was the elder brother of Colin Eric Baumgarte who was killed near Ypres on 17 July 1917 while serving with the Worcestershire Regiment (see p.216). Con himself served in the Herefordshire Regiment. His father had been the manager of the Royal Hotel at Symonds Yat but died in 1907; the altar cross at English Bicknor Church is dedicated to his memory, and Con's mother was possibly from English Bicknor. She remarried after his father's early death and was the Mrs. Pitchford who lived in Coughton Cottage in the early 1920s; she was a keen supporter of the Walford Womens' Institute. Soon after the First World War Con changed his surname to Lewis. He ran the Coughton post office in a bungalow (no longer in existence) on the Fowbridge side of Coughton corner for many years until the late 1960s.

Con Lewis also acted as postman in the area, although this job did not need the stamina required by his predecesssor in the 1930s. The latter collected mail from Coughton and delivered it around the Howle Hill and Deep Dean areas in the mornings, before having a break in a small hut situated in the quarry area of Coldharbour (now Peacehaven) on Forest Green. After this he collected mail from the post box in the wall there, then walked down Bulls Hill to the post box near Holcombe Lodge, along the pathway by Marks Well to the Howle Hill box, round by the Chapel on Howle Hill and past St. John's Church across to Deep Dean where there was another box, then finally back, past The Firs (near Cobrey) and Coughton, to the Coughton post office. The postman blew a whistle as he went, so that people could

Con Lewis and his bungalow—
the Coughton P.O. and shop.
(Courtesy of Walford W.I.)

bring out any letters for posting and he would supply a stamp for 1 1/2d. This was a similar system to that used in the big cities before postboxes were installed.

After Con's retirement the business was transferred to the shop that then existed in Coughton Place. This is mentioned in the Walford Women's Institute local histories of 1954-55 and 1965 as being run by Mr. and Mrs. Penrey. After their departure the shop, combined with the post office, was kept successively by Mrs. Nankivell, Mr. and Mrs. Reynolds (1971), Mr. and Mrs. Burton, Mrs. Wool (who introduced videos for rental as well as the grocery and greengrocery sales) and, finally, Sharon and Bernard who came in 1988 and were still there when the shop and post office finally closed in March 1990. Unfortunately nobody could be found to take on the post office on a two-day-a-week basis from their own home. This has meant that people must travel to Tudorville or Ross post offices to deposit savings, and to cash child benefit or pension allowances, which are both important services to the public and a major source of revenue for post offices.

The post office at Howle Hill led a less continuous existence with the first mention in the 1885 trade directories when a Mrs. Miles Morgan was receiver. She lived at Gardener's Green but the location is uncertain. At the time of the 1871 census there was a shop at Gardener's Green run by Elizabeth Cox, wife of Amos, while Richard Young was named in the directories from 1870 to 1902 and, according to these, was at Lime Tump in 1890, and later 'just off Howle Hill' from 1895 onwards. As far as can be ascertained the post office was, at the turn of the century, located at The Wensleys, one of the little group of

The Wensleys. (Photo by Virginia Morgan 1992, courtesy of Barry Whitby)

cottages off the top of Sharman. This could have been known as Old Wenslows Cottage and in the 1881 census Frances, the wife of Edwin Whittingham, is listed as a 'small shopkeeper' there.

After 1902, for a few years, the sub-postmistress was Mrs. Annie Spencer (the grandmother of Mrs. Joyce Roberts) probably in the house opposite the Wensleys, now called Springhill but previously Jubilee Cottage; the letterbox is still present and operational.

George William Young then took over, most likely at the house now known as The Old Post House. Finally the post office was operated by Mrs. Caroline Sarah Spencer, who later remarried becoming Mrs. Collier. She is listed as sub-postmistress in 1926 and served for 23 years, to be followed by her daughter Mrs. Carrie Evans, known as 'Carry the Post', for a further 32 years, giving a grand total of over 50 years service between them. During these years the post office was first situated in the house opposite The Old Post House, called Malvern View, and, after an interval, in The Old Barn which had been renovated into a house and shop. Eventually the post office closed on Howle Hill at the end of July 1979. At the time the comment was made in the parish newsletter 'it will never be the same again'.

Another shop in the village area of Walford was that of the confectionery and bakery business of the Morgan family, which was in existence in one form or another for just on a hundred years. The first mention of the business is in the 1851 census, with William Morgan 'confectioner and biscuit maker' at Parbrook, and Mrs. Charlotte Morgan continuing the confectionery side from 1885 (after William's death in 1884) at their house in Whitings Lane. Their son, John, is mentioned as 'baker' from 1891, after his retirement from the police force in 1888. He had been stationed in Walford as a policeman from 1880, living in Road Cottage which adjoins the old bakery building.

Charlotte died in 1901 and John shortly afterwards, in 1907, after which the business was carried on by John's widow, Ellen, until she re-married in 1918. Osman Morgan was then in charge, but continued to live at The Glebe, opposite Walford Primary School, rather than next to the bakery. He is last mentioned in 1937 and then, in the 1941 directory, there appears another William Morgan, who was known as Danny.

Older parishioners remember that two vans were used to deliver bread around the area (Leys Hill, Sharman, etc.) and that Danny Morgan used to deliver three times a week down Bulls Hill. Ray Cawthorn (of Walford) worked with Danny when he was a lad of 13. 'In 1950 I used to walk from Norrland Place to work as a Baker's Boy for William Morgan (known as Danny) for five shillings a day. I used to start work at 7 a.m. on weekends and holidays. I would begin with greasing 300 tins while Danny made the dough. When Danny went in to have his breakfast I used to stand over the dough to push it back down when it was rising. After breakfast Danny would come back in the Bakehouse and I would then cut the dough into one pound lumps and he would shape the bread into loaves. These were baked in two batches. In the afternoon we would deliver the bread around the surrounding area. I remember one family with three boys that lived on Coppett Hill and who used to have 12 loaves every Saturday. I also helped him deliver on Mondays, Wednesdays and Fridays after school'.

At Christmas the window of the shop was decorated and Christmas cakes displayed. The shop also seems to have sold groceries, at least during the 1880s and 1890s. Although the shop closed in the late 1930s the bakery business and the delivery round continued until 1955, when the round was sold and the bakery sold to become a private house known, appropriately, as The Old Bakery.

Morgan's are making "Extra-Special" Buns.

Forget those unappetising Buns that you have had before and just try Morgan's. Notice how lovely and large they are . . . . and how light. Just take a bite . . . . yes, and then another . . . . . all those fine currants are the best money can buy.

If you want Hot Cross Buns made well, in a cleanly manner, and from the finest ingredients, then make sure you order a big bagful from Morgan's NOW.

O. MORGAN, The Bakery, Walford, Ross.

Advert for Morgan's 'Extra-Special' buns in the Ross Gazette
for 26 March 1931

At one point, just before the Second World War, a shed next to The Old Soundings was used as a butcher's shop, by Russell Preston, on two days a week.

Another butcher was a Thomas Parry of Bulls Hill, listed in the 1841 and 1861 censuses. (A Thomas Parry of Daycroft—not the same one but possibly related—appears in various directories between 1891 and 1902 dying, aged 67, in 1904.) Other butchers at one time or another were Henry Phelps, who combined some butchery with farming between 1870 and 1879, and James Tomkins of Rock Villa (now called Bramble Bank), also a butcher and farmer, in the late 1890s and early 1900s.

The family pig was an important part of the economy in earlier days, and the pig-killer, or 'pig-sticker', was needed when the day came for the dispatch of the cherished animal. During the 1920s and 30s, Thomas Beach of Springherne Cottage, Bulls Hill, carried out this task and passed his skill on to his son Isaac. Isaac, who lived at Marks Well Cottage, travelled all over the parish with his commission. Many adults, children then, will remember the desperate squeals of the pig before its death, and the considerable activity that followed with searing the hair, cleaning the skin, making the black puddings from the fresh blood and the washing and plaiting of the chitterlings (the intestines). Neighbours would share the choice 'fry' with each other, and

Top: Walford village centre in the 1920s. (Courtesy of Fred Druce, Ross)
Lower: Walford village centre in 2001. (Photo by Bridget Vine)

Margaret Wilce remembers that these offerings were covered with a membrane, the veil or caul. By tradition the lengthy salting and preservation of the ham and bacon was carried out by the menfolk.

As far as other shops are concerned trade directory entries, although very useful for the longer-established and larger businesses, were not exhaustive, probably because contributors had to pay for their entries. Quite frequently a small shop was kept in one room of a house, mostly for groceries, tobacco and sweets. Joyce Roberts' mother, Mrs. Clara Stacey, kept one while living at Pear Tree House at the top of Bulls Hill until the family moved in 1916.

Over on Howle Hill in the 1930s and through the Second World War, Mrs. Green (mother of Harry Green) is remembered as selling groceries and tobacco from a small stock kept on a shelf in her back kitchen at Fairview, behind the Brethren Chapel. Bob and Fanny Childs (parents of 'Row' — Rowland Childs) kept a rather bigger shop in Shop Cottage, now demolished, but which stood on the site of the present Kiln Green House; local people remember it trading into the early 1950s.

Bob Childs also kept a very productive market garden on the other side of the road and sold the produce in the shop. In addition he had a greengrocery round in the Lydbrook area on Saturdays. According to 'Row' Childs' reminiscences, quoted in the Walford Women's Institute Local History of 1954/55, a very well-stocked general store was kept by Henry Bodenham at Hill Farm at the top of Leys Hill from around 1867 to 1905.

In addition to the above, the directories mention the following:

William Greenaway, Wensley's Cottage, Old Hill	c.1850 to 1875
Amos Penn (and his wife), Coughton	c.1855 to 1870
Henry Phelps, The Hill	c.1850 to 1870
John Gwatkin (father and son), New Buildings	c.1850 to 1870
Mrs. Kate Yemm, The Mill, Walford (1914) and Porters Lodge (1926)	c.1913 to 1934
Frank Morgan, Ivy House, Bishopswood, (later Stafford House, and now Riverside House)	c.1922 to 1934
('Gran' Morgan sold sweets from here)	

Several others are mentioned once or twice in the trade directories. Shop Farm, at the far end of Pear Tree Lane, off the top of Bulls Hill, does, at one point, seem to have been a shop, but not since the 1840s. The name, however, is perpetuated in the converted barn known as Shop Farm Barn.

Shop Cottage, Kiln Green, in 1984 (now demolished).
(Photo by Virginia Morgan)

Most of the small shops appear to have been concerned with the sale of groceries. This presumably was because these would have been the heaviest items needed frequently, as most households grew their own vegetables and fruit, at least until the end of the Second World War. Some deliveries of groceries were made from Ross or Lydbrook. A frequent procedure was for one week's order to be delivered and the following week's order collected, and the houses around Hill Court, without shops in the near neighbourhood, certainly used this system. From Howle Hill some people walked in to Ross via the route of the old turnpike road (between Chase and Penyard woods) to place orders or to collect items. Butchers' meat was sometimes fetched although, again, it could be delivered. Names remembered are Tom Stewart from Ross, and a Mr. Buffey from Drybrook; the latter also operated a mobile butcher's shop, just after the Second World War, around the Howle Hill and Forest Green areas.

Joyce Roberts, in her reminiscences, *Life on Howle Hill in the 1920s*, remembers that many of the daily requirements were delivered. 'Milk was delivered each morning by Mrs. Young, carrying a churn with a pint and half-pint measure, which would then be measured into the customer's jug. Morgan's of Walford delivered bread, and other supplies of bread and Chelsea buns etc. came from Mr. Hatchard and Smith's of Drybrook. In earlier days bread was baked by Merrick Phelps at the Crown Inn. Tim Barnett delivered fish once a week, carrying bread and balancing a basket with great skill on his head. Coal was often fetched from the Forest of Dean. Many cottagers would fetch it by pony and cart, making a supply for winter assured'.

Some names of milkmen, from the directories, are as follows:

Alfred Griffin of Coughton from 1909 to 1914

Arthur Young of the Old Post Office, Howle Hill from 1922 to 1941, possibly later

Cyril Williams of Marling Pitts, Howle Hill from 1934 to 1941 and his niece, Yvonne, is remembered as delivering milk with a pony and cart around 1946

Many older residents remember 'Joe the Milk' (Joe Lewis) and his wife, Doris, who took over the established round from Mr. and Mrs. Winnall of Ross, and delivered papers, milk and eggs all round the parish area from 1964. When they retired in 1998 their daughter continued the Howle Hill round until the beginning of 2001. Keith Fowler of Wilton still delivers milk in most of the rest of the parish area. Another dairyman, Alan Flynn, lived near the hairpin bend on Leys Hill and kept milk for sale in a cold-store adjacent to the road just above the bend. He made deliveries in the Goodrich and Whitchurch areas.

Once bus transport became available people were encouraged to shop more in Ross and Lydbrook and thus patronised the smaller, local shops less. In essence this pattern has been repeated now that car transport is almost universal, with the supermarkets taking the place of the individual shops in the town centres and 'one-stop' shopping proving, on the whole, much speedier and more convenient. The latest development has been the innovation of a Farmers' Market, once a month, in the Ross market-place, where small businesses can sell such items as locally grown and prepared wine and fruit juices, meat, eggs and other produce.

An integral part of the social life of the parish has been the many public houses and inns. These pubs have been thoroughly documented in a recent publication entitled *The Pubs of Ross and South Herefordshire* by Heather Hurley (published in 2001) and more detailed information can be found there. The 1840 Tithe Map of the parish, with its accompanying Apportionment (dated 1843) has been invaluable in tracing the details of the various hostelries. Similarly the census and trade directory details provide valuable information.

The 'New Inn (and Garden)' was in the centre of Walford village, and is mentioned on the Tithe Map, with the owner listed as Thomas Bright, and the occupier as James Higgins. Fairly recently this was the Police Station and is now a private house called The Old Soundings.

On the opposite side of the Walford road (B4234) there is a public house, the Mill Race, formerly the Spread Eagle. A local lady believes the original name derived from the influence of the Romans in this district, and is a perpetuation of their eagle symbol. The Spread Eagle dates from the 1860s. The 1881 Census records the family of the landlord, Robert (Bob) Smith who was also a woodturner and master mill-wright. There were seven children, the eldest, Charles, also a woodturner. Bob himself was born in Longhope, Gloucestershire, but all the children were born at Walford. He was there from 1881 to 1925, and the famous 'Bob's Rumpus' annual celebrations, held in the field adjoining (to the north), are described in the chapter on the social life of the parish. Ivor Worsfold, who was licensee of the Spread Eagle from 1959 to

BED & BREAKFAST — BAR LUNCHES
SNACKS — BASKET MEALS

THE

SPREAD EAGLE INN

CARAVAN OVERNIGHT STOP

WALFORD, Nr. ROSS-ON-WYE, HEREFORDSHIRE
Telephone Ross-on-Wye 62891

An advert for the Spread Eagle displaying the inn's sign

1966, has kindly supplied details of his term there. The brewery did repairs soon after he and his wife, Kathleen, took over and it was found that the kitchen floor sloped so much that the table legs had to be cut to provide a level working surface. The skittle alley was constructed and two tin baths were put there, after football matches, to be available for the players. Ivor was one of the founders of the Walford football team, part of the Ross League, in 1959 and became its chairman; he also started up a darts team. In 1961, when renovations were being made, Ivor Worsfold placed a 'time capsule' in a Kilner jar buried between false walls behind the bar.

Travelling south along the B4234 towards Lydbrook the Inn on the Wye, the Albion Inn and the Kerne Bridge Inn are on the left, the last two almost opposite the site of the Plough Inn between the road and the river. The Inn on the Wye has been recently extended and modernised (c.1995), a welcome change from the boarded-up building that was the previous Castle View Hotel.

In 1881 the Albion appears to have been an outlet for George Davies' various occupations—'grocer, beer retailer and coal dealer'—but it closed after 1941. The Kerne Bridge Inn was opened shortly after the opening of the railway (1873), with the Kerne Bridge Station nearby. The annual auctions of the tolls for the nearby road bridge (built in 1828) were held at this Inn for several years. This was a popular meeting place until falling trade forced John Martin-Slater to sell in 1992, and the licence was not renewed. In 1993 the new owners, John and Alison Hamilton, redecorated and refurbished the elegant

Kerne Bridge Inn c.1920s. (Courtesy of John Martin-Slater, Bristol)

house, and opened it as a 'Bed and Breakfast' guest house under a new name, 'Lumleys', but it is now in new hands. Local people will remember the petrol pumps that used to stand in the forecourt of the Inn.

The records of the Plough Inn are scanty, but it appears to have been situated on the side of the road opposite the junction of the Leys Hill road with the B4234. It is listed on the tithe map details as under the ownership of Mary Nourse, with the occupant William White. However the 1841 census notes William Jenkins as the publican there.

The last 'pub' in Bishopswood on this route south was situated at the present Drybrook House, once the Drybrook Inn (although one reference gives it the name of The Travellers' Rest), to the north of the Bishopswood Post Office and Stores. The 1841 census records Thomas Williams as publican, and in 1851 George Taylor was the innkeeper. The latter is noted in the same role until the 1867 directory, and in 1858 a Mrs. Taylor was both a farmer and a beer retailer.

At Coughton there was a Travellers' Rest, situated at the present Barn House on the east side of Coughton Street. This is a fine old house, with an ancient detached barn, which retains its character as there have been no major changes to the structure. In 1841 Esther Attwood was the occupant and victualler (the owner William Watkins), and her occupation continued until at least 1858. There is a reference to the effect that the Vestry meetings were held in the Travellers' Rest in the 1860s. However the 1871 census lists William Phillips with his wife and family of four there, with 'one family Servant (general) aged 14'. William Phillips was described as a 'Miller's Labourer', but by the next census (in 1881) he was a 'Farmer of 12 acres'. Almost opposite this house there was an old building, until c.1965 called the Old Pike House, or the Pig and Whistle. Older parishioners recall home-brewing of cider in the barn of Barn House, and convivial gatherings afterwards in the Pig and Whistle, an informal drinking haven.

Moving from Coughton to Castlebrook, beyond Cobrey on the minor road to

The Pig and Whistle or Old Pike House,
Coughton, in the early 1960s.
(Courtesy of Walford W.I.)

Pontshill, there was, it is thought, another Travellers' Rest at Castlebrook, but this is easily confused with The Travellers' Rest at Deep Dean. The 1871 census names William Onions as the occupant of the latter—'Haulier and Inn-keeper', and ten years later he was still the innkeeper but also a wood cutter. The establishment was called the Deep Dean Beer House, and later the Travellers' Rest Inn.

On Howle Hill there was a public house known as The Crown, for which Mrs. Joyce Roberts has kindly supplied the following account. The Crown was founded in 1857, and from the 1860s to the 1890s the property was run as a licensed inn. It was owned by Major John Stratford Collins and among the landlords was George Morgan, related to Mrs. Roberts' mother by marriage. It is believed that before this time the property comprised two cottages called Kiln Cottages for lime-stone workers. In 1897 the property was purchased by Francis Wintle of Mitcheldean Breweries (the Forest Brewery). Mr. Fred Stacey took over the tenancy in 1919 and was landlord until 1950. The tenancy was then transferred to his daughter and her husband (Joyce and her husband Gilbert Roberts). At this time the owners were the Cheltenham Original Breweries. In the late 1950s the Crown became a Free House and was purchased by the Roberts, who lived there until 1977. After they left custom fluctuated, with an improvement when the inn began providing good, home-cooked meals to accompany the alcohol intake. However it became uneconomic to continue to run the pub, and it closed in 2000.

The alternative drinking place on the high ground was the New Buildings, Forest Green, a Free House built in 1790. From at least 1861 John Gwatkin,

The Crown Inn, Howle Hill, around 1952. (Courtesy of Joyce Roberts)

*The New Buildings, Forest Green, with John Gwatkin and his daughter
Lucy Gwatkin, c.1910. (Courtesy of Margaret Wilce, Ross)*

carpenter, and his family lived there. He became a builder and later acquired an
off licence. In 1898 he was granted permission to sell beer and cider at the
premises. Behind the pub there was a sawmill, a smithy, a carpenter's shop, a
cider mill and a dairy. After John Gwatkin's death, in 1916, his daughters,
Laura and Lucy, continued to run the public house; they did not allow women
in the bar, but asked them to sit in a front room. The sisters were succeeded by
'Kit' Shuttleworth and his wife and, in 1957, Alfred Bundy bought the premises
from the Alton Court Brewery with a 20 year 'tie' on their products. After his
death his widow, Mrs. Dorothy Bundy, was the landlady until she died, aged
95, in 1993. Many local people will remember enjoyable evenings there with
her son, Charlie, playing his old gramophone records, and their haunting
melodies filling the simple, unadorned saloon bar. The New Buildings are no
longer licensed and are a family home.

There were also smaller beer or cider houses, one off the west side of the
lower part of Bulls Hill, at the small hamlet, long since gone, called Pusty or
Pewsty. In 1841 this, the New Inn, was kept by Benjamin Jenkins. Another
small beer house was said to be situated at Marks Well, between Howle Hill
and Bulls Hill. The larger houses brewed their own cider, and a fine cider mill
stood at Marling Pitts (Howle Hill) as an example. Before the installation of
safe drinking water it was thought that it was wiser to drink home-brewed
alcohol than the often contaminated well-water!

As this history goes to print it is sad to report that the hilltop taverns have
all closed, with only the Mill Race and the Inn on the Wye open for relaxed
social interchange with a drink and a meal.

CHAPTER IX
Housing

The earliest figures available for the number of houses in the parish come from the Hearth Tax assessments of the 1660s and 1670s. This tax was levied at a rate of one shilling (5p.) per hearth each half year, on the occupiers of all houses, except for householders who were exempted by reason of poverty from Church and Poor Rates, or whose houses were worth less than £1 per annum. The tax was levied from Michaelmas 1662 to Lady Day 1689 and was thoroughly unpopular, mainly due to the fact that houses could be entered twice yearly for inspection if a written return had not been made. The Window Tax, imposed later, was more acceptable as this could be assessed from the outside.

The figures Faraday gives for the Hearth Tax in Walford parish (Table 1) are of particular interest where the total number of houses is given in addition to those charged. The table shows, on the whole, a gradual rise in the number of taxed houses over the period. Discrepancies are largely due to a combination of varying criteria for charging and how strictly these were applied. Comparison with other local parishes indicates that a larger proportion of houses in Walford

	1662 (M/m)	1664 (L/d)	1664 (M/m)	1665 (L/d)	1671 (M/m)	1673 (L/d)
Charged hearths	101	114	101	100	126	*
Charged houses	38	54	41	40	52	62
Exempted houses	*	*	*	*	54	*
Total number of houses in Parish	*	69	*	*	106	*

* = figures not given   M/m = Michaelmas 29 Sept.
L/d = Lady Day 25 March

Table 1. Walford Parish Hearth Tax figures compared between 1662 and 1673 extracted from Faraday's article: 'The Hearth Tax in Herefordshire'
(TWNFC, 1973)

No. of chargeable hearths per house	No. of houses chargeable			
	1665		1671	
Over 10	1	(15 hearths in the house of Robert Kirle)	1	(15 hearths in Walford Court)
10	0		0	
9	0		0	
8	1	(Robert Stratford)	1	
7	1	(John Lee or Lea)	1	
6	1	(Richard Clarke)	1	
5	1	(John Mayo)	2	
4	0		1	
3	4		10	
2	11		11	
1	19		24	
	39		52	
	Exempted houses			
	*		54	
Totals:	*		106	
Hearths that were stopped, defaced or concealed	4		3	
* = figures not given				

Table 2. The Hearth Tax Figures for Walford for Miachaelmas 1665 and 1671. (Figures given by Harnden for 1665 and Faraday for 1671)

parish appear to have been exempt from charges: over 50% according to the figures for 1671 (Table 2).

The Window Tax assessment available for Walford in 1776 is not as helpful in assessing the number of houses but lists a total of 34 houses as having four or more windows. The house of the Misses Clarke, Hill Court, at Hom Green, had 72! Assuming houses of four or more windows are roughly equivalent to those with two or more hearths in 1671 (28 out of a total of 106), this would give a proportionate figure of around four times this number of actual dwellings; that is 140 or so. This analysis would fit reasonably with the figure of 152 given in the 1801 census. This assumption allows for new buildings, indeed two houses are entered in the list as being new, one belonging to Mrs. Elton and another to Mr. Harris, having 11 and 10 windows respectively, but no names or localities are given.

Population figures (Table 3) as derived from the official census figures, or as quoted in the local Trade Directories, vary between 1,000 and 1,500 for the civil parish of Walford between 1851 and the present day, with the residents in the parish of Bishopswood (ecclesiastical) numbering approximately 400.

The corresponding figures given for inhabited houses are just below 300 for the *whole* parish (civil) until the Second World War, with about a third of these

Acreage	Year	Inhabited Houses	Households	Uninhabited	Building	Total Population	B'wood only
	1801	152	159	5	*	728	
	1811	187	207	7	3	888	
	1821	227	255	6	0	1060	
3,720	1831	244	245	13	3	1155	
	1841	272	*	19	0	1227	
4,241	1851	271	*	23	3	1217	
	1861	280				1204	590
	1871	286	299	9	*	1303	446
	1881	269	297	29	1	1179	405
		B'wood 96					
	1891	257		12	1	1116	386
		B'wood 91	*	B'wood 7	B'wood 1		
	1901					1071	315
	1911					1025	380
4,340	1921	246	250			1080	412
4,998	1931	290	292			1142	417
	1941	(Census not taken)					
	1951	336	340			1136	320
	1961	387				1153	
	1971	380				1072	
	1981					1088	
more boundary changes	1991					1119	
	2000	560 appx. (from (electoral roll) of which 365 were in Walford, 150 in Bishopswood and 45 in Hom Green				There were 1,086 voters in Walford Parish in 2000 * = not given	

Table 3. Numbers of Households and Inhabitants of Walford Parish for 1801 to 2000, extracted from the Census Returns and local Trade Directories

in Bishopswood. Since then there has been a considerable amount of house building and the number of dwellings has risen steeply. A rough count taken from the electoral roll for the year 2000 gives a figure of about 366 houses for the Walford section, 150 for Bishopswood and approximately 45 in Hom Green. However, the population has not risen in line with the increase in houses, reflecting both the trend towards smaller families these days and the greater number of people who live alone.

The Tithe Map of 1840 and its Apportionment are invaluable as a source of evidence indicating where houses were situated and the size of the plot of land associated with the house. Larger houses, farms and artisan houses (smithy, inn, carpenter's shop etc.), were situated along the general line of roads at the time or else on the flatter land which was better and more suited to arable use. The latter is located in the Wye and Castlebrook valleys, and on top of the plateau where Great Howle forms a central point. The smaller cottages were mostly built on the steep and often wooded slopes in between. A rough count gives about 30% of the dwellings in the former category and 70% in the latter.

This is in marked contrast with the distribution of housing in the parish today. Most of the newer housing has been built either near the roads, especially along the Wye valley road to Lydbrook, or on sites such as the Cedar Grove/Priory Lea development, which used to be the buildings and garden of a hotel. This is most probably because planners and builders today prefer to use sites for several houses at a time and with easy connection to main services (roads, electricity, water, etc.)

It is quite probable that a fair number of the small cottages were originally built by squatters. The distribution of the cottages and the amount of ground around each house (about an acre) are both fairly typical of this type of house. Such cases have been documented in northern Herefordshire and the nearby Forest of Dean. There was a tradition that anybody who could build a shanty and have a fire going in it before sunrise had the right to remain there. This applied to buildings put up on manorial waste land and in forests, and the right to occupation was established by bye-laws, with formalisation of their title following later.

Belle Vue Cottage, Bulls Hill, around 1930.
(Courtesy of Miss Elizabeth England, London)

Sunnyside, Howle Hill—before and after renovation.
(Photos by Virginia Morgan and Bridget Vine)

Not all the slopes in the parish have cottages sited on them; the sides of Chase Hill and Penyard Hill and the area of most of the Bishopswood estate being notably clear. However, the hillsides around the present Leys Hill, Bulls Hill and Sharman Hill roads and, to a lesser extent, the Deep Dean road, are well covered in dwellings. Some can be associated with quarries and limekilns, such as the group of older cottages at the top of Sharman Hill, of which Wenslow Cottage is one.

Many of these cottages appear to have been built in the late 1700s and early 1800s, and are basically similar in type, for example Belle Vue on Bulls Hill. Typically they are 'two up, two down' (or 'one up, one down') with a steep (sometimes spiral) staircase leading into one of the upstairs rooms, and having a lean-to, either at the back or at one end of the building. The latter could be a store or scullery or just an extra room. However, in common with most parts of the country, as the older owners die and the cottages are sold, the new owners extend and modernise, sometimes until the original cottage is unrecognisable. Often so little is left of the original that to all intents and purposes it is a new building. An example is Sunnyside, on Howle Hill, where the only wall of the old cottage scheduled to be retained, fell down.

Not much new building has been permitted recently in the open countryside by the planning authorities but there have been several conversions of redundant barns into dwelling houses.

Quite a number of the houses, possibly as many as 40, which appear on the Tithe Map have actually disappeared. There was a group of dwellings near the top of the Oxlet path which are now in ruins or have disappeared entirely and there are no signs left of the little hamlet of Pewsty (or Pusty), which lay off

Kiln Green Barn—an example of a barn conversion.
(Photo by David Walshaw, courtesy of Alan and Jackie Burley)

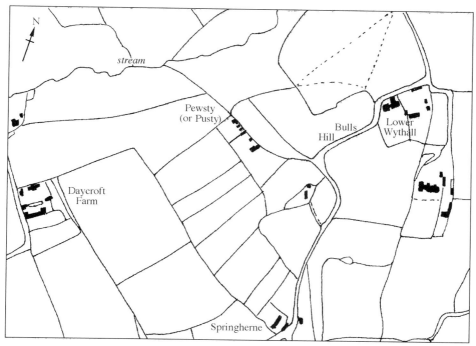

Location of Hamlet of Pewsty, Bulls Hill.
(Drawn by Sheila Walshaw after the 1840 Tithe Map)

the lower section of Bulls Hill. The latter appears on maps until around the turn of the century, but disappears thereafter.

Another example is the ruined remains of a dwelling on the rocky shelf below Holcombe Lodge (formerly Rock Farm), Bulls Hill. Other houses, often through a lack of vehicular access, were deserted and became derelict. If, and when, an access was eventually made some of the houses came back into use. Jacob's Ladder, above Whitings Lane, Leys Hill is an example of this. Although condemned as long ago as the 1950s it remained occupied until 1975. Eventually it was re-occupied in 1991 after modernisation of the cottage and the extension of a vehicle access to serve it and the cottage next door.

A fair number of houses were built between the time of the 1840 Tithe Map and the 1904 OS map. The latter was the basis chosen for a parish survey of older houses, conducted by the Walford Parish Residents' Association in the year 2000. About 200 questionnaires were sent out and some of the material from those returned has been included in this section. It is hoped to lodge the questionnaires which were returned with the Herefordshire Record Office where they will be available for reference.

Some houses started life as two or more 'tenements'. Tump House, just the other side of the road from the house at Walford Sawmills is an example. The site of Peacehaven at Kiln Green (previously called Coldharbour) originally boasted three tenements, and one of these became the garage of the present house, the bulk of which is a converted barn. Another place where a barn has been incorporated into the house is Wenslow Cottage on Howle Hill where it provides a living room larger than other rooms in the rest of the house, together with a sleeping gallery. Middle Park Farm, on the northern slopes of Howle Hill, is yet another example.

It is clear from the 1840 Tithe Map that there was very little in the way of a 'village' at Walford and none at Bishopswood at that time. The 'big house' of Walford Court and the nearby church existed, together with the Vicarage, now Hunsdon House. Close to the latter was the dwelling now known as Flaxley House, the buildings of Brook Farm and also some others that have gone. Among those was the small toll cottage just round the corner in the Lydbrook direction (on the north side of the road), together with a group of other buildings opposite Walford Court, more or less where the Village Pound has been rebuilt. Also in this group, though now separated by the line of the old Ross to Monmouth railway, were the four dwellings and carpenter's shop at Parbrook with Lower Warryfield a little further away.

Where the current village of Walford lies there was only the corn mill, the New Inn (now the house called The Old Soundings), the dwellings called Chestnut Cottage ('Chusnut Cottage' on the 1843 Tithe Apportionment accompanying the Tithe Map) with Newall Cottage alongside, and a blacksmith's house and workshop where Gordon Villas now stand. Gradually other houses were built and the blacksmith's workshop was moved to a building next to the mill. The Spread Eagle (forerunner of The Mill Race) is first mentioned in the Trade Directories in 1863.

Coughton (Coketon or Coughton Street as it was variously called) was a hamlet, with the Travellers' Rest inn, smithy, mill, the 'big house' of Coughton House, toll cottage and various other cottages, some of which no longer exist.

Howle Hill, although at one time or another it has had most of the official attributes of a village (church, chapel, school, shop, post office and public house), now depends more on Walford or Ross for such services, even though the houses form as big a group as Walford village proper. Another such group of houses is that at Kerne Bridge at the bottom of Leys Hill which probably largely developed as a result of the building and opening of the road bridge in 1828 and the railway station in 1873.

Hom Green is the only other settlement in the area of any size, but has only been part of Walford civil parish since 1931. Under the Local Government Act of 1929 the boundaries of the Ross Town parish were extended and the detached portion of Ross Rural parish which resulted was added to Walford. The boundary is now roughly from the river Wye just this side of Lower Cleeve Farm across to Vine Tree Farm on the Ross-Walford road. Some extra houses have been built or converted from existing buildings over the last 100 years but no major expansion has occurred apart from the housing at Green Meadows.

Newer developments in the area started with the building of Norrland Place, at the bottom of Bulls Hill, which was completed in 1947. Eight houses were built initially with a further two later and another

The 'Swedish houses' at Norrland Place, Walford.
(Photo by Chris Barron)

quite recently. The original eight houses were made of wood and are referred to as the 'Swedish houses'.

Coughton Place followed in the early 1950s and provided 26 houses and 16 flats. The initial phase of the sheltered housing development of Fowbridge Gardens was opened in April 1960 by the Lord Lieutenant of Herefordshire, the Right Honourable Viscount Cilcennin PC, as this was the first housing of this type in the county. The secondary development of two-bedroomed bungalows was opened in 1992. When the properties were first occupied rents were 45s. and 26s. 6d. at Coughton Place and Fowbridge Gardens respectively.

The private hotel opposite Fowbridge Gardens, formerly known as The Cedars (and later as the Walford House Hotel), was sold in the late 1980s and converted into flats, with the mews made into maisonettes. The fine 'Pleasure

Sheltered housing at Fowbridge Gardens, Walford.
(Photo by Chris Barron)

Grounds', with the magnificent cedar trees, were developed for housing in the 1990s; first for the Cedar Grove houses and then the Priory Lea estate. The Cedar Grove houses are described as 'executive houses' by estate agents, with the Priory Lea ones, while not quite so luxurious and expensive, are classed as 'modern detached family houses'. So too are those houses in the Green Meadows development at Hom Green, which were built on the site of an old engineering works.

The housing at Green Colley Grove was built in two phases as 'affordable housing', on a green-field site opposite Walford Sawmills, with fine views across to Goodrich Castle. The site of the former Nelson's Garage, next to the Mill Race, was cleared in 2001 and five residences built (three detached houses and a pair of semi-detached dwellings). Four more homes are being built on the site of the former Symonds builders' yard and a further four on part of an adjoining field. Additional dwellings are being constructed in the gardens of existing houses nearby.

While not strictly speaking 'houses', the caravan site at Bishopswood should be included here. This was originally the kitchen garden for the first Bishopswood Mansion House, together with the head ghillie's house (Wye Tower) and the laundry complex. The house attached to the latter is now known as The Old Post Office and a large copper, a relic of the laundry operations, was found during the demolition of the outbuildings behind it. Opened as an all year round caravan site in the early 1950s with mobile vans, the site has gradually been extended and the caravans replaced by residential 'mobile homes'. The lower part of the old stone and brick walls of the original walled garden remains and the field opposite the Bishopswood post office stores and garage is still known as Laundry Bank.

The building material of most of the smaller cottages appears to be stone of differing types. This is mainly either oolitic limestone or Old Red Sandstone. There were several quarries in the immediate neighbourhood including the parish quarry, Cockshoot, on the Walford side of Kerne Bridge and several masons and builders in the community are recorded in various census returns. However, there were so many places where stone has been abstracted that it is unlikely that the parish quarry was much used as a source for house-building material.

Bricks were being made locally by the 1840s and this continued until around 1900 although few houses were built entirely of brick until recently. Some houses have one or more walls of brick; Brick House on Forest Green is one example. Originally of stone, but now with two walls of brick, it is situated next to the site of the old brickworks sold by Kemps of Ross in the 1960s. The other local brickyard was at Hom, just on the Ross side of the present Brickyard Cottage and its neighbour Rose Cottage, which are described in the Ross Tithe Map details as 'smiths's shop and cottages', with James Ruck, Charles Pye and William Harry as occupiers.

Brick chimney at Riverside House (formerly Stafford House) Kerne Bridge. (Photo by David Walshaw)

Ashlar and rubble stone used in Chestnut Cottage, Walford. (Photo by David Walshaw)

Among the earliest brick residences in the parish are Gordon Villas which were built before 1884 and probably originally called Oriel Villas. A house on Bulls Hill, Red Hall (formerly called Four Winds and before that Hill View) is brick-built. Brick was preferred for chimneys as it was more fireproof than stone and chimneys in the smaller cottages tended to be built on the outside of the house rather than projecting out into the rooms.

Barn House, Coughton, mentioned in reference books as being originally built in around 1600 as a two-bay, timber-framed building, is unusual amongst the smaller local properties which were typically stone-built.

The building stone used for the small houses and cottages was often a mixture of 'ashlar' (or squared stone) for the corners and 'rubble' (unshaped stone) for the walls. This can be seen where the houses have not been rendered and white-washed; probably amounting to about half the total number.

Local roofing materials seem to have been slate or tile with thatch rarely being used. One known exception, however, is Porters Lodge at the bottom of Sharman Hill, which had a thatched roof in the early years of the 20th century when it was known as Jesimine, but called Jasmine Cottage.

Many householders used to make their own cider from the apples grown in the local orchards, sometimes borrowing their neighbour's equipment. Upper Whythall and Marling Pitts both had cider presses and so did Barn House at Coughton.

Electricity, piped mains water and indoor toilets are all amenities that were installed comparatively recently in the scattered cottages. Most dwellings had large rain water tanks to collect roof water and these still exist at Tump House. This house is built against a steep hillside and the tanks were installed underneath the main house. They were made of metal, and, when the mains water was connected in the early 1950s, the tanks were made into storage sheds with access from the lower side.

Jesimine Cottage, Coughton, around 1910, with Mrs. Elizabeth Gardiner,
née Whittingham. (From a postcard by G.W. Young, Ross,
courtesy of Betty Yemm)

Before the provision of piped mains drinking water, many older residents remember carrying water from the abundant wells and springs in the area. Current house names such as Marks Well, Rogers Well and Wellhead all indicate the location of some of the wells. Parish field names from the Tithe Map also indicate the location of many of the local springs, for example Spout Meadow, the Waterfall Orchard and Spring Meadow.

The Bishopswood Estate provided water to its estate houses and some others from the reservoir near the estate Home Farm. Water was pumped up by means of a water-powered ram from the ponds down by the old mansion house. When the ram became uneconomic to repair in 1974, a mains pipe was laid to Bishopswood House from the Howle Green reservoir on the top of Howle Hill, with some properties, such as The Old School, having to pay to be connected.

The Castle Brook at Coughton was a major source of water for much of the rest of the parish, with a pumping station and treatment works near Coleraine Farm. This proved inadequate to keep pace with increasing demand and the Walford Parish Council newsletters of 1975-6 detail breakdowns in supply (without warning) and the use of water tankers to top up the Howle Green reservoir. Eventually a new pipeline was laid to pump direct from the river Wye to Castlebrook and this was completed just in time before the drought of 1976. Further extra water supplies were to come from the Wigpool reservoir in Gloucestershire. The Coleraine plant ceased functioning about ten years ago and is now derelict and vandalised. Nowadays the water supply is pumped from the Wye near Lydbrook up to the Wigpool reservoir for treatment before being pumped back to the Howle Green reservoir. The main water pipes were renewed in 1997-8 throughout the area as a lot of water was being lost through the old and leaky pipes.

Piped water had been laid on to most properties in the 1950s, and bathrooms were installed for the first time, with sewage disposal via septic tanks. Until the building of the Cedar Grove/Priory Lea development, sewage from Coughton Place and Fowbridge Gardens had been processed in a small sewage plant behind Fowbridge. This was not large enough to deal with the extra effluent from the new houses and eventually a large pipe was installed to take all waste down to a holding tank behind Norrland Place. From here it is pumped to Ross (the pipes run along the line of the road as far as The Vine Tree) for treatment and disposal at the Lower Cleeve plant. The school and Norrland Place are also attached to this system and the new houses on the Symonds' yard site and the adjoining site are being connected to it, but other houses opposite the school and those at Coughton corner still have individual septic tanks. The new housing at Green Colley Grove, further away in Walford village, was provided with its own Biodisc system. Outside privies are no longer needed, but in some cases (for example at Wye View, above the Walford Sawmills) the small separate buildings still exist.

The first houses to have electricity in the area were those at the bottom of Leys Hill. Mrs. Mary Hann, when she bought Hazelhurst house in 1931, installed electricity there and any houses near the line of the cable between Kerne Bridge and Hazelhurst had the chance to be connected. Later in the 1930s electricity was installed more generally throughout the area although not all houses were wired to the supply at this time. The poles up Bulls Hill were installed in 1939.

Power cuts used to be frequent but following improvements to the overhead cables some years ago the supply has become much more reliable. A programme of tree cutting has recently been carried out which should further improve matters. There are several high-voltage power lines in the parish, with a concentration of pylons in the Coughton area. Unfortunately, the cost of burying the lines is enormous. The pylons and cables do tend to spoil the views; they are also problematical during field cultivation and road repairs and their positioning has ruled out many possible sites during the recent search for a suitable children's play area near Coughton.

It is noticeable that many of the older cottages are tucked away in sheltered places, built in the days before insulation and double-glazing made it possible to live in comparatively exposed places which command spectacular views. The houses today are a mixture of old, very new and middle of the 20th century architecture, and on the whole form an attractive feature of the area.

The parish of Walford is well endowed with grand houses. As W.H. Cooke notes in his *Continuation of Duncumb's History and Antiquities of the County of Hereford*, 'From the fertility of its soil, and its vicinity to the Forest of Dean and the navigable River Wye, Walford has been during many generations divided into estates, cultivated by separate and substantial owners of the class of farming gentry formerly denominated yeomen...'. For the purposes of this account, the larger estate houses will be described first, followed by some of the more historic, larger houses. In a few cases these categories will include farmhouses but more information can be found about these in the chapter on agriculture.

Bishopswood Mansion

In 1801 William Partridge, a Monmouth ironmaster, bought the 1,300 acre Bishopswood Estate from the Marquis of Bath. His son John commissioned the architect Jeffrey Wyatt to design an imposing mansion near Lodge Grove Brook; this was completed *c.*1824. An accidental fire on the night of 29 November 1873 gutted the house. The *Gloucester Journal* of 6 December records that only a few valuable old pictures were saved, 'the library was totally destroyed as well as the room which contained the family plate, the latter now lying in the ruins, a molten mass'. The shell of the house was sold to Jacob Chivers, a colliery and tinplate works owner, in 1874. He carried out some restoration but the next owner, Harry L.B. McCalmont, M.P. for East Cambridgeshire, completed the work. When he put the whole estate (totalling 2,015 acres) on the market in 1898, the sales particulars described the beautiful antique oak staircase and a 'wood screen' in the mansion which had been 'removed from Wandsworth Manor House stated to have been built about 1670 by Sir Christopher Wren'. The carving on the panels and balusters of the staircase, and the arches of the screen were attributed to the famous Grinling Gibbons. In 1901, William Otho Nicholson Shaw was the estate owner, followed by Sir George Bullough in 1906. In 1910 Robert Holme Storey

Bishopswood Mansion. 1844 picture from estate map by William Price

became the new owner. There was a second fire at the mansion *c*.1918 and the site was cleared. Now only the Coach House and the ancillary Lodges (Upper, Lower, Grove, Suff and Yat) remain, all occupied as private houses.

Bishopswood House (formerly called **Lower Coppice** and **The Coppice**)
It is thought that the original house was built before 1840 as it is shown on the tithe map as Lower Coppice House and Garden owned by John Partridge and it was probably occupied by the Revd. Mr. Robert Wood Collins. Until the Vicarage was built (now Beverley House), the incumbents of All Saints Church, Bishopswood lived in this house, paying a 'nominal' rental. Jim Bromhead, the son of the long-serving Bishopswood School headmaster, notes that 36 baptisms were carried out before the church was consecrated, so it is likely that these would have taken place here.

Some of the sales particulars state the house was built 'about 1875' and there is also mention of considerable improvements being made to an existing house. After the second fire at the mansion The Coppice became the chief residence of the estate owners. However, Mr. and Mrs. Storey moved to the Home Farm when they sold most of the estate in 1948 and 1949, and in 1950 Bishopswood House was on the market with 26½ acres. Major Thomas Stanley Chambers was the purchaser and subsequently bought several pieces of the former estate land. In 1978 Mr. and Mrs. William Brooks became the new owners of the house and a large acreage of woodland.

The house is stone-built with a slated roof, and commands a magnificent view over the Wye Valley.

Cubberley
The present house was only constructed in 1971 but there had been a mansion on the site for many years. It is believed that the original house was a farmhouse which 'grew' over the years as it was on three levels. The style was early

Cubberley c.1965. (Courtesy of Walford W.I.)

Georgian with small-pane windows. When the fourth Lord (Ronald) Greville bought the property in 1970 he commissioned the architect, the Hon. Claud Phillimore, to recondition the house. However, on the advice of the architect, the owner decided to pull it down and erect a completely new Regency style country house. It had the spaciously proportioned rooms typical of that period, with landscaped parkland, grounds and formal gardens. In 1981 John Joiner and his family moved into the house, selling in 1991 to the folk singer, Roger Whittaker, who owned it until 2000. In 1991 the estate comprised around 50 acres of pasture and woodland.

Old Hill Court (also called The Hill or Old Hill)
A beautiful black and white timbered house of considerable historic interest, it is said to have been the residence of William Crulle (or Kyrle), son of Robert Crulle of Alton and Hom Green, as early as 1318. The present owners believe it was built in approximately 1480. It was the home of the Clarke family, descendants through Alice, née Kyrle. It remained in the Clarke family until the death of Miss Jane Clarke in 1806, when it passed to her cousin Kingsmill Evans who also inherited Hill Court and other estate properties. In more recent times the property was part of the estate of the Trafford family and the many occupiers have included the Revd. Aldrich-Blake in around 1867, Miss Shand in the 1880s—a churchwarden, which was unusual for a woman at that time, and Lieut.-Colonel L. Frewen in the 1940s until he left in 1947.

Photo of Old Hill Court c.1955. (Courtesy of Walford W.I.)

Hill Court
The original rectangular, two storied, brick-built house was completed in 1708 by Joseph Clarke, the brother of Richard who had initiated the project in 1698. After Joseph's death in 1748 his son Richard extended the house but he died in 1748 before the alterations were finished. As explained above, the house passed

into the hands of Kingsmill Evans, second cousin to the Clarke family, who improved and enlarged the gardens in the early 19th century. Leaving no heirs, Hill Court passed to a nephew, Captain Kingsmill Manley Power, in 1851. Following Kingsmill Manley Power's death in 1888, Major Lionel James Trafford bought the property. The sale particulars describe the mansion as Queen Anne, 'occupying an excellent position in a beautifully timbered park, with a famous elm avenue planted by the "Man of Ross"' (John Kyrle).

On Major Trafford's death in 1900 he was succeeded by his brother, Guy, who had married Miss Dorothy Moffatt, the daughter of Harold Moffatt of Goodrich Court. On the death of her brother in 1916, Mrs. Dorothy Trafford inherited Goodrich Court and the two united estates comprised nearly 2,000 acres stretching across several parishes. Under her aegis Felsted School in Essex was temporarily accommodated in both Hill Court and Goodrich Court during the Second World War. In 1946 Goodrich Court was pulled down, and until her death in 1954 Dorothy Trafford resided at Hill Court.

Miss Cicely Trafford (deceased) was born there in 1908 and recorded her memories. She described the house as 'a large house ... the wings were rather bumptious really, huge rooms. There were 15 bedrooms and seven reception rooms, but the drawing room was very large. When I first remember it there was no electricity nor central heating, and in the winter it was really cold. The plumbing was a bit weird too; sometimes it made a noise like someone playing a clarinet'. On the death of her brother, John, in 1978, the tenant farmers were given the opportunity to purchase their farms, and the house, with nearly 100 acres, was bought by Christopher Rowley in 1983. It passed out of his hands in 1994 when the house and land were bought by Rehau Plastics Ltd. as their company headquarters. An avenue of lime trees has been thinned recently and replanted with a more suitable species. The aspect is still very impressive.

A dovecote is recorded in the Herefordshire Council Sites and Monuments list. This is situated south of the house and is octagonal in plan with a pyramidal roof terminating in a small cupola or glazed octagonal lantern dated to the 18th century.

Hill Court, c.1954. (Courtesy of Walford W.I.)

Lower Wythall (sometimes spelled **Lower Whytehall**)
A very old black and white half-timbered house which was originally the farm-house for the Wythall Estate. It is thought to be older than Upper Wythall and both properties were built in the lifetime of William Stratford, during the 1500s. The property was sold by Ferdinando Stratford to the Dew family in around 1623 and remained the residence of a branch of that family until 1823 when John Stratford Collins restored it to his paternal estate. The property was occupied by Eira and John Dodd who were tenants of Miss Collins (who lived in nearby Upper Wythall) for several years but they left for Australia in 1963 after a particularly cold winter; there was no mains water and no central heating. The property was sold by Miss Collins around 1970. The house changed hands several times with each owner improving the property: an annexe was added, the drawing room extended, and the position of the front door was altered after 1963. The present owners, Dr. and Mrs. Wyllie, have lived there since 1986. The house is described in the report of the Royal Commission on Historical Monuments in South West Herefordshire and also in W.A. Cooke's *Continuation of Duncumb's History*.

Engraving of Upper Wythall from A History of the Mansions and Manors of Herefordshire *by Revd. C.J. Robinson*

Upper Wythall
This fine secluded mansion is described in Revd. C.J. Robinson's *A History of the Mansions and Manors of Herefordshire* as 'an almost unique example of an untouched timber house built in Tudor times. Rare skill has been shown not merely in the selection of the oak, but also in the clever manner in which joists and beams, struts and ties have been framed together. The staircase winds round a single lofty stem, which forms, as it were, the mansion's main support'.

The house is said to have been built by William Stratford during the 1500s who had acquired lands at the Howle by his second wife, Ann (née Wallwyn) and held Upper and Lower Whitehall. The descent to the Collins family was through the marriage, in 1680, of William Collins with Mary (1659 to 1739), third daughter of Robert Stratford and eventually the heiress of John Stratford. In 1859 the tragic death of Edith Stratford-Collins (wife of John and daughter of Philip Jones of the Cleeve, Ross) was reported in *The Illustrated London News* edition of 13 April 1859: 'At Ross, Herefordshire, a few days since, as Mrs. Collins was endeavouring to entice a stag which had escaped from its domain to return to the paddock, the animal furiously rushed upon her and struck her to the ground. After some time the unfortunate lady attempted to return to the house, when the animal renewed the attack and so serious were the injuries inflicted upon her person that she ultimately sunk and died. The stag was slaughtered shortly after the accident'.

In around 1500 the estate totalled about 250 acres, and was part of the Manor of Walford Court through small quit rents. These were fixed annual rents which released a tenant from feudal duties to a manorial lord. They continued until 1922 when they were abolished. The house remains in the ownership of a branch of the Collins family.

In addition to these larger, estate houses, there are several other houses in the parish of historic importance. These include:

Arbour Hill

The present house was built in 1934 and the Folly within its grounds is a structure of considerable interest. This is a mound with a stepped ramp up to its summit and an open-windowed chamber underneath. The Folly was formerly in the grounds of the neighbouring Lincoln Hill House (or Lincoln House) and is thought to have been commissioned by an invalid admiral who, in Victorian times, liked to be pushed or carried up the ramp to look at the view. Another local story is that the ladies of the house liked to sit in the lower part of the Folly to do their embroidery. In the 1883 sale particulars for the Lincoln Hill estate, this building is described as 'a Castellated Summer House, approached by a Battlemented Terrace, the views from which are varied and delightful and include the picturesque scenery of the Wye Vale ...'.

Bishopswood Grange

This house was probably built around 1840. The core of the building is the same as the original, but the staff quarters have been demolished, and the kitchen and other areas remodelled.

Bishopswood Leigh

At the time of the Tithe Map this was a house and shop, and the present owner thinks that the building more than doubled its size in the 1890s.

Coughton House from estate agent's sales particulars around 1996

Coughton House

This property is said to be the original farmhouse for Coughton Farm (next door) and it might have been the original Coughton Manor House. It is a stone-built Georgian house, and looks like a gentleman's residence of some prestige. It is thought that it was built in 1750, and there is a fine tulip tree in the grounds which, it is affirmed, was planted in 1779.

Doughton Cottage

This fine house is set back from the Ross / Walford Road and commands extensive views across the plain. There is a date of 1823 on the west-facing elevation and local trade directories and census entries give the house various names: Chase Cottage in 1841, Chase Wood in 1851 with subsequent entries alternating between these names. From 1909 it was called Doughton Cottage. Julius B. Isbell (one of the benefactors of the Plymouth Brethren Chapel and Sunday School on Howle Hill) lived there in 1861 and from 1862 to 1871 the Misses Collins lived there. John Knight (deceased) lived at Doughton Cottage before building and occupying a new bungalow in the grounds of the neighbouring Purland Chase. The present owners have lived in Doughton Cottage since 1978. The Herefordshire Council Sites and Monuments Record notes that there was a tunnel near the house, which measured approximately 15 x 5.4 metres and was built of stone with inserted brick relieving arches. The far (north) end had collapsed and been filled in to accommodate the driveway to the house. The driveway is shown on a map dated 1845.

Forest Lodge

A stone house with a commanding position at the top of Bulls Hill. During the time that Revd. Rhys Williams lived there (from 1913 to 1934), there was a serious fire in the early 1920s and the house was razed to the ground. Joe Lewis (now living at Pontshill) remembers that the fire engine had to come from Ross and Jack Gwatkin used his big horses to help the fire engine get up the hill, and '... lead was running off the roof'.

Glen Kerne (on Leys Hill near Kerne Bridge)

In 1873 this house was known as the Walford Saw Mills and Turnery Company, and the business was sold in that year. In 1882 there were two cottages on the site.

Greystone House (formerly The Eyrie)

A square stone house with commanding views to the west. In 1890 the property comprised five acres, including a quarry and woodland.

Hazelhurst

Situated near the B4234, this stone house was built between 1840 and 1855, and extended in 1870. It was the home of Edward Otto Partridge, the second son of John Partridge of Bishopswood. Miss M.B. Philips, a generous benefactor to the parishioners of Walford and Bishopswood, then lived there with her cousin, Miss Harriet Cockshott. Mrs. Mary Hann purchased the property from General Ashmore in January 1931 when it totalled 50 acres, and she employed two gardeners to look after the five gardens. Hazelhurst became a

Hazelhurst House, Bishopswood, around 1913.
(From Herefordshire Country Life, January 1981)

private school in 1973/4 and later a nursing home in 1987/88, with ancillary, privately-owned, semi-detached bungalows.

Hill House (formerly called **East Hill**, **The Hill** and **White House**)

Noted in the 1841 census as White Hill with Mary Bond as the owner/occupier, the property has since been in the hands of a variety of owners, several of these clergymen. In 1895 John Northey Wilkes, a substantial landowner, lived there, and his widow remained there until her death in 1916. The house was for several years converted into flats but is now occupied by a single household with the associated coach house as a separate dwelling.

Holcombe

This is a substantial stone-built house on Bulls Hill with the date 1887 inscribed on the north facing wall. A dwelling on this site is noted on the 1840 Tithe Map details as belonging to Edmund Turner of Ross, the maker of the Kyrle Boot. His shop entrance is still evident in the High Street. The Butt family lived at Holcombe between 1907 and 1919 when the house was sold to Mrs. W.G. Glendinning. It is said that the Butts were related to the famous contralto singer, Clara Butt.

Holcombe House around 1920. (Courtesy of Richard and Jenny Hales)

Hunsdon House

This was the first vicarage for Walford parish church and was built around 1704. It is a Queen Anne house and used to be surrounded by Glebe land. To authenticate the age there is a carved stone under the eaves with this date. A former clerk to the Parish Council, Stanley Lance, lived there and the present owners generously passed the Village Pound, part of the property, in trust, to Walford Parish Council in 1987.

Kerne Lodge

Previously called Kerne Villa or simply Kerne, this house is just to the east of the B4234. Directory entries note occupants here from 1851. The house was the home of Robert Pashley and his wife, and his parents before him. Robert Pashley took a kindly interest in many parish matters and on his death, in 1956, left a generous legacy for the benefit of pupils of Walford School. (A pen portrait on pp.230-232 describes his life.)

Purland Chase

Originally part of the Bollin Farm, this large house was situated to the east of the main Ross to Walford road. In 1866 Joseph Turnock, manager of the Alton Court Brewery, purchased the land and had the house built. In 1886 he sold the whole property to Frederick Wigan who, in turn, sold to Miss Frances Maria Harvey in 1902. The Harvey family are noted in local directories as resident until 1950, but there was a serious fire in August 1923. The Walford Women's Institute local history account (1954/55) reports this disaster: 'when the whole roof was affected. Much valuable silver, jewellery pictures and furnishings were destroyed, and also a pet dog. Water from Ross main proved quite inadequate and in two hours little was left of the house but the main walls. The house was rebuilt'.

As previously mentioned, John Knight lived in neighbouring Doughton Cottage and bought the house and 13 acres of land in 1965. The large house was in a poor state and, as vandalism was proving a problem, he decided to demolish the building, preserving two walls to be integrated into the new bungalow he built on the site. He was a long-term supporter of the

Purland Chase House prior to demolition in 1965.
(Photo by John Knight, courtesy of his executors)

Herefordshire Nature Trust and Vice-Chairman of the Ross branch for 14 years and it was found, on his death in 1998, that he had bequeathed the property together with the 13 acres of land and woodland to that organisation.

The Queach

This property is situated near the top of Leys Hill. The original house was built before 1855; it was advertised for sale in the first issue of the *Ross Gazette* on Saturday 9 June 1855 as a 'newly erected commodious Dwelling House'. Subsequent sales particulars describe the house as 'nestling on a sheltered eminence well protected from the north and north east winds'. Later a 'Cottage Ornée known as the Queach' was advertised to let for two to three months; this was in *The Times* of May 1878. The present owners were concerned about settlement cracks and in 1986/7 the insurers insisted that the house be demolished as there was evidence of severe subsidence. The cost of a new house was financed by them, and this is situated in the walled garden of the original dwelling. The Herefordshire Council Sites and Monuments Record mentions a warren nearby with the following details: 'there were five mounds in the 30 to 50 year old forest. Four of these were long and low, and considered to be pillow mounds and a local inhabitant said they were thrown up around 1880 as rabbit warrens. The fifth was circular and approximately 1.65 metres high with a slight ditch at the base'.

The Queach; from a photo of the original house, date unknown.
(Courtesy of Roy and Jackie Cope)

Tan House

This half-timbered house was originally a 'one-up, one-down', cruck roof construction in the section nearest the road with the front door facing west and with no windows upstairs. There is a bread oven in the south east corner but it is not clear whether this was integral with the first dwelling or built in when the house was later extended to three times its original size. The main beam which supports the cruck beam (in the kitchen) has the date 1517 etched on it but as the whole house has been built from materials from other buildings, this may not be an indicator of its age. As cruck roof construction ceased after 1680, the first part, nearest the

Tan House, Coughton.
(Courtesy of Walford W.I.)

road, must be earlier than this. An undated reference to a 'rubble cottage' on the site has been noted. The house was part of the Hill Court estate until the late 1700s, and there was a field away from this site in the same ownership.

The whole house is shown on the Tithe Map and described as The Tan House in the ownership of Kingsmill Evans, and occupied by William Howells. In the records of the monuments in the parish described in the Royal Commission for Historic Monuments report there is the following description: 'COTTAGE, on the S. side of Coughton and nearly 1 mile N. E. of the parish church, is partly timber-framed'. Recent owners of the house (from 1960) were Leslie Reid and his wife, Enid, who died in 1980 and 1993 respectively. Mrs. Reid is mentioned in the 1965 Women's Institute local history as 'our energetic Treasurer'. The present owners are her grand-daughter, Helen (who was born in the cottage) and her husband Clive Goodwin.

Walford Court

A grey stone-built building situated opposite the parish church, this important house was the property of James Kyrle. He was the younger son of Walter Kyrle, who was, in 1483, the mesne lord of Walford Court Manor and of the Hill estates. (A mesne lord was a lord who held land directly of the Crown and who was above other lords in status). James Kyrle also owned lands in English Bicknor and Ruardean. The widow of James' grandson, also Walter, married Philip Scudamore and their only child became Lady Kyrle. It is thought that the rear part of the house was built in about 1500 and the front part re-built in the early 1800s. A historian, writing in 1879, notes that this dwelling was 'put into a position of defence in the Civil War ... seated upon a petty eminence above a level on the left bank of the Wye towards the north-east, and in view of

Goodrich Castle. It still exhibits the remains of a small but handsome façade in the Jacobean style, with a terraced front and balustraded steps ascending to the entrance. It is at a point where three roads meet, and is surrounded by a wall which may have been from 15 to 20 feet in height, commanding the several approaches, with here and there a salient angle for protection. On the north-western part of the area enclosed by it, the vestiges of works are discernible, and there is a mound on which artillery might have been planted. The interior of the mansion, long since converted to a farmhouse and prior to the pulling down of part of it in 1839, contained about 30 lodging rooms and had several staircases. A sort of hiding-place, or ante chamber in a shed was dignified with the appellation of "the armoury"'.

On a hill to the south is an open field, the Warren, where Colonel Robert Kyrle is said to have exercised his men. The historian adds: 'cannon bullets of various sizes from 6 to 18 lbs have been found on the premises. The mound still remains though almost everything else has been so altered that the description is no longer applicable'. The writer has been told that another cannon ball was found near the river.

The 1841 census records the farm as 'Cort Farm' with several subsequent farmers noted in the Trade Directories, including the Roberts family from 1921 to 1975. As with the many other properties owned by the Hill Court estate, but sold on the death of John Trafford in 1978, this farm and farmhouse were sold to the tenants. Until recently the house was the centre of a working farm but was sold as a private dwelling in 2001 and the farm buildings advertised for

Walford Court, from Memorials of the Civil War in Herefordshire (Vol. 2)
by Revd. John Webb

Walford House Hotel, formerly The Cedars Hotel, in the 1960s.
(Courtesy of Walford W.I.)

sale as industrial premises. In the sale details the house was described as 'a Grade II listed country residence with mature gardens and paddocks of approx 2.5 acres'. A room in the house, with an oriel window is called 'Cromwell's Chamber' because, it is said, he slept there one night.

Walford House (previously called **The New House**, **The Cedars**, and the **Walford House Hotel**)
This property, situated on the main Ross to Lydbrook road, is a stone-built house first noted in the directories in 1841 when Samuel Compton was resident. In 1851 it passed into the hands of the Allaway family, and in May 1875 it was advertised for sale. William Allaway, and his brother James, both ironmasters, lived there in succession and from 1922 the Misses Humphreys lived there. The property, situated in six acres with conservatories, vineries and extensive gardens, was a very desirable residence. More recently it was a private hotel, The Cedars, which was later called the Walford House Hotel. The magnificent cedar trees are still standing. In 1989/90 the hotel and grounds were sold to developers to create two housing estates: Cedar Grove and Priory Lea.

Wyelands
Formerly situated on the west side of the Ross to Lydbrook road, just before the county border, this house was demolished in 1970. It stood near the site of the existing Severn and Trent water works and was the residence of William Partridge, the eldest son of John Partridge of Bishopswood. In the latter part of the 1800s he was Deputy Lieutenant for the Counties of Hereford and Monmouth. Arthur Henry Rowlatt, formerly of Alexandria, died there in 1890.

There is a memorial in Bishopswood church to Admiral Francis Starkie Clayton who lived there until his death in 1913. The inscription also honours his two younger sons, one of whom was killed at the Battle of Jutland in May 1916. Captain Carr lived there after the Second World War until Sidney Littler bought the house and used the premises as a depot for salvaged naval equipment and furniture. The house was subject to flooding and Mr. Littler had it demolished and built the existing bungalow on built-up land immediately to the north-east.

Three smaller 17th-century dwellings are mentioned in the Royal Commission for Historic Monuments Inventory. The first, The Soundings, now called **The Old Soundings**, is a cottage opposite the Spread Eagle Inn (now the Mill Race) and ¼ mile S.S.E. of the parish church. The second is a house, formerly called Hazebrook and now **Coughton Forge**, situated 200 yards east of Tan House which has been rebuilt except for the west wing. It was described in the Tithe Map Apportionment as a Smith's Shop. Both of these dwellings are 'of the 17th century and of two storeys; the walls are of rubble and the roofs are tile or slate covered. Condition good or fairly good'. The third dwelling is mentioned as **Spring Herne Cottage**, 'a cottage opposite Spring Herne (on Bulls Hill) and 1,100 yards east of the parish church, is partly timber framed.'

The names of the houses and cottages in the parish are given in the Register of Electors, 2000. Some of these which might indicate age, ownership, location or the occupation of former inhabitants, are listed below:

Bank Cottage	Lime Tump	Smithy Cottage
Bramble Bank	Markswell House	Southbank
Brickyard Cottage	Maytree Cottage	Springfield
Cherry Tree House	Old Kilns	Stoneyway
Collier's Cottage	Parbrook Cottages	The Mill House
Doctor's Place	Quarry House	The Old Cider Barn
Drybrook House	River View	The Old School House
Edgehill Farm	Roger's Well	The Old Workhouse
Jacob's Ladder	Salt Box	Triple View
Lime Kiln Cottage	Shop Cottage	World's End

Chapter X
Education

Prior to the mid-19th century schooling for the poorer children in the parish was limited to that provided by the Church authorities, through the Sunday School movement and the National Society, the Chapel sponsored schools and also one supported by a private endowment. There may well have been a 'dame' school, where a few pence provided child-minding for hard-working parents.

This situation was repeated in other parts of the country although in the North the Sunday Schools, first appearing in the 1780s, began to improve literacy significantly. Lack of time, money and candle-light were disincentives to study, but social reformers like Dr. James Kay-Shuttleworth set about redressing the situation. The superior educational provision in parts of Europe, in 1870, when literate Prussia triumphed over comparatively illiterate France gave political impetus to the movement to provide the basic skills of learning for the children of this country.

This chapter describes the two larger schools in the parish, the elementary school in Walford village, and the free school built in the hamlet of Bishopswood. Walford School was state-supported and opened in 1874, as a result of the demand for education for the poorer children, whereas Bishopswood National School had been built in 1846 at the expense of a local iron-master and land-owner, John Partridge of Bishopswood. The smaller Chapel and Sunday Schools, and the endowed school, are described in other chapters.

The free school at Bishopswood was associated with the nearby All Saints Church (Church of England) and was administered under the auspices of the National Society for Promoting the Education of the Poor in the Principles of the Established Church. This was a voluntary organisation, and together with the rival non-conformist British and Foreign Society, sought to provide basic education for children. However, in 1870, under the Forster Education Act, compulsory attendance at school was introduced, and made mandatory in 1880.

Over 2,568 school boards for the new state-supported schools were established throughout the country over the next few years.

Voluntary schools had received some grant-aid from the Treasury from 1833 but from 1839 this was made conditional on official inspections of the schools' performance and attendance records. In 1870, with the inception of compulsory education, these grants were reduced, so that the Church and non-conformist schools had to rely more on local subscriptions, school fees and assistance from their central bodies. The state schools, on the other hand, were rate aided, received grants as above, and also charged tuition fees. Inevitably Bishopswood School ceased to be free. Both types of school had to employ a Certificated Head Teacher, who supervised non-certificated assistants, pupil-teachers and child monitors. The state-funded school buildings had to conform to a certain standard, with ventilation, heating and sanitation facilities adequately provided.

The annual inspections, by His/Her Majesty's Inspectors (H.M.I.) continued in both types of school, but the chief difference between them lay in the religious instruction of the pupils.

Administration

Elementary schools were administered by school boards elected by local rate-payers. Non-sectarian teaching was mandatory, with some freedom allowed to individual boards as to the extent of the religious instruction. On the other hand the voluntary schools were governed by managers, with the local incumbent very prominent among them; religious education was central to the ethos of the schools. At Bishopswood there was an active choir, and dedicated observance of the Church of England formalities.

The curriculum in all schools receiving Treasury grants had to conform to a rigid routine laid down in the Revised Code of 1862. This aimed at 'cheap and efficient' education but had severe effects on the children; it was summarised as 'payment by results'. Under this system grants to school administrators were subject to satisfactory results in the 3 Rs only and to minimum attendance figures related to the number of children on the roll. Grants for other subjects were not, initially, available, and the result was rote-learning and coercion of the pupils in reiterated lessons, with considerable anxiety, on the part of staff and pupils, as the dreaded inspection by the H.M.I. drew near. These mechanical methods of teaching were delivered to six standards, with children from age 6 advancing after successful results. Table 1 (opposite) illustrates the expectations from each standard. Brighter children were kept back, and the slower ones bullied into mastering the skills. Historians record that sometimes pupils had to memorise the requisite page in the reading book and, whilst the H.M.I. was posing questions in arithmetic, the class teacher would make signals behind his back to the bemused students; this was an attempt to achieve success—and the grant.

	Standard I	Standard II	Standard III	Standard IV	Standard V	Standard VI
READING	Narrative mono-syllables	One of the narratives next in order after mono-syllables in elementary reading book used in the school	A short paragraph from an elementary reading book used in the school	A short paragraph from a more advanced reading book used in the school	A few lines of poetry from a reading book used in the first class of the school	A short ordinary paragraph in a newspaper or other modern narrative
WRITING	Form on blackboard or slate, from dictation, letters capital and small, manuscript	Copy in manuscript character a line of print	A sentence from the same slowly read once and then dictated in single words	A sentence slowly dictated once, by a few words at a time from the same book, but not from the paragraph read	A sentence slowly dictated once, by a few words at a time from a reading book used in the first class of the school	Another short ordinary paragraph in a newspaper, or other modern narrative, slowly dictated once by a few words at a time
ARITH-METIC	Form on blackboard or slate, from dictation, figures up to 20; add and subtract figures up to 10, orally, from examples on blackboard	A sum in simple addition or subtraction and the multiplication table	A sum in any simple rule as far as short division (inclusive)	A sum in compound rules (money)	A sum in compound rules (common weights and measures)	A sum in practice or bills of parcels

Table 1 Revised Code, 1862, showing the syllabus for the examination in each standard, from A History of Education in Great Britain *by S.J. Curtis*

Initially the school leaving age was 10 and children could leave if they had passed the top standard, or even if they had put in a certain number of attendances; if not they had to stay on until 13. This meant that the brightest children left earliest, to enter employment, without the chance of further education unless they joined the evening classes that had become popular.

In 1899 the compulsory leaving age was extended to age 12. In 1918 it rose to 14, in 1947 to 15 and in 1972 to 16.

Fees were paid in both the schools in this parish, and this 'school pence' (max. of 9d. per child per week) could cause financial difficulties in the larger families. In the schools under review it was usually around 3d. per child per week, but in cases of extreme hardship the managers could waive even this payment.

Consequently the 'Free Education' Act of 1891 was popular, and in 1895 the 'payment by results' code was abolished. The discrepancy between the expenditures of the two different types of school is illustrated by national statistics in 1871 and 1881; in Church schools the average cost per child, per annum, was £1 5s. 9d. in 1871; this had risen to £1 14s.10d. by 1881. The voluntary subscriptions from Church people had doubled in this period. In 1876 the grant to managers of voluntary schools was raised from 15s. to 17s. 6d. per child per annum, and a larger grant was available if local subscriptions could equal this Treasury grant. In many areas the board schools were accused of profligacy; the average cost per child, per annum, in 1881 was £2 1s. 11d. For additional costs in their schools, all that was needed was an application for an increase in the rate assistance. A note in 1904 lists the grants paid to Walford School: 81 scholars @ 22s. = £89 2s., and 31 scholars @ 17s. = £26 7s. For Pupil Teacher 1st year: £1. Fee grant: 112 @ 10s. = £56. Total = £172 9s. (The fee grant was awarded as, by this stage, 'school pence' payments by parents of school children were not demanded).

Bishopswood School	
1871-1880	William Barnett
Jan. 1881 - Nov. 1864	William Blurton
Jan. 1885 - Oct. 1885	Miss K. Darlington
Nov. 1885 - Sept. 1886	Mr. Cook
Oct. 1886 - June 1892	Robert Goodacre
July 1892 - Apr. 1924	Harry Gilbert Halliday
Apr. 1924 - May 1925	Mr. T. Miles
May 1925 - June 1925	Mrs. Grace E. Powell
June 1925 - May 1945	Albert Cecil Bromhead
June 1945 - July 1945	Mr. Tillotson
July 1945 - Dec. 1949	Miss F.E. Willetts (from Oct. 1949, after her marriage, Mrs. Tovey)
Jan. 1950 - Dec. 1950	Mr. H.L. Hoggard
Jan. 1951 -	Miss Helen Brown

Walford School	
Jan. 1874 - Jan. 1891	James Howell
Feb. 1891 - Jan. 1914	Mr. A.E. Bellamy
Nov. 1914 - Aug. 1916	Matt Richardson
Sept. 1916 - Mar. 1919	temporary heads
Apr. 1919 - Aug. 1923	Matt Richardson
Sept. 1923 - Oct. 1923	Mrs. M. Caudle
Oct. 1923 - Sept. 1939	Charles H. Tarry
Oct. 1939 - May 1943	Sidney Lewis Taylor
June 1943 - July 1943	Mrs. Marian L. Payne
Aug. 1943 -	Robert C. Cross

Headteachers of Bishopswood and Walford Schools until 1951. (Privacy protocol does not permit access to school logbooks within the past 50 years)

In 1902 an Education Bill redressed the imbalanced situation for the voluntary sector; both Walford and Bishopswood schools came under the jurisdiction of the Local Education Authority (L.E.A.) which was controlled by the newly created Herefordshire County Council. Rate support was made available to both schools and secondary education was financed. Five years later the extended education scholarship system improved the chances for the brighter pupils as secondary schools were required to offer 25% of their free places to their 'feeder' schools.

The log books of these two larger parish schools reflect many of the problems and also the good times; the financial backing of John Partridge, and subsequently Miss Mary Beatrice Philips of Hazelhurst were vital in the early days of Bishopswood School. Walford School benefitted from the support of the Manley Power and Trafford families, and in recent years from significant gifts by Robert Pashley of Kerne Lodge. He was a school manager for many years, and always took a keen interest in the welfare of the pupils. Robert Pashley died in 1956; an account of his many contributions to the Parish will be found on p.230-232.

Buildings

Walford School is built on one acre of glebe land conveyed by the vicar of Walford, Revd. Arthur Stonhouse, with the consent, and seals, of the bishops of Hereford and of Worcester 'for the purpose of erecting a school for poor children in the Parish'. The Trust Deed of Transfer is dated 11 June 1872.

The building, including integral housing for the head teacher, cost over £900. It was designed to accommodate 140 pupils. The architects were Messrs. Haddon of Malvern and a local firm, Messrs. Pearson of Ross, built the school. There was initially one large classroom (to be divided later by a moveable glass partition) and an infant room. For many years there were no significant alter-

Walford School in 1954. A drawing by Jeremy Whitehouse, Ross, when a pupil. (Courtesy of Walford W.I.)

Walford School-yard—date and identities not known

ations, although the vigilant inspectors insisted on cloakroom provision and improved ventilation through additional windows. The gallery in the infant room was removed as educational theory encouraged more active learning for the very young pupils; the gallery was a series of tiered benches.

In 1949 a HORSA hut was installed in the playground (acronym for Hutting Operation for the Raising of the School leaving Age); this was to house the canteen for the recently introduced school dinner provision. It was soon to double as a classroom. A portable 'Terrapin' hut was later sited to the south of the main building to provide another classroom. In 1989 the long awaited permanent extension was begun; the hut was removed, and a spacious hall erected, together with a classroom, kitchen and indoor toilet facilities. This was opened in January 1990. The canteen building was demolished, together with the outside lavatory block. In 1997 a mobile classroom was installed, and a year later an efficient office block and secure side entrance constructed to the north of the original building. During 2000 a further classroom, for the reception children, was built, the library resited and another 'Terrapin' hut installed to the east of the new hall. The school is well decorated, comfortable and well equipped to accommodate the increasing number of children in attendance.

Bishopwood schoolchildren ready for Maypole dancing, c.1947. (Courtesy of Basil Brown, Mitcheldean)

When the school was first built, the playground, or 'yard', was unsurfaced. Despite an inspector's recommendation that a causeway should be laid from the road to the classroom, conditions were unsatisfactory, particularly in winter. In another scheme to meet the inspector's demands the yard was surfaced with dust and ashes. The entry in the log-book (September 1904) is eloquent: 'The school yard is in a worse state than it was before since the dust and ashes were spread over it; the dust rises in clouds during the whole time the children are stepping on it; it has yet to be rolled, and unless this makes a wonderful difference to the present state of things, the playground will not be fit for the children to use'.

Eventually the playground was properly surfaced (in 1949) but the writer recalls the children practising their races along the narrow grass strip adjoining the tarmac. Those on the field side had the disadvantage of avoiding the fence struts. The outside amenities improved dramatically when the 5.5 acre field beside the school ground was purchased in 1970. This was made possible through Robert Pashley's generous legacy. With this fine field sports and competitive games can be enjoyed and in the summer it is an additional playground.

The school building at Bishopswood was completed in 1846, the year after the adjoining All Saints Church was consecrated. The site slopes steeply away to the west and the outside lavatories were down the slope. There were two classrooms, with fine high ceilings; the larger room used for the older children. The building was enlarged before 1873 to accommodate 130 children. Two fireplaces at either end of the building heated each room, with the coal-store underneath the infant room. As at Walford the inspector deprecated the use of the gallery for the infant scholars; in his 1901 report he writes: 'I much wish the Managers could see their way to remove the gallery in the Infants Room and to substitute as many kindergarten desks as may be wanted'.

The church is very close and was frequently used by the pupils for divine service on the main observance days. During 1940 it was used as additional

Amended Scheme of Work proposed for the year ending May 31st 1901.

Recitation:

Standard I. "The Windmill". (H.W. Longfellow)

     " II. "Wynken, Blynken & Nod". (Eugene Field).

     " III. "Mad River" (H.W. Longfellow).

     " IV. "Richard I at his Father's Bier". (Mrs Hemans).

     " V–VII. The Fall of Cardinal Wolsey. (Shakespere)

Grammar:

Standard. I. Pointing out Nouns.

     " II. Pointing out Nouns & Verbs.

     " III. Pointing out all parts of speech and forming simple sentences containing them.

     " IV. Parsing easy sentences and by examples to show the use of each of the parts of speech.

     " V. Parsing and Analysis of simple sentences. The method of forming Nouns, Adjectives and Verbs from each other.

     " VI & VII. Analysis of Complex Sentences and Parsing of same. Meaning and use of the most common Latin Prefixes in the formation of English words.

Geography. IV. Physical & Political Geography of England

     V–VII. British Isles & British N. America

Object Lessons.

Infants & Standard I. Birds, Cuckoo, Woodpecker, Spiders, Snail, Potato, Mushroom, Coal, Suet, Feet of Animals, Large animals useful to man, Insects useful to man, The Farmyard, Loaf of sugar, Chalk, a Brick, Clay, Water, The Cat, The Dog, The Horse (3 lessons), The Rabbit (3 lessons), The Honey Bee, Wheat.

Standards II & III. Paraffin Oil, Parts of a Flower, Pea Blossom, Evergreen Plants, Holly & Ivy, Vegetation and Cultivation, Ploughing, Digging, Draining, Harrowing, Rolling, Buds (a spring lesson), Plant Food, The Mole, The Hedgehog, Chalk and Lime, The Compass, a River, How to prevent Paraffin Lamp Accidents, Geographical Terms (Parts of Land & Water) Use of a map.

The Scheme of Work for 1901 (and opposite). All projected work on the curriculum had to be outlined and approved by H.M.I. (From Walford School Logbook, courtesy of the headmaster)

teaching accommodation when the numbers peaked with the influx of evacuees with the infant class held in the vestry and a junior class round the font.

Successive head teachers had no housing provision, until local fund-raising efforts (1926 to 1931) funded the construction of the School House, built near the B4234; Albert Cecil Bromhead (known as Cecil) was the first occupant. There was some help with financing this from the Church authorities along with other subscriptions. The only level ground for drill, dance or games was the asphalted apron in front of the Church.

Despite the comparative lack of amenities one pupil remembers the glorious 'dinner play-times' when, unsupervised, the children played in the woods which surrounded the school. The beautiful setting has changed with the substitution of many deciduous trees with conifers but the remote school, now a comfortable family home, must be remembered by many local adults with affection.

Curriculum

Bishopswood School enjoyed a few years of unfettered teaching before the strictures of the hated Revised Code. Even after it had been abolished the annual inspection, over a wider range of subjects, continued as a condition of grant-aid. This, of course, now affected both schools under review, and there are many examples in the logbooks of the schemes of work; these had to be approved by the H.M.I. on the occasion of his inspection, and copied into the logbook, alongside a copy of his report.

The anxiety generated by the inspection is revealed in an entry for June 1889 (Bishopswood); 'On Tuesday and Thursdays during the past month examinations as nearly as possible like those of H.M.I. held to give the children nerve to undergo their fast approaching ordeal'. The Walford inspection for 1885 was generally satisfactory but there is a critical note; 'songs presented to the Inspector must be entirely secular in character'. The emancipation from the code is revealed in another entry (September 1896); 'From now on the children of all the Standards will be taken together for Physical Exercises when the weather will permit of their being out of doors'. In the early days drill was practised, largely through mechanical exercises. In one entry the master used this discipline as a means of restoring order: 'as irregularity of attendance has greatly affected the discipline and progress was obliged to devote the greater part of the morning to drill etc. to get order' (11 December 1874). As the curriculum broadened, games were introduced; the kindly farmer, Evan Jones of Daycroft Farm, allowed the children to use the adjoining field for sports and races, and the site of the Norrland Place houses, tenanted, at that time, by Jack Roberts of Walford Court, provided another games area. One logbook item of 1950 mentions the ten minute walk to the playing field; this was situated on the other side of the railway line, beyond the level crossing, not far from the Parish Church.

In May 1900 singing including 'tonic sol-fa' was introduced. A 1904 inspector's report on Walford School is enthusiastic: 'This is a thoroughly good school, well-disciplined, well-organised and well-taught'.

In June 1910 the master and an uncertificated assistant were teaching 80 children with Standards I to VI in the large classroom; the infants were in the adjoining room. A school library was started in 1922 with a nucleus of about 70 children's books 'presented in answer to an appeal'. These were augmented by Robert Pashley when he brought 17 volumes of Dickens in 1931.

Needlework had always been a mandatory subject for the girls, with drawing for the boys. One report by the directress of needlework dictates: 'in Standard 5 a thread should not be drawn in tucking and in Group E a fair-sized hole in stocking material should be darned'. As time went on practical subjects like cookery and woodwork were introduced, with the Walter Scott School Centre in Ross open to senior pupils from both schools. In the early days the older girls from Bishopswood went to Goodrich for cookery.

The curriculum at Bishopswood appears to have been innovative in many ways. In August 1875 the master notes: 'the children like the geography but not the grammar lessons'. In 1881 the decision was made to teach 'table arithmetic instead of animal physiology'. A spelling bee was given to the top standards, and in March 1889 the headmaster introduced incentives to quicker mental arithmetic. In his words: 'Children dismissed at 12a.m. by mental arithmetic. A question asked. The child who answers first goes. Satisfactory result. This done every morning'. In March 1901 a special lesson was held on the completion of the census forms. When the weather was very hot the pupils would have their 'simultaneous reading lessons taken outside under the shade of the trees'. One year (1909) the Drawing H.M.I. visited and 'the whole school, including infants, took drawing till 3.30p.m. number present 101, after signing the afternoon registers'. Music and drama were encouraged. Some years later (1932) Revd. Harold Hutton was the incumbent, and a manager. In addition to his frequent scripture lessons his sister, Miss Jessie Hutton, gave a talk on musical appreciation to the lower school and infants 'illustrated by gramophone records'. Nature walks in the surrounding woods were initiated by an enterprising lady head teacher, and from 1927 county-based folk dancing festivals were attended; a team of eight girls (aged 12 to 14) came second in their class in June 1930.

*Senior children from Walford School, with Mr. Handley and Mrs. Tarry,
on the sands at Blackpool, 1964. (Photograph taken by Miss Mason)*

With the school's strong association with the Church of England there were annual Bible and Prayer Book Examinations, with a Diocesan Inspector asking questions, and requiring both verbal and written responses. One laconic comment by the examiner reads: 'the worst [results] were very little below the best'. The tone of the school was also reported; in March 1932 the note was more lively: 'It is a real pleasure to renew acquaintance with such a live school'. Despite the emphasis on religious studies, children of other faiths were allowed to absent themselves from scripture lessons.

The 1902 Education Bill aimed at the improvement of the intellectual and physical well-being of children. Science teaching replaced the tedious 'object' lessons of the past, and educational visits (which qualified as attendances) became regular features in the timetable.

On one occasion Walford pupils visited the Cadbury complex at Bournville, and, nearer home, on another day two classes were taken to Goodrich Castle. In 1945, under the guidance of Revd. T.M. Williams the headmaster took the junior class around the Parish Church. They also visited the wheel-wright's yard 'where Arthur Jones explained the various types of work he carried out'. (Arthur Jones was the late Mrs. Barbara Cawthorn's grandfather). The workshop was sited to the north of the village centre, on the site of two houses built in 1979. In 1948 there were visits to view a 'technicolour' film of the olympic games. 1949 was a busy year; in May Miss Mason and Mrs. Tarry took 40 children to the Hereford Music Festival. A few days later the headmaster supervised his class during a visit to Goodrich Court 'which is to be removed to U.S.A. They were taken over the building by Mrs. Trafford'. As at

Bishopswood the school usually closed for one day, in June, to allow staff and pupils to visit the Three Counties Show at its different venues.

Thanks to Robert Pashley's generosity Walford pupils were able to have regular day trips to the seaside. There were also some week-long stays in Blackpool and London. Miss Molly Mason took a few photographs of these happy days.

The children attending Bishopswood School also enjoyed some supervised trips. In 1928 the upper class were invited to 'look over the Moreland England's Glory Match Factory at Gloucester'. During the preceding month the head teacher accompanied the upper standard boys to Kerne Bridge 'to watch a Diver at work in the Wye examining the bridge supports under the water. The diver very kindly explained the structure of all his apparatus to the boys. The visit proved an instructive and interesting one. The party returned to school at 2.30; this visit took the place of the Monday afternoon science lesson'.

Every year the Bishopswood pupils attended Ross Parish Church Carol Festivals, and the school choristers had an annual visit to Weston-super-Mare.

Competitive games entered the timetables of both schools. As early as 1926 the Bishopswood School football team played in a match against Ross at Kerne Bridge. In the Walford School logbooks cricket, skittleball, shinty and football matches are reported; in November 1945 the Walford skittleball team defeated Whitchurch 'in a demonstration game at Ross Council School'. In the following year the Senior Girls were victorious in a shinty match, and the football team gained two triumphs against Whitchurch, with Gerald Stacey

Walford School Football Team in May 1973 (left) and April 1981 (right)
On the left: Back Row: Keith Walker, Steven Ellis, Michael Evans;
Front Row: Stephen Smith, Glen Moreton, Stephen Winney
On the right: Back Row: David Hale, Daniel Margrett, Darren Dobson;
Front Row: Edward Davies, David Whitson, Martin Ruck.
(Courtesy of Mrs. Joan Edwards, coach)

Walford schoolchildren in 1928

scoring three goals in the second match (score 6 : 0). In 1951 a Walford pupil gained the Silver Medal at the County Sports at Hereford for the 100 yards race for the boys aged 11+. In her many years at Walford School Mrs. Joan Edwards, the school secretary, was an enthusiastic sports coach, and the school hosted several matches against local primary schools, making good use of the fine field.

Despite the lack of convenient games facilities, Bishopswood School football team played a match against Ross boys at Kerne Bridge as early as March 1926, and in November 1948 played against their Walford rivals. They joined battle again in the summer of 1951, this time at cricket. There would have been many other, unrecorded, sports activities; fortunately some photographs remain.

Out of School
The pupils from both schools enjoyed a break from school routine to celebrate national occasions. Queen Victoria's Golden Jubilee in June 1887 and Diamond one in 1897, the Declaration of Peace at the end of the Boer War in June 1902, several royal weddings, some coronations and periodical General Elections all merited time out of school. Visits of celebrities are also recorded: in September 1891 the Bishopswood pupils were assembled at 2p.m. and 'marched to the Wye Meadows and saw the Duke and Duchess of Teck and passengers pass down the Wye to Symonds Yat. Each child received a bun on leaving kindly provided by Miss Philips'.

Bishopswood schoolchildren 1918-19. (Courtesy of Margery Spencer)

There were school closures for days of national and local mourning. The 20 May 1910 was the day of the funeral of King Edward VII, and the death of George V in January 1936 was another day of sorrow. Services of remembrance of local residents are noted. On the death of Miss M.B. Philips in January 1898 the headmaster inserted a tribute in the logbook: 'for upwards of 26 years she has been the sole supporter of this school and both teachers and children feel they have lost one they had learned to love and revere as a friend at all times'. The schoolchildren attended a service in her memory at Hazelhurst a few days later.

From 1906 until 1944 Empire Day was observed every year on 24 May. Before the children were dismissed for a half-holiday lessons were held, and patriotic songs sung; this was often followed by a ceremony of saluting the Union Jack. In 1931 Robert Pashley presented medals for the best essays on the theme of Empire.

Local and General Elections provided a day off school as the Walford classrooms were needed for polling purposes.

The eclipse of the sun on 29 June 1927 was observed by Walford School pupils; the whole school met at the top of Howle Hill at 5.15a.m. and after the exciting event they enjoyed tea and refreshments provided by the managers, and after an address by the Revd. Richard Greene had the rest of the day off.

All school closures had to be recorded in the logbooks, as these would be calculated among the assessment of the average attendance figures. In the earlier years many, unauthorised, Sunday School treats and outings drew the children from their desks, but in due course the managers agreed that these should be eligible for a half or whole-day holiday.

The local clubs and societies often held fêtes, with flower shows and associated teas in some cases. The Shepherds' Club is mentioned in 1884 when its

Bishopswood School 1934/35. Left to right:
Back Row: Mr. Bromhead, Roy Morris, Cyril Smith, John Hodges,
Hugh Duberley, Lionel Little, John Larner, Arthur Richardson.
Third Row: John Andrews, Howard Larner, Kathleen Price, Edna French,
Mary Lewis, Harold Spencer, Charlie Jones.
Second Row: Dorothy Jayne, Iris Duberley, Jean Jenkinson, Margery Jayne,
Rebecca Lewis, Joan Richardson.
First Row: Alfie Price, Vera Price, Cecil Bromhead, Betty Hiatt, Jack Lewis,
Dorothy Smith, Donald French.
(Courtesy of Joan Evans, Ross)

annual celebration drew more than half the Walford scholars from their studies. The Primrose Kerne Bridge Habitation League held regular meetings, and occasional concerts, in the Bishopswood schoolroom. The Vegetable, Flower and Fruit Show at Lydbrook Show always attracted the nearby residents with their children. During August 1906, while school was in session, rival events were held on the same day: the Walford Flower Show and the Friendly Societies Sports Day at Lydbrook. A holiday was granted. Later on that month many Bishopswood schoolchildren competed in the Wild Flower Class at the Lydbrook District Flower and Poultry Show.

The Walford Oddfellows' Club featured in the social calendar across the parish. The children from both schools were allowed to celebrate its annual festivities, usually on a Monday in early July. These celebrations combined the divine and the secular: the Oddfellows attended divine service in Bishopswood All Saints Church, and the afternoon was spent at Walford with the Fête, Gala,

Bishopswood School 1936. Left to right:
Back Row: Len Hiatt, Tony Harris, Tom Smart, ?, Reg Price.
Middle Row: Miss Nash, Reg Duberley, Donny Gardiner, Frank Baldwin,
Donald Spiers, Dennis Smith, Ted Hiatt.
Front Row: Joy Matthews, Beryl Webb, Joan Smith, Barbara Teague,
Barbara Duberley, Jean Harris. (Courtesy of Ruby Burford, Ross)

Sports and a 'Club Feast'. The half-day holiday awarded at Bishopswood School is recorded as late as 1910, when a walk is also noted; a similar holiday was always granted at Walford School. An extract from the local paper (21 August 1881) quotes the Revd. C.W.N. Custance's exhortation to the members: 'in enjoining upon his hearers that life is short, he urged upon them also the necessity of preparing in the present for the eternal life. He also gave them some good advice as to their conduct during the day.' The article continues: '... we should not omit to say that the band played very nicely a hymn during the service.'

General

Concerts and entertainments for the children were often held in the classrooms of both schools. From the early years of Walford School the successive owners of Hill Court provided regular treats for the pupils. Teas and games were organised in the summer, and a Christmas tree brought in to school in the winter. One Christmas Eve the logbook records: 'Mrs. Power and sons exhibited a Magic Lantern to the school this evening'. The tradition of a summer treat was continued by Major and Mrs. Trafford. Other tea parties were given by General

Walford School 1939. Left to right:
Back Row: Bevel Howls, Ernest Beach, ?, Desmond Samuels,
Bernard Howls, Robert Chinn.
Middle Row: Valerie Meredith, ?, Richard Yemm, Margaret Morgan,
Betty Paine, Doreen Whitehall, Violet Hornice.
Front Row: Jeffrey Jones, William Holloway, Margaret Gwatkin, Violet
Samuels, ?, Barbara Peacock. (Courtesy of Margaret Wilce, Ross)

and Mrs. Hutchinson of Upper Whythall, and in late July 1914, a 'breaking-up' tea was given by Mr. Ferdinando Stratford Collins of Lincoln Hill.

The large schoolroom at Bishopswood also served as the venue for 'tea-drinking' and tea parties on many occasions. In December 1889 Mrs. McCalmont of Bishopswood House gave a Christmas treat to the 'whole of the Day and Sunday school children to the number of 135. After tea the Misses Philips amused the children by solos upon the Banjo and Machete'; the machete was a small four-stringed instrument, originating in Portugal.

There were many other distractions. Truancy was always a problem, and the delights of the circus in Ross were irresistible, particularly one year (May 1884) when this was accompanied by a waxwork show, a wild beast show and a fair. The Walford Head admonished boys who had been absent at Ross races; they were 'much discountenanced and checked by the Master'. At Bishopswood there were seasonal absentees among the older boys who were employed as beaters on the estate. The Head not only disapproved of their 'irregular' attendance but also of the disturbance caused around the secluded school.

Bishopswood schoolchildren in 1949.
(Courtesy of Basil Brown, Mitcheldean)

Welfare

From 1906 Local Authorities were empowered to feed needy children out of the rates, and a year later all children were medically inspected on entering and leaving school. These regular visits, by the Medical Officer of Health (M.O.H.) with follow-ups by the school nurses, were complemented by examinations and treatment carried out by school dentists. In 1908 the Walford School well had been contaminated, and all drinking water had to be carried from the Vicarage (now the Old Vicarage), so the M.O.H. visit in 1909 was very timely. As a precaution, in both schools, the premises were disinfected on several occasions to try to stem the diptheria epidemics of 1906 and 1908; immunization procedures began in 1941. Despite vaccination some smallpox cases occurred at Lydbrook and Kerne Bridge in 1893 and 1896 and Bishopswood School was closed at once. These closures of the schools were ordered, often by the medical authorites, for up to three weeks in an attempt to eradicate communicable diseases. Another safeguard was to exclude individual children in contact with notified cases. There are sad accounts of fatalities in the years from 1877 to 1926, with diptheria the worst killer. Four children died from influenza in the winter of 1890 and whooping-cough killed two other Walford pupils in late 1915. Measles was another scourge, with five epidemics at Walford and six more at Bishopswood. Scarlet fever and chicken-pox also necessitated school closures, with mumps recurring. In 1950 there were three cases of poliomyelitis among Bishopswood pupils. In addition to these serious problems there were frequent coughs, colds and chilblains resulting from bitter winter weather.

Walford School 1954, Class 4. Left to right:
Back Row: Mr. Bob Cross (Headmaster), Simon Pitcher, George Marshall,
Raymond Watkins, Graham Lewis, Jeremy Whitehouse, Francis Jones, ?,
Raymond Margrett, Malcolm Austin.
Third Row: Mary Watts, Valerie Cleal, Rosemary Williams, ?, Deborah Davies,
Diane Beckham, Diane Chard, Joan Davies, Shirley Davies.
Second Row: Sheila Turner, Julie Backhouse, Maureen Maguire, Carol ?,
Audrey Spencer, Enid Davies, Susan Evans, Anne Cawthorn
Front Row: David Goode, Neil Christopher, Stanley Wheeler, Johnnie Edwards,
Ronnie Powell, Bernard Morris, Ronnie Sinclair.
(Courtesy of Sheila Turner, Sheffield)

School milk, free for the needy, was supplied from 1936, and Mr. Margrett of Hope Mansell is noted as the contractor to Bishopswood School in 1946. Hot midday meals were supplied under the School Meals Service from 1944, with special arrangements being made for collection of the containers from the Ross Schools Meals depot until other facilities were available.

Attendance and the weather are the topics most frequently described in the logbooks, and to some extent these were inter-dependent.

The 'numbers on the registers, or roll, fluctuated at Walford between 23 (January 1874) and 140 (August 1904) and at Bishopswood it was similarly variable. There the maximum was 123 (March 1897) falling to 37 (1951). However attendance figures could be half the number on roll, for a variety of reasons. An attendance officer was employed to interview parents of 'irregulars' and the School Board could apply fines to parents of persistent absentees. These sanctions seem to have been disregarded; in June 1893 the Walford Head was despairing, as the inspection drew near: 'the Master lays before the Board a list of the irregulars in attendance at every one of their meetings but for all the purpose it serves it is not worth the paper it is written on. The work will have to be left undone or undue pressure used when the children are at school'. Both schools had incentive schemes in the form of prizes awarded to the pupils with the best attendance in each class. In the early days Miss Philips gave boots and shoes to the children with the best record. Walford followed Bishopswood's example, some years later, in awarding a half day's holiday in the period following a month's attendance figures in excess of 90%.

The weather was frequently a justifiable reason for non-attendance. In March 1887 the master arrived at Bishopswood School to find five children awaiting admission in the snow; they were sent home. That school's location made conditions very difficult. 1887 was an exceptionally wet autumn, and in October 1891 'a terrific gale' brought many trees down. Dark afternoons made lessons impossible and singing would be substituted. In December 1910 'very stormy and wet near Pritchard's spring, road flooded, Master had to clamber over hedges to get to school'. A few days later; 'four feet of water between Pritchard's spring and Hazelhurst'. In March 1916 there was a 7 foot snow drift on the road towards Howle Hill from Bishopswood, preventing access to the school. On 9 December 1929 the flood was over the Kerne Bridge toll gate. The dreadful winter of 1947 was a trial to all parishioners. At Walford School the lavatories froze in February, and there was serious flooding when the snow finally thawed. The heavy March gales blew down the shelter in the yard. Classroom temperatures were recorded as 40 degrees F. (4.4 degrees C); one entry, in winter 1891, comments: 'too cold to keep the children at their lessons constantly'. On many mornings the teacher's first task was to remove and dry the children's boots and stockings.

Poverty was another factor; in winter the simple explanation for absence was 'bad boots'. One 1876 entry mentions that the father of the family is ill and the mother and the children had been removed to the workhouse (this would have been the Union Workhouse in Ross). In July 1903 a very poor attendance is noted 'owing to children being kept at home to mind the baby while their mothers are working in the hayfield'. Seasonal tasks like gleaning, hop-picking, gathering fruit or potatoes were all reasons for staying away from school. On other occasions the older boys were employed to drive a cart, or lead a horse; one such illegal employer was the attendance officer himself. The years of depression also took their toll. Many families left the parish at Michaelmas (29 September) in 1875. With the possibility of a prolonged strike in 1920 the Vicar asked the Walford schoolchildren to bring wood to school for fuel; 'there was a good response'.

The First and Second World War years are featured to a lesser extent. The Zeppelin air raid over London in September 1915 brought two children to

Bishopswood School-house (now a private residence) in 1990.
(Courtesy of Jethro Kirk, Hereford)

Kerne Bridge, and in the same year several children at Walford School were playing an improvised game—'English and Germans', throwing stones—as a result of which two children were hurt. The Head took action: 'the whole militant forces on both sides were caned'. During both wars considerable efforts were made organising blackberry collecting for jam-making, and the schools were closed on occasions to allow the pupils to help with the haymaking, pea picking or potato harvesting at nearby farms. Vegetable seeds were brought in by Robert Pashley, and a quarter of the school-house garden at Walford was 'given over to the children'. A pig-sty was built at the bottom of the garden. There were regular inspections of the children's 'respirators' by the A.R.P. wardens, and gas mask drill added to the school routine.

Evacuees, with their teachers, came from Birmingham to both schools in September 1939, with more from West Ham, London, in June 1940; most remained until 1945. These numbers were difficult to accommodate and the timetables had to be extended, sometimes teaching in shifts. In the holidays recreational activities were organised for the evacuee children, and the Lord Mayor of London's Fund provided treats for all the pupils.

Countless other items of interest are to be found in these fascinating logbooks. For reasons of privacy information within the last 50 years is not available, but many people will remember the 1974 centenary celebrations at Walford School when the headmaster produced a play enacting the history of the school. Another recent celebration, that for the Millennium, was marked with the presentation, by the Parish Council, of an engraved spoon to every child living in the parish under 12 years of age, and also to pupils at Walford School who were resident outside the parish.

Walford School continues to thrive, with lively children, an interesting curriculum, improved amenities and buildings. Bishopswood School is a memory for many, with only the three logbooks left to provide an insight into 110 years of school life.

The children and the staff make a school. The long periods of service of many of the teachers at both these schools are a testimony to the warmth of their regard for their pupils over the years.

An event at Walford School, possibly a children's race, in June 1911.
(Courtesy of Margaret Wilce, Ross)

CHAPTER XI
Recreation and Social Life

Before these high-tech days of home entertainment with videos, widescreen digital television and surround-sound hi-fi, households made their own entertainment or arranged events for all the community to enjoy. People nowadays seem to lead much busier lives with less time available to spare for the organisation of (or even attendance at) clubs and societies. There used to be many more village organisations than there are today and the churches also had a wider, well supported, social programme. Church related social groups are

The Howle Hill String Band in c.1894. From left to right:
Back Row: Morgan Bevan, ? Hargest, Jim Young, Will Young - violins
Middle Row: J. Toomer (check coat), ? Brown - piccolo,
Russell Bodenham - cornet, H. Phelps - trumpet, William Symonds - double base
Front Row (seated): Robert (Bob's Rumpus) Smith - cello,
Charlie Smith - harmonium, (Courtesy of Walford W.I.)

fewer in number and those such as the Mothers' Union are mentioned in the chapter on churches and chapels. Many other activities centred around the inns and public houses and as these have disappeared so, unfortunately, have the associated sports and social clubs.

In the late 1800s the Howle Hill String Band provided much local musical entertainment in the community. The band was formed around 1894 under the musical directorship of the Revd. Kentish Bache, vicar of Walford and were regular entertainers at a range of local events.

Bob's Rumpus was an annual event held from about 1880 until the First World War on the second Monday in July and was named after Robert Smith, the landlord of the Spread Eagle in Walford for 44 years. This was the Festival of the Loyal St. Michael's Lodge of the Independent Order of the Oddfellows (a Friendly Society) which was founded in 1880. At 11 a.m. the Trafalgar band of Lydbrook led the procession of club members, in full regalia, from the Spread Eagle in Walford to Bishopswood Post Office and then back again. Collections were taken along the way to pay for the band.

A traditional roast dinner of duck, green peas and new potatoes was then provided at the Spread Eagle for the members of the lodge and afterwards followed a range of entertainments and activities open to all including skittles, tug-of-war, dancing and, of course, much drinking to help the proceedings along—until well after dark.

Walford Athletic Club, 1930. From left to right:
Back Row: Jack Miles, Sam Cooper, Charles Tarry, Mr. Golding,
Andrew Symonds, Stan Lewis, Harold Phillips
Middle Row: Joe Young, William Lewis, George Williams, Robert Pashley,
Len Bridgeman, Will Symonds, Phil Wright
Front Row: Gordon Symonds, Charlie Morgan. (Courtesy of Margaret Wilce)

The Spread Eagle was very much a focus for social activity in Walford in the first half of the 20th century. There was often no formal arrangement of social events; someone simply had an idea and then everybody joined in to make it happen—and a good time was had by all. The Spread Eagle was also the location for the weekly meetings of the Buffalo Lodge which was formed in 1919 and ran until 1943.

Hospital Sunday was held annually on the first Sunday in August and started in the 1920s when Bob's Rumpus was no longer held. This was also arranged by the Oddfellows Lodge but was a much quieter event. Members of the local churches and other village organisations joined a procession through the district and collections were taken along the way, all the proceeds being donated to the Ross Cottage Hospital, The event continued until the Health Service was nationalised in 1948. (More details can be found in the chapter on the Care of the Sick and the Poor.)

Walford Athletic Club held an annual sports meeting from the beginning of the 20th century until 1939 which was probably the biggest annual event in Walford at that time. The members came from Goodrich, Bishopswood and Walford, totalling 27 originally. Initially the meetings were held on Easter Monday but due to frequent bad weather at Easter time were later moved to

The sports ground at Kerne Bridge flooded one Easter Monday in the 1950s. (Courtesy of Walford W.I.)

The Coronation of King George V was celebrated in 1911 with a village get-together at Walford school—the tables set with helpers ready. (Courtesy of Walford W.I.)

Whit Monday. The venue was originally Kerne Bridge meadow and the choir and local bands also used the opportunity to hold competitions. The event gradually became larger with teams attending from Birmingham and Wales and the venue was moved to the meadow near Walford church. The attractions included all the usual athletics events along with whippet and horse racing, motorcycle racing and long distance races. Several thousand attended and one year £180 was taken at the gate. Admission was one shilling for adults and sixpence for children.

The community celebrated various Royal events. Walford residents celebrated Queen Victoria's Golden Jubilee in 1887. Fund raising enabled a meal to be provided comprising beef, cheese, bread and cider. Harold Bodenham of Hill Farm provided the food for ten pence per head. Sports events were held in the field adjoining Andrew Symonds' builder's yard (opposite Walford school) and during

Jubilee Service at Walford in 1935. William Symonds in foreground. (Courtesy of Walford W.I.)

Jubilee Celebration 1935. The procession from the church to the school in Walford. (Courtesy of Walford W.I.)

the day six cannon were fired by William Allaway of Walford House. Members of the Howle Hill String Band (violin, bass, viola and piano) provided music.

The community also celebrated The Silver Jubilee in 1935. A committee was set up to provide the entertainment and catering and a house-to-house collection was made to raise the necessary funds. The day commenced with a church service at Walford led by the Revd. T. Williams and the congregation then walked to the War Memorial where the National Anthem was sung and prayers read, whilst a Guard of Honour was formed by Walford ex-servicemen. The Lydbrook Band then led a procession to Walford School where a celebratory meal was served. Salmon was donated by Robert Pashley and beef and ham were provided by Danny Morgan, the baker. In order that as many as wanted could attend, transport was arranged for the elderly and infirm. After the meal various entertainments took place including a tug of war and a range of sports. Tea was provided for everybody and a Jubilee Medal and Mug, provided by Robert Pashley, was presented to every child in the parish. To round off the day, a village dance was held in the Walford school room.

The Coronation of King George V1 was celebrated two years later in 1937. The Jubilee committee was reappointed and arranged a day of celebration along similar lines to that organised in 1935. The Parkend Band led the procession from Walford church to the school where a marquee had been erected for the children's teas. Several sittings of 100 at a time in the school ensured everybody had a good feast. An evening dance was followed by a firework display and the singing of 'Auld Lang Syne' and the National Anthem, whilst up on Howle Hill a large bonfire was lit to celebrate the occasion.

The Coronation of Elizabeth II in 1952 was watched on the television sets that were now owned by many households, and the Walford School headmaster, Robert Cross, arranged a television viewing in the school for those without a set. The Parish Council initiated the idea for a community Silver

The Coronation of George VI in 1937: a group of well-wishers at Walford War Memorial. From left to right: Mr. J. Rogers, Mr. F. Griffin, Mr. Lloyd, Revd. T. Williams, Mr. R. Pashley, Mr. O. Morgan. (Courtesy of Walford W.I.)

Jubilee celebration held on the public Jubilee holiday, 7 June 1977. Street parties were held throughout the parish and at the Walford village hall the chairman of the Parish Council and Virginia Morgan (then a teacher at Walford school) presented a commemorative mug to every child in the parish.

Walford Village Flower Shows were held from around 1890 to 1924 on the Vicarage meadow, although prizes were also awarded for the best gardens in the district. Unfortunately the event was not a financial success and was discontinued in 1924.

After the First World War the Walford skittle team was formed and affiliated to the Forest of Dean Fellowship Reform League, Walford later transferring to the Ross and District League when it was formed. The team won the league cup several times. There was also a darts team and both clubs were based at the Spread Eagle after the Second World War and enjoyed many matches with teams from other villages. The darts team is no more but the skittle team still continues, now known as the Spread Eagle Nomads, and uses the bowling club facilities in Ross.

The Hom Green Rifle Club was formed in 1932 by Edgar Hawker and ran continuously in the parish until after 1955 with a membership of around two dozen. Initially the club met at the Old Village Hall at Hom Green and later above the stables at Hill Court when John Trafford was the president. There was an indoor and outdoor shooting range at Hill Court where members met

The Spread Eagle Skittle Team, May 1938. From left to right:
Back Row: Tom Green, Fred Yemm, Bert Wheeler, Jock Lewis,
Ervine ('Curly') Lewis, Reg. Howls, Harry Saul
Middle Row: Chesney Jones, George Williams, Eddie Carless, Jim Tonkins,
Charlie Yemm, Tom Bush, Bill Powell
Front Row: Evan Francis, Andrew Symonds, Vince Preston, Mr. Mose.
(Courtesy of Nancy Roberts, Milton Keynes)

Hom Green Rifle Club members in 1935. From left to right:
Back Row: R. Nunn, Len Davies (Treasurer), Dave Hawker, R. Taylor, G.S. Young,
R. Price, W. Palmer, Harry Green, G. Smith (Sub-Captain), Ivor Griffin
Middle Row: Tom Bush, Mrs. G. Trafford, James Hutchinson (Chairman), Edgar
Hawker (Secretary)
Front Row: Di Lerego, Jim Jukes, Jack Edwards, J. Bush.
(Courtesy of Robert Green, Ross)

twice a week and the club was affiliated to the Herefordshire and Gloucestershire Small Bore Rifle Associations. The members consistently won awards in a range of competitions throughout the Midlands, including the Midlands Short Range Championship in 1936, all divisions of the Gloucestershire league and the Herefordshire Individual County Championship (four times). Following the death of John Trafford, the club had to leave Hill Court when the Garden Centre took over their premises. The club now uses an outdoor range at Bromyard in the summer months.

The Walford Choral Society was started in 1930 and ran for about five years. The group gave many fundraising concerts and these enabled a new piano to be purchased for the school. The members also went further afield in the county and on one occasion won a competition in Kington.

The Walford Players—the cast of Aladdin,
performed in 1949 in Walford School. From left to right:
Back row: David Nunn, John Cawthorn, Ronald Woodhouse, Nancy Wheeler,
Violet Samuels, Eddie Cobb, Sylvia Green, George Nunn, Mrs. Gwatkin,
Mr. Gwatkin, Mrs. Thackwell, Elizabeth Cawthorn, Beryl Yemm,
Tony Woodhouse, Raymond Cawthorn, Philip Best.
Middle Row: Pat Lloyd, Heather Lerego, Miss Iris Cole, Miss Moore,
Ann Morgan, Barbara Webb, Dorothy Wheeler.
Front Row: Jill Smith, Evelyn Powell, Pam Cross, Lorraine Robbins,
Valerie Matthews, Jenny Hill, Christine Ollis, Elizabeth Ollis,
Anne Thackwell, Judith Smith. (Courtesy of Marjorie Green, Ross)

The Walford Players—the sailors' scene from Dick Whittington, perfomed in January 1951. (Courtesy of Walford W.I.)

The Walford Players were formed in 1949 by Police Constable and Mrs. Nunn. Eddie Cobb, another policeman, was also involved in organising the group. Originally they were formed to raise funds for the Sunday School Christmas party and prizes and this was achieved for six years. As there was no village hall at this time, their productions of pantomimes and variety shows were held in the school in the Christmas holidays, and drew on local talent and resources. The temporary stage was made from timber donated by John Trafford of Hill Court, processed by Walford Saw Mills and finished at Andrew Symonds' carpenter's shop. In the 1950s the officials were John Trafford as President; Revd. J. Thackwell as Chairman; Monica Ing as Secretary and Robert Ing as Treasurer.

Walford Youth Club was formed in 1948 with Robert Cross, then head-master of the school, as leader of 20 members and Lieut.-Colonel Frewen as Chairman. The club met in the school and the increasing membership took part in a range of activities: table tennis, cricket, air rifle shooting and billiards. In the 1960s the committee comprised Francis Handley (school headmaster), Mrs. Tarry (W.I.), Nurse Watkins (District Nurse), John Trafford, Major Gaskell and Revd. J. Owen. Once the village hall opened in the late 1960s, the youth club met there but unfortunately ran into difficulties and was eventually closed; on

Festival of Britain outing in 1951—a party from Walford Primary School outside Buckingham Palace. (Courtesy of Walford W.I.)

several occasions unruly elements from the Forest of Dean disrupted sessions and finally the police had to be called and a knife confiscated.

Girl Guide and Brownie troops started in Walford in the late 1920s under the leadership of Miss Hope Glendinning and later Mrs. Dorothy Trafford, but the groups were not re-formed after the Second World War. There was a scout hut in Bishopswood just past the war memorial and in 1924 a group of boy scouts went on a Jamboree visit to London.

The Festival of Britain in 1951 was marked by a village party and school trip to London. Robert Cross, the headmaster, had taken the initiative in writing

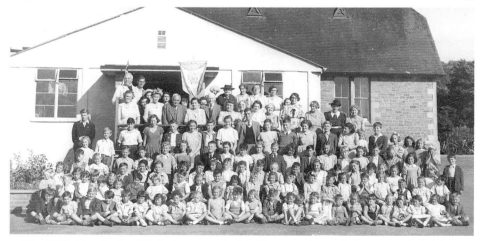

The W.I. Festival of Britain party in 1951—members, helpers and children outside Walford School dining room. (Courtesy of Walford W.I.)

to the Comptroller of the Royal Household to ask if the children might be permitted to enter the forecourt of Buckingham Palace. He received a positive response to his request and a photograph marked the occasion. After this the children visited the South Bank and the Festival Gardens and spent the night at the special Festival camp before returning to Walford the next day. Back in Walford, the Women's Institute arranged a tea party in the school dining room and sports were organised outside. A conjurer entertained those children who had not gone on the trip to London.

No rural community would be complete without its 'W.I.' and there have always been two branches of the Herefordshire Federation of the Women's Institute in the parish, meeting in Walford and Bishopswood. The Women's Institute in Bishopswood was started in 1919 by founder members Mrs. Duberley and Mrs. Webb and has run continuously since then. Before the village hall was available, meetings were held in the club room of the Kerne Bridge Inn. The Walford group started in 1917 and Mrs. Dorothy Trafford was the first President followed by Miss Harvey, Miss Hope Glendinning, Mrs. Cutfirth, Lady Almond, and Mrs. Dorothy Tarry in the 1950s. The group disbanded in the early 1990s but reformed again in 1998 under the Presidency of Mrs. Shirley Eastwood of Howle Hill.

From the 1960s, an Annual Church Fête was held at Cobrey Park, the home of William and Peggy Chinn. In 1965 the sum of £350 was raised and used to purchase a new carpet and install oil fired central heating at Walford church in time for the Christmas services. Also that year a Harvest Supper was held at Cobrey Park. The Walford parish council news sheet for July 1976 noted: 'a

Walford W.I. members around 1936 at Holcombe House, Bull's Hill home of Mrs. Glendinning. (Courtesy of Walford W.I.)

Walford W.I. in 1949 in preparation for the county picnic— a dress rehearsal for Kenilworth—*in the vicarage garden with Revd. J. Thackwell (Courtesy of Walford W.I.)*

new feature for this year is the fancy dress competition ... organised by Mrs. J. Perry and Miss Sandra Chinn ... open to anyone of any age are four classes: the best tramp, the best ghost, the best princess and the best robot'. In the 1990s the location of the fête moved to the field adjacent to the Village Hall but the event has not taken place since 1999.

Walford Football Club was formed in 1959 and won the Ross and District A & B Challenge Cup in 1965. The team is notable in having been founded by, amongst others, a woman, Joan Edwards of Walford, who didn't want to be left at home on Saturday afternoons when the rest of her family were out enjoying themselves. The team was the first to be formed in the village for over 20 years and her husband, Dennis, was captain for several years. Mrs. Edwards not only helped with the team's administration but never missed a match. For some years the club held an annual Boxing Day fancy dress football match, played with a rugby ball, in the field behind where the Walford village hall now stands. Most of the team dressed as women and after the match everyone retired to the Spread Eagle where food and drink were plentiful.

On 17 June in the Millennium Year, 2000, Walford School held a fête and school reunion. During the course of the afternoon every child in the parish under the age of 12 years, and also Walford School pupils living outside the

Walford Football team in 1965. From left to right:
Standing: Harold Miles (Treasurer), Eddie Price, Michael Palmer, Ray Cawthorn, Tony Mace, Peter Davies, John Cawthorn, Dennis Wilce
Sitting: Stan James, Lionel Phillips, Gerald Baynham, Dennis Edwards (captain), Richard Brookes, Cliff Skidmore, David Newall.
(Courtesy of Walford W.I.)

parish, were given an engraved, commemorative spoon by the Chairman of Walford Parish Council, Ted Sainsbury.

There are two village halls in the parish, one in Walford and the other in Bishopswood. The story of the village hall in Walford is summarised in the heading in the *Ross-on-Wye Advertiser* of 22 April 1970: 'Walford's patience rewarded after 58 years'. In 1911 Robert Pashley had asked the parish council to make a contribution towards a parish room and this sparked the idea of providing a village hall for the community. The First World War then intervened and afterwards, in the 1920s, even the sum of £50 could not purchase what was described as 'a tin room' for use as a meeting place. A small fund was started and added to over several years but unfortunately become static at £140. Then the Second World War interrupted the project's progress.

In the 1950s events towards achieving the project took a positive turn. Land for a village hall site was promised by John Trafford of Hill Court and in 1953 a parish hall committee was formed and fundraising began in earnest. Ted and Sylvia Allen were assisted by, amongst others, Cyril and Betty Kettle from Norrland Place and Alice Watkins (the District Nurse at the time). The committee sought community endorsement for the project from Wilfred Chinn, then chairman of the Parish Council, Revd. J. Thackwell, Robert Pashley and Sir James Almond, church organist at the time.

A whole series of events was arranged to raise funds including jalopy racing, professional wrestling and a fair from Much Cowarne. There was even a pop concert by a group called 'the Soulents' who later became famous as 'Mott the Hoople'; their drummer was a local lad, Terry Griffin. The Walford Women's Institute local history of 1965 records: 'there is one building we hope will materialise in the near future and that is the new village hall. This has been a pipe dream for many years and goodness knows how many W.I. cakes and sandwiches have contributed to the funds'.

By 1966 the fund had reached around £3,500 and a government grant doubled this sum to a total of over £7,000 which was, at last, sufficient to build the hall. The building contractor was Reg Davis of Wigpool, Mitcheldean. In December 1969 the Robert Pashley Memorial Hall, Walford village hall, was opened and since then has been extended by the addition of a committee room.

Prior to the opening of Walford village hall, community events were held in the village school. This had limitations particularly in that the furniture was only suitable for children and events could usually only take place in the school holidays.

The opening of the Robert Pashley Memorial Hall, 1969.
From left to right: Major J. Gaskell, Ted Allen (Sec.), Francis Handley,
Wilfred Chinn, Reg Davis (building contractor). (Courtesy of Ted Allen)

Once the hall was opened, more community activities took place. Ted Allen and Bob Cross started up a 'scratch' cricket team which used the field at the side of the hall. A sequence dancing group has met in the hall since 1971 and started its life as the Old Time Club. The hall now hosts Pre-school and Toddlers' groups, and there are regular meetings of other groups for older folk.

The 'old' Bishopswood Village Hall, from sale particulars, 1999

During the late 1800s, at the far end of the parish in Bishopswood, in the days of Bishopswood Mansion, an Annual Ball was held at the house which was a very grand affair. More usually, the residents of Bishopswood used their school building for social functions until its closure in 1956. Children's 'treats' were often held there in addition to the teas held at Hazelhurst, Bishopswood Grange, Great Howle and other venues in the parish.

From 1957 the Assembly Rooms once belonging to the Albion Inn were used for social functions which were arranged by a village hall committee. The Albion Inn had closed at around the same time as the school and the Assembly Rooms were bought by the committee (later the Bishopswood Community Association) which was initially chaired by Sylvia Moon. The building needed to be put into running order and many fundraising activities took place so that the necessary repairs could be paid for. By 1967 sufficient money had been raised to enable the addition of a kitchen and toilet facilities. The fundraising was continued in order to maintain the building and one Hallowe'en the Revd. Owen opened a grand sale complete with a real witch! The hall was decorated inside and out and a local signwriter, John Blake, painted and donated a name board for the outside of the hall. Up until 1998 this 'old' Bishopswood village hall, built in the First World War, was the focus of social activity. In December 1998 the site was sold and the proceeds contributed to the building fund for a new hall.

In 1977 the committee of the newly formed Bishopswood Community Association, including Monica Edmunds amongst others, arranged a celebration for the Silver Jubilee of Queen Elizabeth II, an event held in the grounds of Hazelhurst House. This raised sufficient funds to provide teas and a barbecue along with sports competitions. In the evening a fancy dress competition was held at the Kerne Bridge Inn and the evening was rounded off by

The 'new' Bishopswood Village Hall. (Photo Bridget Vine)

a huge bonfire and firework display in the grounds of Hazelhurst. The committee continued to prosper under the chairmanship of Mrs. Dorothy Hann and arranged a wide range of events including social evenings, an annual pantomime and fête held jointly by members of the church and village hall. There was also an annual bonfire around Guy Fawkes' Night and barn dances.

In around 1988 the Hereford and Worcester County Council had offered the community association land for a new village hall near the canoe launch site, provided that public facilities were available at the building. The funds needed to build a new hall proved a daunting prospect but the Bishopswood Village Hall Committee, led by Dr. Colin Price, raised the £300,000 necessary— including the proceeds from the sale of the old hall—to provide a new building which was built in 2000 as a Millennium project. (Several of the grants obtained could only be used for a new building and were not available to refurbish and modernise the old hall.) The hall is proving a popular venue for a range of social functions and has up-to-date facilities including computing equipment and a large, modern, kitchen.

Bishopswood did not have as many sports clubs as there were in Walford but there were cricket and football teams which played in the Wye meadows, and darts was played in the public houses. The Bishopswood Amateur Football Club (B.A.F.C.) was active in the 1930s and until the early 1950s. They were

Bishopswood Amateur Football Club around 1949. From left to right:
Standing: Jack Lewis, George Clark, Ervine Lewis ('Curly'), Michael Morris
(Goalkeeper), Frank Frogner (p.o.w.), Geoff Lawrence, Ernie Harper,
Mr. Clark
Sitting: Dennis Fluck, Derek Lewis, Dennis Edwards (Captain),
Dennis Bundy, Alan Price. (Courtesy of Joan Edwards)

fortunate to have a keen young Secretary in the latter years—Joan Smith, later Joan Edwards of Walford.

On Howle Hill the Crown public house, run by the Stacey and Roberts families from around 1919 until 1977, provided a focus for social activity in that part of the parish. The Howle Hill Football Club was formed in the 1920s under the Chairmanship of Fred Stacey (Joyce Roberts' father) and was also based at the Crown. The team used to change for their matches and take their post-match baths there. Whist drives were regularly held in the big barn at Great Howle farm to raise funds for the football team. Cribbage and darts teams played regularly at the Crown and outside skittles matches were held in the pub garden. Unfortunately the Crown ceased trading in the year 2000 and has now become a private residence, the community thus losing this social asset.

Joyce Roberts of Howle Hill remembers how 'entertainment was very much self made' with the children enjoying picnics, marbles, hoop racing and

Howle Hill Football Team, 1911-12. (Courtesy of Harvey Hemms, Ross)

conkers. Evenings in the cottages were spent darning and mending, making patchwork quilts, playing cards, snakes and ladders, draughts and other board games, making music on the piano or harmonium. Television was unheard of in the 1920s but was more widely available by the 1950s. As domestic chores were not relieved by machines washing, cleaning etc were all done by hand and took much time. Other activities such as wine making and preserving were carried out by all the family.

Today there are fewer village organisations than previously and at the start of the new millennium only one public house, the Mill Race, remains open in the parish. The two village halls provide indoor venues for a range of events whilst the extensive network of footpaths (including part of the Wye Valley Walk) and bridleways provides for the outdoor leisure activities of walking and riding.

CHAPTER XII
War and Peace

In respect of the First and Second World Wars, there are three major war memorials in the civil parish: the memorial at the entrance to Walford Church is Grade II listed and has the Road of Remembrance (an avenue of lime trees) behind it; a second stands at the foot of Bishopswood Hill, opposite the Old Post Office, and the third is outside St. John's Church on Howle Hill. Inside Bishopswood Church there is also a commemorative marble tablet and a wrought iron screen and archway.

Some parishioners are remembered on all three memorials, usually because of having lived or been brought up in one parish and having worked in the other, for example Fred Jenkins and Albert Powell.

Many names are on two memorials, as the people attending St. John's Church lived in both Bishopswood and Walford (ecclesiastical) parishes with the dividing line up Leys Hill, along the 'Dirty Road' and past St. John's Church itself. William Wall is a slightly different case, as he was living in Brook Farm before enlisting, and his wife later took a job at Bishopswood House and lived in an estate house near the New Buildings at Forest Green. As Brook Farm is in Walford parish and the other house is in Bishopswood, he is remembered on both memorials.

J. Morley (St. John's memorial) and J.H. Weaver (Bishopswood) are, as far as can be ascertained, one and the same person. Born Joseph Morley, his mother was widowed early and later remarried—to John Weaver who lived next door on Howle Hill. Regimental details and dates correspond exactly, although the name given on the civil memorial at Bishopswood gives him as James Weaver.

Several additions were also made to Bishopswood Church to commemorate the 18 men who died in the First World War: an oak reredos, a chancel screen and arch were erected and the oak choir stalls replaced by oak seats. The reredos is positioned at the back of the altar and is an ornately carved oak panel depicting Christ's crucifixion. A sandstone cross was erected at the south of the village also in commemoration of these 18 men. After the Second World War, eight further names were added to the war memorials.

The Road of Remembrance at Walford Church is an unusual form of war memorial. Instigated by the Revd. R.D.R. Greene, the vicar of Walford just after the First World War, one lime tree was planted for every man lost from the parish in that war around a new access road to the church and along the side of the churchyard extension. Each of the trees, 24 in total, has an engraved stone slab at its base with the details of the serviceman for whom it had been planted to commemorate. The churchyard extension, the Road of Remembrance and

Above left: Bishopswood War Memorial. (Photo by Bridget Vine)
Above right: St. John's, Howle Hill, War Memorial. (Photo by Bridget Vine)
Below: Walford's War Memorial. (Courtesy of Walford W.I.)

Parish of S. Michael's and All Angels,
WALFORD.

CONSECRATION AND DEDICATION
OF
Churchyard Extension, The Road of Remembrance & War Memorial
SUNDAY, JUNE 21st, 1925.

WALFORD CHURCH COUNCIL.
Road of Remembrance and Churchyard
Extension Fund.
Chairman : Rev R. D. R. GREENE, C.F.

WALFORD WAR MEMORIAL FUND.
Chairman :
Mr. G. R. TRAFFORD J P.

1914.   1918.

"Greater love hath no man than this, that a man lay down his life for his friends."

To the Glory of God and in Memory of the men who gave their lives in the Great War.

K. Bevan	R. A. Butt	F. Hughes	H. W. Symonds
J. Morgan	F. C. Butt	E. Hughes	J. O'Brien
E. H. Chapman	L. Morris	H. Wilshire	G. Jeans
F. A. Jenkins	W. Morgan	R. G. Hayward	A. Powell
G. M. Woolley	W. Wall	C. C. Husbands	A. A. Hawker
H. L. Napier	C. E. Beaumgarte	H. G. Roberts	T. H. Tomkins

R. D. R. GREENE, Vicar,
G. COLLIER,
J. YOUNG,   } Wardens.

Printed at " The Ross Gazette " Office.

Order of Combined Service of Consecration, Dedication and unveiling at Walford Church in 1925. (Courtesy of Walford W.I.)

the War Memorial outside the gates were completed in 1925 and on 21 June the Bishop of Hereford, the Rt. Revd. Taylor-Smith, a former Chaplain General to HM Forces, consecrated the churchyard and dedicated the Road of Remembrance, as well as unveiling the War Memorial. Over the years two trees have had to be replaced and the memorial stones were renewed and recarved in 1997 by Paul Daffurn of Howl Green. He also recut the inscriptions on the Bishopswood War Memorial.

Table 1 (this page and opposite) - Walford Parish First World War Casualties
Abbreviations: d.= died, d.o.w. = died of wounds,
F&F = France and Flanders, k. in a. = killed in action

Name	Memorial(s)	Service details	Age
ASHMORE, Geoffrey	B	Lt., R.E.	41
		k. in a. 4.5.1917 Italy	
BAUMGARTE, Colin	W	L/Cpl., Worcs. Regt.	22
		k. in a. Ypres 19.8.17	
BEAVAN, James	B	Pte., Border Regt.	Not known
		k. in a. F&F 12.1.17	
BEVAN, Kenneth	W(service stone)	Pte., K.S.L.I.	19
		d. Farnham 5.4.15	
BUTT, F. Claude	W/St. J.	Rfm., London Rifle Bgde.	19
		d.o.w. Le Cateau 6.7.16	
BUTT, Richard	W/St. J.	2nd Lt., K.S.L.I.	24
		k. in a. Ypres 9.1.16	
CHAPMAN, Edward	W	Lt. Col., Yorkshire Regt.	40
		k. in a. Suvla Bay 7.8.15	
CORBETT, Charles	B	Pte., Worcs Regt.	18
		k. in a. Cambrai 30.11.17	
EDMUNDS, Reginald	B	Pte., Herefordshire Regt.	not known
		k. in a. F&F 1.8.18	
EVANS, H. Ernest	B	Pte., Herefordshire Regt.	27
	(service stone Walford)	died at home as result	
		of injuries 10.6.20	
HARRIS, Frederick	B/St. J.	Lt., Royal Field Artillery	24
		d.o.w. 19.9.15 Poperinghe	
HAWKER, A. Allen	W	Sgt., Grenadier Guards	26
	(also at Homme Church)	k. in a. Queant 9.9.18	
HAYWARD, Rowland	W	A.B., Royal Naval Detachment	28
		k. in a. Cambrai 15.12.17	
HUGHES, Ernest	W/St. J.	Pte., Gloucestershire Regt.	29
		d.o.w. France 28.6.18	
HUGHES, Frederick	W/St. J.	Pte., Border Regt.	not known
		k. in a. Redan Ridge 18.11.16	
HUSBANDS, Clifford	W/B	Pte., K.S.L.I.	19
		d.o.w. 21.9.17 F&F	
JEANS, George	W	Cpl., Essex Regt.	28
		k. in a. Arras 2.9.18	
JENKINS, Fred	W/St. J./B	Pte., Herefordshire Regt.	26
		k. in a. Suvla Bay 9.8.15	
LEWIS, Sidney	B	Lt. Cpl., South Wales Borderers	29
		d. F&F 1.11.18	
LITTLE, Charles	B	Pte., K.S.L.I.	30
		k. in a. F&F 2.9.18	

MANSFIELD, William	B (service stone)	Pte., K.S.L.I. died in Bath as a result of injuries 3.9.20	28
MATTHEWS, Edward	B	Pte., Herefordshire Regt. k. in a. Palestine 6.11.17	21
MORGAN, John	W (service stone)	Pte., K.S.L.I. d.o.w. Lincoln 25.5.15	26
MORGAN, William	W/St. J.	Sgt., K.S.L.I. k. in a. Arras 9.4.17	27
MORLEY, J. (see Weaver, J.)	St. J.		
MORRIS, Leonard	W/St. J.	Sgt., K.S.L.I. k. in a. Arras 8.4.17	not known
NAPIER, Henry	W	Major, Sherwood Foresters drowned 17.11.15	39
O'BRIEN, Jesse	W/St. J.	Pte., Lancashire Fusiliers k. in a. Ypres 27.9.18	38
POWELL, Albert	W/St. J./B	Pte., K.S.L.I. k. in a. Salonika 6.9.18	38
ROBERTS, George	W/St. J.	Pte., K.S.L.I. k. in a. Marne 29.5.18	24
SYMONDS, Harold	W/St. J.	Pte., K.S.L.I. k. in a. Marne 30.5.18	22
TAYLOR, Hugh	B	L/Cpl., Herefordshire Regt. k. in a. Egypt 6.11.17	not known
TOMKINS, T. Hubert	W	Pte., R.A.S.C. died Abancourt 15.4.19	27
WALL, William	W	Pte., Kings Liverpool Regt. d. Egypt 28.5.16	34
WEAVER, J. (Morley J.)	B	Pte., Connaught Rangers k. in a. France 26.11.14	24
WHEELER, Charles	B	Pte., South Wales Borderers k. in a. F&F 1.8.17	22
WHITING, Robert	B	Pte., Herefordshire Regt. k. in a. Gallipoli 10.9.15	21
WILSHIRE, Harry	W	Pte., K.S.L.I. d.o.w. Arras 9.4.17	not known
WOOLLEY, George	W	Pte., K.S.L.I. d.o.w. Etaples 5.10.15	19

Tables 1 and 2 list the casualties from the First and Second World Wars, with brief service details. This information was collated by Sheila Walshaw. Further details, both on the memorials and those commemorated, is available from Herefordshire Record Office.

Table 2 - Walford Parish Second World War Casualties
Abbreviations: d.o.w. = died of wounds, k. in a. = killed in action

Name	Memorial(s)	Service details	Age
FLOWER, Cecil	B (service stone)	L/Cpl., Royal Military Police died Bishopswood 8.12.46	39
JENKINS, T. James	W	Radio Officer, R.N. Ship sunk 1.7.41 *H.M.S. Malvernian*	26
KEITH, Edward	B/St. J.	Leading Aircraftman, R.A.F. died 3.9.45	not known
KIDDLE, Robert	B	F/Sgt., R.A.F. k. in a. 21.1.45	not known
LARNER, John	St. J.	Ordinary Seaman, R.N. Ship sunk Feb. 1944 *H.M.S. Tweed*	25
MASON, Daniel	B (service stone)	Aircraftman, R.A.F. died 16.4.43	31
MORRIS, L. Gwynn	B	Pte., Royal Fusiliers died 28.2.44	24
MORRIS, Norman	W	Wing Cdr., R.A.F. k. in a. 21.1.45	30
PERKINS, Reginald	W/St. J.	Sgt., R.A.F. k. in a. 11.7.41	24
PRICE, Frank	B	Rfmn., Cameronians k. in a. Rieste 1.5.45	not known
PUDDLE, Ralph	W/St. J.	Pte., Durham Light Infantry d.o.w. Beirut 24.9.42	24
RUSHWORTH, Alfred	St. J.	Pte., K.S.L.I. k. in a. Tunisia 24.4.43	25
STOREY, Roy	B	Lt., K.S.L.I. k. in a. Italy 13.2.44	30
STOREY, Thomas	B (private grave)	Pilot Officer, R.A.F. killed 28.11.1939	30
YOUNG, Richard	W/St. J.	Pte., Kings Own Yorkshire Lt. Infantry k. in a. Monte Cassino 28.12.43	23

During the First World War there were Home Defence groups formed by men in reserved occupations or over military age. The local group met to attend drill practice. The ladies were busy knitting and sewing and probably helped at neighbouring Goodrich Court which was used as a convalescent home, whilst Mr. and Mrs. Guy Trafford of Hill Court assisted with the transport of wounded servicemen from Southampton to various hospitals. The Edison Swan Cables works at Lydbrook was then an ammunitions factory.

Walford Church before the erection of the War Memorial and construction of the Road of Remembrance. (Courtesy of Walford W.I.)

Following the end of this war, a celebration of the peace was held in Walford. Plans were made to erect an appropriate memorial to those who had lost their lives, the community joining in the fundraising efforts.

The Memorial gives a record of all those who lost their lives, and inside Walford church a stained glass window was erected by the Butt family as a memorial to the brothers Richard Acton and Frederick Claude Butt, who lived at Holcombe and were both killed in the war. The Second World War was commemorated by the erection of the Memorial Gates at Walford church at the entrance to the Road of Remembrance and with names added to the memorials. The wrought iron gates were the gift of Lieut.-Colonel L.D. Frewen, DSO, formerly of Old Hill Court and the stone piers were presented by the parishioners through the War Memorial Committee. Both were dedicated on 24 Sepember 1950 by the Revd. Prebendary P.A. Lushington, Rural Dean, to commemorate those who died in the Second World War.

The stone providing information for the Road of Remembrance. (Courtesy of Sheila Walshaw)

The activities of the civilian population were more numerous in the Second World War. Walford Platoon, along with Goodrich and Glewstone Platoons, formed the Z company, 6th Battalion of the Herefordshire Home

Guard. The first commanding officer was Lieut.-Colonel Frewen of Old Hill Court, followed by Major Glendinning of Holcombe. The Walford Platoon was led by Lieut. Bond and then Lieut. Spencer. Mr. Tomkins, a First World War veteran and Standard Bearer to the British Legion, was Platoon Sergeant. An Air Raid Patrol group of 11 wardens was led by Sgt.-Major William Evans of Triple View,

The Road of Remembrance at Walford church in 1954. (Courtesy of Walford W.I.)

Howle Hill. A room at the vicarage became the first aid post and emergency fire station. Sgt.-Major Evans and others organised whist drives in St. John's schoolroom, the funds from which went to a comfort fund for soldiers on leave.

Although several bombs were dropped in the parish, there was no loss of human life but several farm animals were killed on the Ross side of the parish. A former resident, Edward Vickers, remembered around 29 bombs dropped on the parish and a crater on Howle Hill was claimed to be the largest in South Herefordshire. Jean Reeves of Balls Farm, near Hom, recounts: 'during the Second World War when Mr. and Mrs. Dukes rented the farm, three bombs were dropped, one very near the house'. Bernard Howls of Coughton recalls that there was an ammunition dump in Cockshott Quarry, near Kerne Bridge.

The Leys Hill chapel register records that in 1940, a German plane jettisoned bombs in the area, two of which dropped within 80 yards of the chapel

Walford Peace Celebrations after the First World War in 1919.
(Courtesy of Nancy Roberts)

*Mrs. Margaret Stratford Collins opening a fête at Wythall in aid of the
War Memorial Fund around 1920. (Courtesy of Walford W.I.)*

building. The chapel remained intact and nobody was injured but there was
some damage to nearby properties.

Margaret Wilce remembers how her father, an A.R.P. warden in Walford,
spotted an airman bailing out of an aircraft in the area: 'the searchlights

*Memorial Gates at Walford Church to commemorate those killed in the
Second World War; photo dated c.1950. (Courtesy of Walford W.I.)*

followed the young airman down into the trees at Bishopswood. Father and others tried to find him but failed. During the next day the story of what happened rapidly spread around the area. The airman despite the darkness had managed to find his way out of the Oxlet woods and had found Chadwyns farmhouse where Daphne Jones lived with her father. Without really knowing who he was, Daphne took the airman up the lane to the nearest house with a telephone so that he could contact his unit and tell them he was safe. My mother was extremely disappointed my father had not found the parachute as she was an excellent needlewoman and would have made good use of the fabric'.

The Womens' Land Army was an important organisation vital to the continuation of agricultural work whilst the men were away in the forces during both World Wars. Apart from the picture below, it has not been possible to find information about a Land Army presence in the parish during the First World War. During the Second World War the administration for the South Herefordshire area was carried out by Sgt.-Major William Evans (father of Bill Evans and Phyllis Marshall, née Evans), of Triple View, Howle Hill, from the War Agriculture Office in Ross. Young women from other parts of the country arrived there and were allocated to farms around the area, either being billetted at the farms where they worked or in hostels. In Walford there were mainly German prisoners of war working on the farms or helping in gardens who were brought out to work on a daily basis from their camp in Ross by Webb's bus.

Walford school supported the 'Salute the Soldier' campaign and helped raise funds for the war effort. The Walford school log books for the war years

Land Army girls at Great Howle Farm during the First World War. The farm was then owned by Mr. and Mrs. Harris. Mr. Harris is possibly the second on the right in the front row. Mrs. Lane, from London, wears a peaked army hat in the middle row. (Courtesy of Jack Roberts, Cinderford)

have several entries in relation to war activities: monthly respirator inspections, visits to the school by the A.R.P. warden, the school windows being treated with a special material to prevent the glass splintering, sandbags being delivered for use against incendiary bombs and several holidays were given to enable the children to assist with crop harvesting and haymaking. (The log books also that show that in 1917, during the First World War, the school was closed twice to enable the children to collect blackberries to make jam for the navy.)

The Bishopswood schoolchildren were equally industrious. The school log books give account of many holidays being extended: 'so that the children would be useful on the land'. Potato harvesting, pea picking and hay-making on the local farms all helped the war effort.

As mentioned in the chapters on Education and River, Road and Rail, Walford received quite a number of evacuees. Children came from Birmingham and London and families were also evacuated to the area. Local residents such as Robert Pashley accommodated children during their stay. A Mrs. Hart in Ross was the Chief Billeting Officer for the young evacuees.

There was a Ross Spitfire Fund to which the parish contributed and War Savings were collected in the local schools and at the Women's Institute meetings. At the outbreak of war a Comfort Fund was started and all men who joined up from the parish were periodically sent items such as sweets and cigarettes. The fund was supported by a range of activities including whist drives and skittles evenings which were also beneficial social activities.

Second World War evacuees arriving at Walford School, around 1939
(Courtesy of Adeline Tarry, Derby)

After the war had ended, the Comfort Fund became the Welcome Home Fund. When the majority had returned from the war, a presentation and celebratory dinner was held at Walford School. Robert Pashley provided salmon and others contributed poultry for the meal. A presentation cheque was also sent to the ex-service men and women who had been active in the nursing services during the First World War.

The British Legion was founded in 1921 with the general principle of inaugurating and maintaining 'in a strong, stimulating, united and democratic comradeship, all those who served in his Majesty's Navy, Army, Air Force or any Auxiliary Forces'. The Walford men's branch was formed in 1933 but closed in 1996. Jack Edwards was Chairman for many years and regular meetings and an annual dinner were held at the Spread Eagle in the early part of the 20th century.

Several members of the Legion served in both the World Wars:

Major J.C. Beckham	M.C., M.M. (awarded in the First World War), R.A.F.
H.G. Bond	M.C. (awarded in the First World War)
C.H. Lewis	
L. Puddle	M.M. (awarded in the Second World War)
Capt. R.J. Finlow	R.D., R.N.R., Captain of the *Queen Mary* when used as a troopship in the Second World War
J.O. Rogers	

Queen Elizabeth the Queen Mother was the National Women's President of the British Legion at the time of her death and the women's section in Walford was formed in 1965 with 30 members, Mrs. Hutchinson being President; Mrs. Jackson, Chairman; Mrs. Harris, Secretary; and Mrs. Baldwin as Treasurer. The membership subscription at that time was four shillings and sixpence and a badge cost one shilling and sixpence; today the membership is £3.50p. Walford is one of the 10 branches in Herefordshire which is now part of the West Midlands Counties area. The current Chairman is Cicely Edwards and there are 24 members.

Initially the members met in the school but meetings transferred to the village hall when it opened. Up until about 1990 the group arranged an annual fête in the grounds of the Cedars Hotel (home of Mrs. Jackson) and subsequently at Hill Court. Over the years the ladies have raised many thousands of pounds for the benefit of the organisation and hold an annual Poppy Concert in November in Walford village hall at which the Drybrook Male Voice Choir sing. Each year at the 11th hour on the 11th day of the 11th month, the members lay a wreath on Walford war memorial and throughout the year put flowers at the base of the memorial.

FOUR PORTRAITS

THE REVEREND MR. THOMAS DUDLEY FOSBROKE
1770 - 1842
- vicar, historian and antiquarian -

Thomas Dudley Fosbroke was born at Billericay, Essex, in 1770, the son of the Revd. William Fosbrooke. He was educated at Billericay and Petersfield, Hampshire, before entering St. Paul's School, London, in 1779. With a scholarship he obtained a place at Pembroke College, Oxford and graduated with a B.A. in 1789 and an M.A. in 1792. In the latter year he entered the Church, following the family tradition, and was made a Deacon. Two years later he was curate at Horsley, Gloucestershire. In 1796 he married Mary (née Howell) from that parish; they had four sons and six daughters.

In 1810 the family moved to Walford where for 20 years he struggled on a curate's stipend. In 1830 he was made the vicar of St. Leonard's Church, Walford. He had, both as curate and vicar, been responsible for Ruardean Chapelry which had been served by Walford benefice from 1535, and organised Sunday Schools there. This joint benefice arrangement ceased in 1842 when Ruardean separated from Walford eventually becoming, in 1875, a Rectory.

The Revd. T.D. Fosbroke was a scholar and a historian. With a large family finances were stretched, and he observed, wryly, of his choice of career 'in a wordly view, unhappily for myself, my habits of application might have procured me remuneration in another profession'. At one period he claimed to devote eight hours a day to research.

The results of this application were many. After many hours in the British Museum he produced a volume describing monastic life *British Monachism* in 1802. This was followed by a collection entitled *Abstracts of Records and Manuscripts respecting the County of Gloucester* in 1807. He edited John Gilpin's *Observations on the River Wye* and *A Commentary on the New Testament* by Whitby. As a regular contributor to the *Gentleman's Magazine* he met its proprietor and, with his encouragement, the learned curate embarked on his *Original History of the City of Gloucester* published in 1819. In 1820 he changed his name from Fosbrooke to Fosbroke.

In addition to his parochial duties, his research and his writing, he coached students; a letter (written in June 1818) to his publisher reported progress: 'now my pupils are gone I am getting on quick'.

In 1821 another historical account came off the presses entitled: *Ariconensia or Archaeological Sketches of Ross and Archenfield illustrative of the Campaigns of Caractacus etc. with other matters never before published.* This was printed in Ross in 1821. The book has many descriptions of Walford and Bishopswood people and places.

His next achievement was a two-volume *Encyclopaedia of Antiquities* published in 1825 and until seven years before his death he continued researching historical and topographical subjects. In an edition of sermons connected with freemasonry he noted that the publication depended on prior subscriptions. He explained that 'private expense the Author cannot incur, through duty to his large family; nor does he write for exhibition, but for the pleasure of writing and diffusing information'.

He supported John Partridge's scheme to build the Kerne Bridge, despite the fact that this would counter the proposal by Kingsmill Evans to site a new bridge near the Goodrich ferry crossing. A letter (written on 25 January 1825) made the then curate's view very clear: 'Mr. Fosbroke is decidedly of the opinion that the risk of inundation to a very serious degree will be incurred by placing the bridge at Goodrich, and that no such risk (without forfeiting a single inconvenience) will ensue from adopting the situation of the Quern'. The letter continued: 'Mr. Fosbroke begs Mr. Partridge's pardon for this probably unnecessary intrusion but it can do no harm and Mr. Fosbroke has a warm feeling to render any service however humble to his Ruardean parishioners'. It is perhaps significant that he was chosen to lay the foundation stone for the bridge at the Kerne in August 1826.

The Revd. Fosbroke's open mind and wide interests must have been beneficial. At Ruardean, in 1822, he had allowed Isaac Bridgman, the curate of Holy

Trinity church, Drybrook, to give a weekly lecture in the Church. Also, on one occasion, the churches were opened to the evangelical preacher, Rowland Hill, the British reformer and initiator of the Penny Post in 1840.

The vicar's health deteriorated and a letter to the *Hereford Times*, (written in 1889 by Mr. T. Sherwood Smith), recalls his difficulties: 'The interesting old Church at Walford was served for very many years by the eminent antiquary, Thomas Dudley Fosbroke, Vicar. In the latter years of his life he was partially paralysed and had to be lifted into the pulpit and propped up with cushions; one of his sons and sometimes a daughter stood by his side to turn over the leaves and keep him supplied with snuff by means of a spoon.'.

The Reverend Fosbroke died on 1 January 1842 and was buried within the chancel of the Church he had served so long. The monumental inscription commemorates not only his work as a scholar, antiquary and local historian but continues 'for his Christian and social virtues he was deservedly esteemed and beloved'.

MR. ROBERT PASHLEY
1880 - 1956
- benefactor, school governor and parish councillor -

Robert Pashley was born at Kerne Lodge, near Bishopswood, Walford in 1880. He was educated at Clifton Preparatory School, Bristol and Westminster. He married Mary (née Marrian) in 1902; there were no children. In September 1914 he enlisted as a private in the Bedfordshire Regiment and served in France with the Machine Gun Corps. He fought in the Somme Offensive and was invalided out in January 1918. He is remembered for his contribution to many parish and county affairs, his service on behalf of Walford Church, his support for the youth of the parish and his remarkable ability as a salmon angler.

He was first elected to Ross and Whitchurch Rural Council in 1907, serving until 1953 when he resigned on a point of principle. He was elected to Herefordshire County Council as the representative of Ross Rural and Walford Division and in 1938 he became an Alderman. In the same year he financed the construction of two semi-detached houses near the top of Howle Hill, Nos. 1 and 2 Sharman Cottages; these were built to provide homes for the two oldest families on Howle Hill. In due course the council took them over, and they are now privately owned. For several years his support for Walford Church involved serving as a Churchwarden and Secretary of the Parochial Parish Council. From the inception of the Walford British Legion in 1933 he was its Vice-President and in recognition of his services he was appointed a Patron. He was Chairman of Walford Parish Council for several years, and a Governor of Walford School. For many years he acted as a Governor of Ross Grammar School and also, from 1954, of Monmouth School.

His support for the youth of the parish, combined with his enthusiasm for sport, (as a young man he had been a keen footballer and cricketer), led him to promote many athletic activities locally. During the inter-war years he organised several sporting functions at Walford as President of the Athletic Club and generously subscribed to their prize funds and was Vice President of Ross Youth Club. In his later years he took a keen interest in the education of the pupils at Walford School, often dropping in to listen to a lesson in the headmaster's classroom. During the restricted times of rationing, during the Second World War, he frequently provided hot cocoa for the children and, as Margaret Wilce remembers, saved his sweet allowance until he could give each child a small bar of chocolate.

His benevolence towards Walford School provided a pantomime visit every winter; he donated several prizes, brought magazines and books for the library, and gave oranges, crackers and a new, silver sixpence to every child at the Christmas Party. Ice creams and prizes at the school Sports Days were other treats.

One of his hobbies was breeding and exhibiting Old English (fighting) game birds and bantams, and he gained several prizes at Crystal Palace poultry shows. His main hobby was salmon fishing and some amazing catches are recorded to indicate his prowess: in 1926 535 fish, total weight 7,557 lbs. In 1932 (within four and a half days) 53; in 1933 (when he had a half-share in the Hill Court and Goodrich waters) 461; in 1936 (when he had a larger share in the same waters) 678. On a single day in 1935, 30 August, he caught 16 fish; the heaviest weighed 19 lbs. Until 1938 he waded into the river, or fished from the river bank, but in his later years arthritis became a problem and he fished from a punt. Towards the end of his life he had to be lifted in and out of the punt by his ghillie. He only used a trout rod for fly fishing for the salmon, with a Mallock reel, and as his ghillie put him within easy reach of the fish he did not have to cast long distances. His skill earned him two titles: The Wizard of the Wye and The Napoleon of Salmon Fishers.

He was generous with the results of his catch; not only did every household in the parish receive, at the start of the season, a portion of fresh salmon, delivered by his ghillie on a frail, but smoked salmon was given to the families (the portion dependent on the size of the family) later in the year. On the annual school trips to the seaside (which he funded) Mr. Pashley asked the ladies of the village to help in the preparation of hampers packed with salmon sandwiches for the staff and children. He even delivered buckets of eels to the school to be shared amongst the pupils' families.

Robert Pashley died at his home, Kerne Lodge, on 1 July, 1956, after some months of failing health. When his will was proved it was discovered that his concern for the children of the parish was to continue. In the words of the will he wished to 'advance the education and promote the welfare of the children of Walford'. A substantial sum was left to provide the customary annual treats, prizes for leavers, books and other educational aids that the Education Committee could not provide, but, in addition, he included financial assistance for past pupils when setting out on their careers. The money was invested and the fund is managed by Herefordshire Council Trustees. The bequest also funded the purchase of a five-acre field, adjacent to the school playground, for improved sports facilities.

The Village Hall opened in Walford in 1969 bears his name, the Robert Pashley Memorial Hall, a fitting tribute to a man who supported, in so many ways, the interests of the parishioners of Walford and Bishopswood.

MISS MOLLIE MASON
1903 - 1998
- primary schoolteacher -

Born on 1 March 1903 Mollie was the third daughter of Edwin and Annie Mason (née Oakley). She was christened Mary Isabel but was always known as Mollie.

Her father was the licensee of The Pheasant at Upton Bishop from 1900 until his death in 1962 when Mollie's eldest sister, Ada, took over the licence.

Miss Mason taught for 12 years at Upton Bishop Voluntary Aided School, near Ross, followed by one year at Vowchurch School but from the end of May, 1934, she began teaching the Infant Class at Walford Primary School and continued there until her retirement in July 1968.

She was a warm, kindly and charismatic teacher. Her teaching methods were sound. 'Times tables' were learned by rote; reading was helped with flash-cards and the older children would stand round her desk, in small groups, reading aloud. Each child had a small tobacco tin with his or her plasticene for modelling in the afternoon periods, and great care was taken to preserve the artistic effort when the boards had to be tidied away. It was a happy classroom; Miss Mason expected good behaviour and, without shouting or repression, she achieved it. She was consistent, firm but fair, and this inspired confidence and trust in her young pupils.

She loved music and played the piano for the morning school assembly. In her own classroom the children would give spontaneous performances, singing

233

or reciting, and each contribution was applauded. Her enthusiasm was not confined to the Reception Class; she organised school choirs and, with Mrs. Tarry, regularly took children to the Hereford Music Festivals.

Jeremy Whitehouse of Ross came to Walford School as an older pupil and recalls his first morning in the headmaster's classroom. He was standing, ill at ease and nervous at the end of Assembly, when Miss Mason passed him as she shepherded her class back to their room. Realizing at once that he was new she put her arm round the shy newcomer and welcomed him to the school.

Mollie Mason bicycled from Upton Bishop to Walford for several years, but graduated to a car. She was very proud of her Morris 1000 (1952 model) with its split windscreen but in icy conditions would take a taxi rather than risk her car. Pupils were honoured to have an occasional lift to school, and she was the one the head teacher asked to take an injured child to hospital, or a sick pupil home.

On her retirement Mollie continued her involvement with people. Raffle-ticket selling or tombola management were her forté and her considerable fund-raising for many Ross charities was acknowledged, in 1986, with the Rotary Award for Community Service.

She never forgot any of the children she taught and would greet them in the streets of Ross with her warm, cheerful smile. On visits to Walford School at the Christmas Party or for the Leavers' Service, she would reminisce with the rapt young pupils, telling them that she had taught their brothers and sisters, their aunts or uncles or their Mums or Dads.

Mollie Mason died on 31 December, 1998. As her friend Lorraine Atkins said so sincerely: 'She was a warm, loving individual who will be sadly missed'.

MR. RICHARD STACEY
1922 - 1998
- a well known local sportsman and valued member of the community -

*Dick (far right), his wife, Vera (2nd left) and his sister, Joyce, (2nd right)
with the Howle Hill Football Team around 1976*

Richard 'Dick' Stacey was born at the Crown Inn on Howle Hill on 20 June 1922 and was the youngest of five children of Clara and Fred Stacey: George, Joyce, Iris, Roy and Dick. He attended Walford Primary School and Ross Secondary School where he showed an early talent on the soccer (association football) field.

Dick was a choirboy at St. John's church on Howle Hill when Mr. Gregson was the choirmaster. The organ was pumped by hand at that time and Dick used to undertake the task of pumping the bellows when requested.

On leaving school he helped Mr. 'Chappie' Webb with a local paper delivery service and then went to work for Chamberlain and Arnold, a grocer's in Gloucester Road, Ross.

During the Second World War, Dick served as a despatch rider in the Royal Army Service Corps in North Africa and Italy. He played soccer in the army team where his skills were noticed and he was asked to sign up to play for Cardiff City on his return from service. After the war Dick attended the club in Cardiff for training, but found he much preferred local soccer and joined Ross United services Football Club. He was a valued and popular player with the club for many seasons.

He went to work at Haywood and Clifford the builders in Ross and then Reeds at Lydbrook from where he retired in 1987.

During his retirement Dick maintained his enthusiasm for local soccer and had a great interest in the local community. He gave willing service to the Walford Parish Council from 1985 to 1995 carrying out a range of duties as the parish handyman.

In 1947 Dick married Vera Price and they had four children: Derek, Gillian, Clare and Valerie. Dick died on 3 May 1998 and is buried in Walford church-yard.

EPILOGUE

Epilogue
Future History

- a summary of the parish at the start of the new millennium -

Number of residents: 1,225 (in 1999)
Number of dwellings: 590 (in 2002)
Number on electoral roll: 1,086 (in 2000)

Parish Council: Mr. Edward 'Ted' Sainsbury (Chairman), Mr. Graham Lovett
(Vice-Chairman), Mr. Richard Chinn, Mr. Sidney Cobb, Mr. Simeon
Cole, Mr. John Daniels, Mr. Eric Drummond, Mr. Brian Edwards,
Miss Lois Hockley, Mr. Michael Hoddinott, Mr. Jamie McIntyre,
Mr. Duncan Stayton, Miss Bridget Vine
Parish Council Clerk: Mrs. Jackie Perry

Walford Parish Residents' Association: Mr. Paul Baker (Chairman),
Mrs. Virginia Morgan (Vice-Chairman), Mrs. Heather Hoddinott
(Treasurer), Mrs. Monica Edmunds, Mrs. Joan Griffiths, Mrs. Margaret
Merrick, Miss Bridget Vine

Parliamentary Constituency: Hereford; M.P. Mr. Paul Keetch
(Liberal Democrat)

Local Government area: Herefordshire Unitary Authority
Walford Parish is in Kerne Bridge Ward
Ward District Councillor: Mrs. Eunice Saunders (Independent)

Ross on Wye Policing Area. Beat Manager: Mr. Phil Berry

Businesses: Burton Pine Furniture, Cartwright Windows, Cobrey Farms, Four
Seasons Plants and Shrubs, Rehau Plastics Ltd., Walford Timber Ltd.,
Warryfield Barn Pine, Plus many others on a self employed basis - not
yet collated in a local trade directory

Churches: St. Michael and All Angels Walford, All Saints Bishopswood
As a result of a Deanery reorganisation, the benefice will be split from
May 2002 with Walford joining the Ross Team ministry and
Bishopswood joining the Borders Groups along with nine other
parishes.. There will be no resident Vicar in the parish.
Churchwardens. Walford: Mr. Paul Baker; Bishopswood: Mrs. Monica
Edmunds, Mrs. Penny Royde

Farms: Arbour Hill, Atlas, Bollin, Chadwyns, Cobrey, Coughton, Daycroft,
Great Howle, Hom, Little Howle, Old Hill, Rose, Vain

School: Walford. Number of pupils: 160 (approx). Head: Mr. Steven Roberts

Shops and Post Offices: Bishopswood Post Office stores and garage

Pubs: The Mill Race, Walford

Hotels: Inn on the Wye, Kerne Bridge - and many B & Bs

Public Transport: Buses

Village halls: Bishopswood, Walford

Clubs and Associations.
Bishopswood: Bridge Club, Brownies, Community Association,
Short Mat Bowls' Club, Village Hall Committee, Women's Institute plus
several groups such as Jumpstart, Martial Arts, Mature Movers

Walford: Churchwomen's Fellowship, Green Colley Grove Residents'
Association, Kerne Bridge Mother and Toddler Group, Village Hall
Committee, Walford Dance Group, Walford Pre-school Playgroup,
Women's British Legion, Women's Institute

Other Facilities: Wye Valley Walk, footpaths and bridleways, fishing,
shooting, mobile library service

Sources and References

Structure format:
These are given chapter by chapter, commencing with reference books, followed
successively by Acts, journals and newspapers, and archives

Abbreviations used

Ariconensia   Ariconensia; or Archaeological Sketches of Ross and Archenfield
Duncumb   Collections towards the History and Antiquities of the County of
        Herefordshire, Vol. III (in continuation of Duncumb's History)
HRO   Herefordshire Records Office
RCHM   Royal Commission for Historical Monuments
TWNFC   Transactions of the Woolhope Naturalists' Field Club
VCH   Victoria County History

Chapter I Archaeology and Geology

Barton, R.N.E. Dr. Five 'Interim Reports on the Survey and Excavations in the Wye
Valley', 1993 - 1997, *Proceedings of the University of Bristol Spelaeological
Society*

Cooke, W.H. *Duncumb*, 1882

Dreghorn, W. *Geology Explained in the Forest of Dean and the Wye Valley*, 1968

Morgan, C.A.V. *The Lime Kilns and Associated Quarries in Walford, Ross-on-Wye*,
1993

Stanford, S.C. Dr. *The Archaeology of the Welsh Marches*, 1980

University of London Institute of Historical Research *VCH Herefordshire*, Vol.1,
1908

Walters, B. Dr. *The Archaeology and History of Ancient Dean and the Wye Valley*,
1992

Herefordshire Council Archaeology Department, Sites and Monuments Records for
Walford Parish, various dates to 2000

Herefordshire and Worcestershire R.I.G.S. Group (Regional Importance of
Geological and Geomorphological Sites)

Chapter II History

Bagnall-Oakley, Mary Ellen 'Notes on a Great Hoard of Roman Coins found at
Bishops Wood in 1895', *Transactions of the Bristol and Gloucestershire
Archaeological Society*, Vol. XIX, and reprinted in *TWNFC*, 1896

Bannister, Revd. A.T. *Transcription of the Camden Miscellany for 1929*, Vol. XV

Claxton, Jonathan Ross Borough and Foreign, unpublished manuscript, 1983

Cooke, W.H. *Duncumb*, 1882

Fosbroke, Revd. T.D. A*riconensia*, 1821

Seaton, Revd. Prebendary Douglas *A History of Archenfield*, 1903

University of London Institute of Historical Research *VCH Herefordshire*, Vol. I,
1908

University of London Institute of Historical Research *VCH Gloucestershire*, Vol. 5,
 Forest of Dean,1998

Clwyd-Powys Archaeological Trust *Offa's Dyke Conservation Statement*, 2000
HRO; various documents including: Perambulation BF 99/8, Terriers HD2/4/23-24

Chapter III The Churches and Chapels
Cooke, W.H. *Duncumb*, 1882
Fitzhugh, T.V.H. *The Dictionary of Genealogy*, 1998
Forest of Dean Local History Society *The Rise of Non-Conformity in the Forest of
 Dean*, 1953
Fosbroke, Revd. Thomas *Ariconensia, 1821*
Lapage, Revd. Michael *The Church of St Michael and All Angels*, Walford, 1985
University of London Institute of Historical Research *VCH Gloucestershire, Vol. 5,
 Forest of Dea*n, 1998
Watkins, A. *The Old Standing Crosses of Herefordshire*, 1930

Various Census Returns for the Parish of Walford, HRO
Claxton, Miss B. Listing of Memorial Inscriptions for Walford Churchyard from
 1663, compiled 1985-1993
Jakeman and Carver's *Directory and Gazetteer of Herefordshire*, 1890
Littlebury's Directory of Hereford, 1867
Report of the RCHM, South West Herefordshire, 1932
Various Walford Parish Records held in HRO
Walford Church Records and Vestry Minutes
Walford Women's Institute W*alford Within Living Memory*, 1954/5 and the Jubilee
 Scrapbook 1965

Chapter IV Care of the Sick and the Poor
Druce, F. T*he Light of Other Days - Country Life Around Ross 1870 - 1940*, 1984
Fitzhugh, T.V.H. *The Dictionary of Genealogy*, 1998
Lawrence-Smith, K. *Tales of Old Herefordshire*, 1990
Morgan, C.A.V. and Briffett, J.M. *The Ross Union Workhouse 1836 - 1914*, 1998

Cassey, E. History, *Topography and Directory of Herefordshire*, 1858
Jakeman and Carver's *Directory and Gazetteer of Herefordshire*, 1890
Kelly's Directories for the years 1895, 1905, 1913 and 1934
Lascelles' Directories for the years 1851 and 1862

Bromfield, Mrs. Nancy, Recollections of the 1920s at Bishopswood
Roberts, Joyce, Oral history Recollections
Watkins, Nurse Alice, Oral history Record
*Reports of the Commissioners for Inquiries concerning Charities in England and
 Wales (County of Hereford) 1837*
Ross and Archenfield and Abbey Dore Deaneries Magazine, 1924
Walford Parish Church Vestry Records

Walford School Log Books for the years 1874 to 1951
Walford Womens' Institute *Walford within Living Memory*, 1954/5 and the Jubilee
    Scrapbook 1965
Various Records held by the HRO: (1) Clarkes of Hill Court F.8
                                         (2) Goff Charity AL21
                                         (3) Charities G.87

Chapter V River, Road and Rail

Awdry, Christopher E*ncyclopaedia of British Railway Companies,* 1990
Bradshaw's *July 1938 Railway, Shipping and Hotel Guide for Great Britain and
    Ireland*, reprint 1969
Bradshaw's *Railway Manual Shareholders' Guide and Directory*, 1869
British Rail *Handbook of Stations*, 1956
Fosbroke, Revd. Thomas *Ariconensia*, 1821
Fosbroke, Revd. Thomas *The Wye Tour*, 1826
Gilbert, H.A. *The Tale of A Wye Fisherman*,1928
Glover, Mark & Celia *The Ross and Monmouth Railway*, 1994
Handley, Brian H. *The Wye Valley Railway*, l988
Heath, C. *The Excursion down the Wye from Hereford to Monmouth*, 1808
Hurley, Heather *The Old Roads of South Herefordshire*, 1992
Jervaise, I.E. *The Ancient Bridges of Wales and Western England*, 1936
Kissack, Keith *The River Wye*, 1978
MacDermot, E.T. (revised. Clinker, C R.), *History of the Great Western Railway*,
    Vol 2, 1964
Morgan, C.A.V. *The Lime Kilns and Associated Quarries in Walford, Ross on Wye*,
    1993
Parr, H.W. *The Severn and Wye Railway*, 1965
Simpson, Helen J. *The Day the Trains Came*, 1977
Smith, William H. *Herefordshire Railways*, 1998
Stockinger, V.R. *The Rivers Wye and Lugg Navigation, A Documentary History,
    1555-1951*, 1996
The Railway Clearing House Handbook of Railway Stations, 1904
William, Stephen *Great Western Branch Line Modelling*, Part 2, 1991

Bromfield, Nancy 'Recollections of a Country Child; The Coracle', *Herefordshire
    Country Life*, Vol. 14, June 1981
Claxton, Jonathan 'The Roads in Walford in 1840', in part in *Walford Parish Council
    Newsletter 30*, 1980
Claxton, Jonathan Ross Borough and Foreign, 1983, unpublished manuscript, HRO
Felsted in Herefordshire, May 1940 - March 1945, printed by George Over
Herefordshire Council, *Bus and Train Timetable, Area 3, Ledbury and Ross on Wye*,
    2000
Kelly's Directories for the years 1929 and 1937
Life on Howle Hill in the 1920s, Oral History Recollection by Joyce Roberts
Maps: 1817 - Price, Henry *Herefordshire*, 1835 - Bryant, A. *Herefordshire*,
    1840 - Tithe Map, 1831, 1887, 1904, 1977, 1984, 1988 - Ordnance Survey,
    1892 - Stooke, *Tourist Map of the River Wye*

Northampton and Banbury Junction Railway; various documents, 1866,
      HRO: F 59/5/15
Quarter Sessions Papers held in HRO for : September 1808 - Plans of Towpath,
      1820 - Stopping up of Turnpike Ross to Paddocks, 1823 - Plan of Road
      between Old Forge and the Lea, 1824 - Intended new road in the parishes of
      Goodrich and Walford, 1833 - Q/RWT/29 - Kerne Bridge to Howle Cross et al,
      Trinity 1855 - Stopping up of road past Hazelhurst
Road Acts for Ross dated 1749, 1791 and 1815, HRO ref for 1815: Q/RWT/10
Roberts, Heather The Bishopswood Estate, 1982, unpublished manuscript
Ross and Monmouth Railway, Plans, sections and book of reference for 1860, 1864
      and 1866, HRO ref for 1860: Q/RW/R30; for 1864/1866: Q/RW/R43-44
Ross and Monmouth Railway, Subscription Contracts, HRO ref: AW 44/48
Ross Gazette, 26th February and 26th March 1931
Ross Turnpike Trust Accounts, 1857 to 1860, by courtesy of Martin Griffiths (Ross)
Seaton, Prebend. D. 'The History of Goodrich', *TWNFC*, 1900, p.213
Shirehampton, W.J.P. *Monmouth's Railways*, Monmouth and District Field Club and
      Antiquarian Society Publication, undated
Tonkin, M. 'Herefordshire Toll Houses Then and Now', *TWNFC*, 1996, p.398
van Laun, John 'The Kerne Bridge in Herefordshire', *Journal of the Railway and
      Canal Historical Society*, Vol XXV, Nos. 2 and 4
Various Commercial / Trade Directories, HRO and Hereford City Library
Walford Womens' Institute W*alford Within Living Memory*, 1954/5 and the Jubilee
      Scrapbook 1965

Chapter VI Agriculture

Clark, John *General View of the Agriculture of the County of Hereford*, 1794
Claxton, Jonathan *Walford Parish Council Newsletters* 1976 - 1980
Duncumb, John *General View of the Agriculture of the County of Hereford*, 1805
Editor *Hereford Cattle Society Breed Journal*, 1996
Hughes, Pat and Hurley, Heather *The Story of Ross-on-Wye*, 1999
RCHM Vol. II, 1932
University of London Institute of Historical Research *VCH Herefordshire*, Vol. I, 1908

Walford Women's Institute *Walford Within Living Memory*, 1954/5 and the Jubilee
      Scrapbook 1965
Trade Directories, Census Returns and Tithe Map Apportionment

Chapter VII Industry

Cooke, W.H. *Duncumb*, 1882
Hart, Dr. Cyril *The Industrial History of Dean*, 1971
Ince, Laurence *The Knight Family and the British Iron Industry 1695 - 1902*, 1991
Morgan, C.A.V. *The Lime Kilns and Associated Quarries in Walford, Ross-on-Wye*,
      1993
Nicholls, H.G. *Iron Making in the Olden Times*, 1866
Paar, Harry W. 'The Drybrook Mystery' and several other articles, all unpublished,
      written 1960 to 2000
University of London Institute of Historical Research *VCH Herefordshire* Vol. I, 1908

Chapter VIII Post Offices, Shops and Trades

Post Office Directory of Gloucestershire with Bath, Bristol and Herefordshire, 1856
Government Census Returns for the years 1841, 1851, 1861, 1871, 1881 and 1891, available in HRO
Life on Howle Hill in the 1920s, oral history record of Mrs. Joyce Roberts
Local Trade Directories, HRO and Hereford City Library
Marriage, Death and Baptism Registers for Walford and Bishopswood
Ross Gazette, 1931
School Records, Monmouth School for Boys
Walford Parish Tithe Map 1840 and Apportionment 1843
Walford Parish Council Newsletter for 1979
Walford Women's Institute *Walford Within Living Memory*, 1954/5 and the Jubilee Scrapbook 1965

Chapter IX Housing

Cooke, W.H. *Duncumb*, 1882
Faraday, M.A. 'The Hearth Tax in Herefordshire', *TWNFC,* Vol. XLI, 1975
Fosbroke, Revd. Thomas *Ariconensia*, 1821
Harnden, J. *The Hearth Tax for Michaelmas 1665 for Herefordshire and comparison with the Herefordshire Militia Assessments of 1663*, 1984
Porter, V. *Life behind the Cottage Door*, 1992
Robinson, Revd. Charles, A *History of the Mansions and Manors of Herefordshire*, 1872
Tonkin, J.W. V*ernacular Buildings*, TWNFC, 1967
Webb, Revd. John *Memorials of the Civil War in Herefordshire*, Vol. 2, 1879

Government Census Returns for various years, available in HRO
Herefordshire Council Archaeology Department Sites and Monuments Record, 1994 to 1999
Local Trade directories between 1851 and 1941 (available in HRO and Hereford City Library)
Report of the RCHM, South West Herefordshire, Vol. II, 1932
The Register of Electors (District of Herefordshire, Walford) 2000
Tithe Map 1840 and OS maps of 1831, 1887, 1904 and 1931
Walford Parish Council Minutes and Newsletters, 1974-77
Walford Parish Residents' Association Millennium House-History Questionnaires, Year 2000
Walford Women's Institute *Walford Within Living Memory*, 1954/5 and the Jubilee Scrapbook 1965
Window Tax for Walford 1776, HRO ref: Q/RTW/16

Chapter X Education and Schools

Bourne, R. and Macarthur, B. T*he Struggle for Education 1870 - 1970*, 1970
Curtis, S.J. *History of Education in Great Britain*, 1948

Bishopswood School Logbooks, 1871 to 1951
HRO, ref: BP58 1,2,3 (Bishopswood School)

Lascelles' Trade Directories, 1851and 1862
Walford Parish Church Vestry Records
Walford Primary School Logbooks, 1874 to 1951
Walford Womens' Institute *Walford within Living Memory*, 1954/5 and the Jubilee
    Scrapbook 1965

Chapter XI Recreation and Social Life
Walford Womens' Institute *Walford within Living Memory*, 1954/5 and the Jubilee
    Scrapbook 1965
Life on Howle Hill in the 1920s; oral history record of Mrs. Joyce Roberts

Chapter XII War and Peace
The Parish War Memorials
Walford Women's Institute *Walford Within Living Memory*, 1954/5
Birth, marriage and burial Registers for Walford and Bishopswood and Ross
Parish Census records for 1881 and 1891
Voters Lists, Walford parish, 1910 and 1914
Commonwealth War Graves Commission (records of burial place)
'Soldiers Died 1914 - 1919'; lists of army casualties (First World War) for each
    regiment
Lists at Family Resource Centre, Myddleton Place, London of Army, Navy and RAF
casualties, First and Second World Wars
The Roll of Honour (First World War)
Regimental War Diaries
Regimental records
Personal record of H.L. Napier (Public Record Office, Kew)
Information from families of those remembered

The Ross Gazette
The Hereford Times

N.B. The Roll of Honour is a large book of all the casualties but was not finished by
the publishers owing to a shortfall in money

Index